英汉概念隐喻用法比较词典

A Usage Dictionary of English and Chinese Conceptual Metaphors

主　　编　苏立昌
副 主 编　李建波
编写人员　苏明妮　金　琳
　　　　　李志华　李　茜

南开大学出版社
天　津

图书在版编目(CIP)数据

英汉概念隐喻用法比较词典 / 苏立昌主编. —天津：南开大学出版社，2009.5(2019.5重印)
ISBN 978-7-310-03124-5

Ⅰ.英… Ⅱ.苏… Ⅲ.英语－隐喻－对比研究－汉语－词典 Ⅳ.H314-61

中国版本图书馆 CIP 数据核字(2009)第 051300 号

版权所有　侵权必究

南开大学出版社出版发行
出版人：刘运峰
地址：天津市南开区卫津路 94 号　邮政编码：300071
营销部电话：(022)23508339　23500755
营销部传真：(022)23508542　邮购部电话：(022)23502200

*

天津市蓟县宏图印务有限公司印刷
全国各地新华书店经销

*

2009 年 5 月第 1 版　　2019 年 5 月第 2 次印刷
880×1230 毫米　32 开本　10.5 印张　392 千字
定价：32.00 元

如遇图书印装质量问题，请与本社营销部联系调换，电话：(022)23507125

本词典的出版得到教育部社科项目（06JA740030）和天津市社科项目（TJYW06-3-003）的资助。

序

英语系主任苏老师告诉我他主编的一本《英汉概念隐喻用法比较词典》要出版，要我给他写个序言，我很高兴地答应了。

这使我马上想起 2001 年，即我刚到南开大学的第二年，老系主任柯文礼教授即将出版《汉英简明百科词典》的事。当时我和老院长刘士聪教授为词典写了序言。那本词典于 2003 年由南开大学出版社出版，直到 2004 年 7 月我任系主任两年已满，一直都在我的案头上，我经常翻看。

所幸南大英语系的事业还在继续，系主任编词典也是一项传统。这不能不说是一件好事。而且从百科词典到隐喻词典，从中也可以发现两点显著的变化：其一是从资料型向研究型的变化。百科是普遍的分类的知识系统，而隐喻则是语言专业的研究范畴，特别是概念隐喻，更是认识人类语言和思维所必需的专业知识的研究内容，对于苏老师的研究专业来说，主要属于认知语言学的研究领域。其二是从自发组织的自选研究项目向省部级研究项目的变化。虽然有无研究项目和项目的等级高低并不一定绝对地决定研究的水平和质量，但像隐喻用法比较词典这样的研究任务，没有一定的项目规划和经费支持是不可能的，至少在保质保量地完成编撰任务和出版方面，会面临许多困难。

隐喻是我们生活须臾不能离开的，也是我所喜欢和关注的，因为这里面的学问很多。

人类的语言，可以按有无隐喻分为两类：一类是无隐喻的，那就是科学的语言，只按照概念思维，没有歧义，平铺直叙，也就没有歧义。一类是有隐喻的语言，那是文学的语言，充满比喻和想象的语言，生动活泼，显豁而鲜活。其实在二者之间，还有两个交叉地带：一个是日常生活领域的语言，多数是有隐喻的，但是并不一定要有隐喻，而且是不自觉的运用，是原始的自然状态的语言，或语言的原始自然状态。另一种就是研究领域，所谓概念隐喻的存身之地了。原则上，日常生活语言是概念隐喻产生的基础，也是后者研究的对象。概念隐喻研究的对象还包括文学语言的隐喻性，再加上科学语言的概念性，也就是说，概念隐喻已经是对于比较固定的概念的隐喻或隐喻性概念的系统化的研究了。从意义系统来说，因为它系统，所以它完整，因为是概念，所以会凝固、定型或趋向于僵化。进一步而言，从历史维度来讲，概念隐喻是一个诞生、变化、僵化以至于死亡的过程。而人类的语言的隐喻性，正是抵抗隐喻僵化而不断转换生成的过程。这也是人类语言的自我隐喻的本质。因此，今日学者心目中的隐喻，正关乎人类的思维与理解，成为继古典修辞学以后解释学的研究对象：

> 只有在隐喻的转换的意义上，我们才可以把思想称为倾听以及通过倾听而进行的理解，才可以把它称为观看以及通过观看而进行的理解。（海德格尔：《理由律》，转引自利科：《活的隐喻》中译本，第 392 页）

隐喻是人类思维的基本方式之一，也是人类语言得以形成的基本保证，它涉及语言的起源、思维的机制、概念的习得、人际交流与相互理解的途径等方面。在西方隐喻的研究开端，固然有柏拉图的隐喻思维和罗格斯中心论的论述，但就现代学科而言，研究隐喻的途径，大概可分为语言学的途径、文学的途径以及翻译学的途径。语言学的途径涉及隐喻的认知途径、概念形成与习得习惯以及有关传授与教育的可能等问题。文学的研究途径，则主要从修辞角度研究文学语言和文学作品中隐喻的应用情况、表达方式及表现力，还有读者理解的可能。翻译是一件更为复杂的事情。它既涉及不同语言中隐喻的对比和比较，以寻求和说明人类隐喻的差异与共同点，又要研究隐喻的转换机制和翻译技巧（就如同纽马克在其《翻译教程》里所表述的那样），并尽可能说明在不同的民族和文化语境中隐喻翻译的复杂现象和表述机制。与之相应的是，隐喻研究对于语言学、文学和翻译在实践和理论上的促进，甚至对于日常生活中人类的有效交际活动，特别是跨文化的交际活动，都发生了积极的影响。不过，一个容易被人忽略的问题是，迄今为止，大部分对于隐喻的研究，都属于专业的范围，受其专业研究与写作方式的限制，局限在专业人士的圈子里，并不能有效地转换为日常生活的知识，而日常生活中人们对于隐喻的应用，仍然在原始的自然的状态中，以约定俗成的方式口口相传，所谓的"百姓日用而不知"了。

也许我们应当指出一点，关于隐喻一类知识，大体会以三种正规教育的途径得到研究或传播：一是研究专著，即专门的分专业的研究成果。它们虽然是专家的研究水平和与时俱进的更新效果，但流传面不广，影响也有限。其二是一般教科书的领域，但教科书只是原理性的、分系统的编排资料，而收容的范围和内容毕竟有限，加之一般的教科书受课程设置的局限，不是所有学校和所有学生都能学习的。尤其是学中文和外语的学生，以及某些在社会上从事语言文字工作的人员，例如作家和翻译家，急于学习和掌握一些隐喻的资料，却反而难以接触到。于是，作为第三种类型的工具书，就应运而生了。从存在方式上来说，只要编写人员功底扎实而且编排得好，工具书可以兼有研究专著的时效、深刻与新颖和教科书的周遍、普及与易懂。从最终的意义和用途来说，相对于其他两种存在方式，一本隐喻词典，正是具有长期稳定和便于查阅的优点，可以一册在手，永远作伴。

该回到眼前这本《英汉概念隐喻用法比较词典》上来了。

通过和主编苏老师简短地交谈，又大略地翻阅了一下词典，细读了其中的一些条目，兹从所得的一些印象出发，简要陈述一下这本《英汉概念隐喻用法比较词典》的优势和特点。

1. 首先是知识分类的系统和体制比较完备。从我看到的有限的几部分内容来看，本词典从人体部位、健康与疾病开始，进入动物、植物和其他生命现象的分类，一直到包括和人类生活密切相关的其他事物的隐喻知识和词汇的分类列举，可谓体大虑周，包罗丰富。大而言之，可说和中国古代的《尔雅》以及现代的百科全书的分类系统，具有异曲同工的妙处。

2. 其次，坚持英汉语言对比和实际的应用，是其突出的特点。众所周知，研究隐喻，若是只涉及某一民族和语言的隐喻系统，虽然也很重要，但并不十分困难，而要进行不同语言隐喻概念的对比研究，而且是系统的对比研究，就有相当的难度。本词典当然不是专著，也不需要从理论上给予各种解释和说明，而是以体例的明晰和较为严格的对照与对应关系，说明了英汉语隐喻的异同（例句的翻译在一定程度上突现了差异性）。特别是文化缺省现象，以附栏的形式专门示出，不仅清晰易见，也使得有关认识的表征趋向于充实和完备。

3. 最后，本词典参考了国内外权威的理论著作和相关词书，创作性地做了新的编排和取舍，根据词典本身的要求和需要进行了合理的设计和操作，作到了体例合理、释义明晰、举例丰富，而且语言生动易懂，便于查阅和自学。除附录以外，在正文部分，按照英语字母顺序排列，单词或短语（成语）下给出不同层次的意思，分别给出例证（英汉对照），而且利用斜体、黑体、下画线等标示出不同的重点和难点，起到了醒目和分别的作用。释义的准确和翻译的对应都是很讲究的。可以说，这是一本用得着、靠得住的英汉语对比的隐喻用法词典，适合教学与研究者使用，也可供翻译和学习者参考。

末了，作为一名先睹为快的普通读者，我要向未来的读者朋友们说，在加深学业、加强交际和了解人类自身及其语言的意义上，而且为了方便和经济计，一部中等规模、便于查阅和利用的隐喻字典，是十分必要和有用的。正是在这个意义上，苏老师主编的这本《英汉概念隐喻用法比较词典》，具有重要的意义，特别是对于语言教学，包括汉语教学和英语教学，以及英汉语比较研究的对外汉语教学，可以说作出了有意义的贡献。更何况在比较严格的意义上，这还是国内首部关于英汉语言中概念隐喻用法的比较词典。对于那些欲先睹为快，急于上手的翻译人员、作家、文秘人员以及其他语言文字工作者，也正是雪中送炭一样的急需。

我也要趁此机会，希望苏老师有更多更好的研究成果！
也祝愿英语系有健康而和谐的发展前景！

王宏印
2008年10月8日
南开大学寓所

前　言

继 1980 年 Lakoff 和 Johnson 的《我们生活中的隐喻》一书问世以后，认知语言学研究取得了新的发展。在语言形式与意义的理论研究方面，人们的视野也由传统的形式句法和意义理论逐步拓宽到更新和更为广阔的研究领域，如认知语言学的语义理论研究领域等。近年来，概念隐喻的语言形式与意义关系的研究，尤其是不同语言之间概念隐喻的语言形式与意义表达模式的关联研究，一直是人们所关注的一个课题。目前，英语概念隐喻的语言形式与意义的研究取得了较快的发展，这主要归功于二十年来认知语言学理论的发展，如意义覆盖、合成空间理论和社会脚本等理论模式的提出。这些理论为语言形式与意义的契合点研究奠定了坚实的理论基础，并引发了一系列的研究成果，如 Lakoff 对概念隐喻与思维间联系的描述，Langacker 和 Turner 对概念隐喻意义构成的认知模式解释，以及 Kövecses 等学者就文化因素对概念隐喻影响的实证研究等等。这些都对我们进一步认识语言、了解语言形式与意义的联系起到了积极的推动作用。

目前，概念隐喻的研究虽然在理论上取得了较大的进展，但现有理论多集中在对概念隐喻意义表达的解释上，对于不同文化中的概念隐喻在多大程度上影响该语言的表达结构，以及概念隐喻与语言表达结构之间存在哪些必然的联系等问题，还无法在现今的理论模式中得到充分的解释。

本词典即是一部根据现有的认知语言学理论模式，通过对英语和汉语两种语言的概念隐喻表达方式的对照、比较，探讨概念隐喻与语言表达模式之间关系的一部工具书。本词典借鉴了 *English Guide: 7 Metaphor*（1995）一书的编写体例，按照 Daniel Rigney《隐喻社会》（2001）一书的概念隐喻理论模式，将概念隐喻分成包括"人生是旅途，社会是生命体系、机器、商场、战场、剧场、游戏、法律体系"

等在内的概念隐喻体系,然后将以上概念隐喻体系模式细分成诸多隐喻用法分类项。在分类项下,将英语和汉语的隐喻用法列举出来,并加以比较。本词典不仅列举出各概念隐喻类项英语和汉语概念隐喻的用法,更重要的是将英语和汉语特有的概念隐喻表达方式标注出来,以利于英汉对比研究。词典同时对英语和汉语文化因素对概念隐喻表达方式的影响做了解释,这些在其他词典中是不曾见到的。词典的编写资料主要来源于基于语料库的权威辞书。

作为国内第一部概念隐喻用法比较词典,本书的出版将对我国目前的外语教学产生多层面的影响。首先,在词汇和语言基本结构教学上,该词典将为英语或汉语语言学习者提供概念隐喻与语言表达方式之间关系的理论依据,解决由于不同文化概念隐喻导致的语言差异给外语词汇和句法结构学习带来的困难,便于语言学习者正确理解和掌握语言意义与结构特征,从而减轻学生外语语言学习的负担,达到较好的学习效果。此外,在篇章阅读和写作方面,该词典将有助于语言学习者正确掌握英语和汉语两种语言概念隐喻形式的表达规律,从而提高学习者对所学语言的理解和运用能力。该词典可以为从事语言教学、科研及翻译工作的人员提供翔实的概念隐喻与语言表达关系方面的语言资料,供进一步研究参考。

本词典为2006年教育部社会科学项目立项和天津市"十一五"社会科学项目立项的主要成果之一。词典出版得到了南开大学出版社的大力支持。南开大学外国语学院王宏印教授慨然为本词典作序。在词典付梓之际,谨此向在词典编写过程中给予我们大力支持和帮助的各位同仁表示衷心的感谢。

编 者
2008年6月16日

体例说明

1. 本词典按二十个主题编写，每个主题下收录相应的词条。收录词条较多的主题下设分类，以利读者查找。主题或分类下的词条按字母顺序排列。
2. 词条与中文释义采用加粗宋体字，释义包括本义与比喻义，以利读者比较两者的相似性。
3. 英文例句和例句译文采用倾斜体；用下划线标注出现在例句中的词条或常用搭配。
4. 对于汉语中隐喻的比较说明部分采用楷体字，相应的汉语隐喻词采用加粗楷体字；出现在汉语例句中的隐喻词用下划线标注。
5. 在比较栏中列出汉语独有的隐喻表达方式并附以译文，以供读者参考。

分类索引

1. The Human Body / 1
   Parts of the body / 1
   Processes in your body / 23
2. Health and Illness / 26
3. Animals / 43
   General words for animals / 43
   Pets / 45
   Poultry / 54
   Farm animals / 57
   Wild animals / 64
4. Plants / 72
   Plants / 72
   Parts of plants / 75
   Cultivating plants / 82
   Growth / 86
5. Cooking and Food / 90
6. Construction / 107
7. Machines and Tools / 119
   Machines & parts of machines / 119
   Tools & working with tools / 126
8. Journeys, Traffic & Vehicles / 135
   Journeys / 135
   Words for roads / 137
   Traffic / 143
   Vehicles / 147

9   Market / 153
10 Theatres and Stage / 162
11 Clothes / 169
12 Games and Sports / 177
13 War / 196
14 Weather / 207
15 Colour / 221
16 Light and Darkness / 229
     Light / 229
     Darkness / 233
17 Temperature / 238
18 Time / 253
19 Space and Container / 261
20 Movement / 287

对比栏索引

Column 1.1 / 3
Column 1.2 / 4
Column 1.3 / 5
Column 1.4 / 8
Column 1.5 / 10
Column 1.6 / 13
Column 1.7 / 14
Column 1.8 / 18
Column 1.9 / 23
Column 2 / 41
Column 3.1 / 48
Column 3.2 / 52
Column 3.3 / 57
Column 3.4 / 64
Column 3.5 / 71
Column 4 / 88
Column 5 / 105
Column 6 / 117
Column 7 / 133
Column 8.1 / 146
Column 8.2 / 152
Column 9 / 160
Column 10 / 168
Column 11 / 176
Column 12 / 195

Column 13 / 205
Column 14 / 220
Column 15.1 / 222
Column 15.2 / 227
Column 16 / 237
Column 17 / 252
Column 18 / 260
Column 19 / 285
Column 20 / 295

目 录

序 / i
前言 / vii
体例说明 / ix
分类索引 / xi
对比栏索引 / xiii
词典正文 / 1
词条英文字母顺序索引 / 296
附录：英语常用概念隐喻 / 313
参考书目 / 316

1 The Human Body

Parts of the body

backbone

1.1 Your **backbone** is the row of small bones that goes down the middle of your body.

脊骨；脊柱

Backbone is used to refer to the determination and strong personality that you need in order to do what is right or deal with a difficult situation.

汉语用**脊梁骨**比喻骨气，如：这个人没有<u>脊梁骨</u>，不要跟他交往。

决心；毅力；骨气；勇气

They wouldn't have the <u>backbone</u> to disagree with him.

他们不会有勇气与他争执。

1.2 The **backbone** of something such as an organization or country is the most important part of it.

某事物的骨干

Ordinary volunteers form the <u>backbone</u> of most charitable organizations.

汉语用**脊梁**比喻支撑事物的中坚，如：人民是历史的<u>脊梁</u>。

普通志愿者组成大多数慈善机构的骨干。

blood

1.3 **Blood** is the red liquid that flows around inside your body.

血；血液

<u>血</u>在汉语中可用来比喻刚烈，如：<u>血</u>性男儿。

Blood can be used to refer to the family, nation, or group that you belong to through your parents and grandparents.

血统；家族；民族；门第

They never fail to remind people that they have royal <u>blood</u> in their veins.

他们从不忘提醒人们，他们的血管里流淌着王室的血。

Like many Canadians, she had some Scottish <u>blood</u>.

像许多加拿大人一样，她有部分苏格兰血统。

1.4 **Blood** is used as a way of referring to violence and death.

杀人，流血（用来指暴力和死亡）

Peace finally came, but a great deal of blood was lost in the process.

和平终于到来，但是在和平的进程中有许多人流血牺牲。

The conflict continued for years, with a lot of blood spilled on both sides.

冲突持续数年，双方都死伤众多。

a ruthless general with blood on his hands

双手沾满鲜血、灭绝人性的将军

1.5 If there is **bad blood** between people, they dislike each other because of something that happened in the past.

仇恨；敌意

Bad blood has arisen between our two daughters because each wants us to retire to their town.

我们的两个女儿之间出现了互相对立的情绪，因为她们两人都要我们在退休之后去她们各自的城镇居住。

1.6 If a crime is committed **in cold blood**, it is done in a cruel calm way, without showing any emotion.

残忍地；冷血地
汉语用**冷血动物**比喻没有感情的人。

Unarmed civilians were shot in cold blood.

手无寸铁的平民被残忍地枪杀了。

1.7 If an ability or quality is **in your blood**, it is part of your nature.

生来就是做某事的

Farming is in my blood.

我生来就要种地当农民。

1.8 You can use **new blood** or **fresh blood** to refer to someone who joins an organization with new exciting ideas or new ways of doing things.

新鲜血液；新生力量；新人
汉语也用**生力军**比喻新加入某种工作或活动，能起积极作用的人员，如：青年人是祖国建设的**生力军**。

We need to bring in some new blood to brighten up our image.

我们必须引进一些新鲜血液来改善我们的形象。

-blooded

1.9 **Cold-blooded** animals have a body temperature that changes to suit their environment.

（动物）冷血的
参见 1.6

A **cold-blooded** action or person does not show or involve any emotions or pity for other people's suffering.

残酷的；无情的

They stand accused of the <u>cold-blooded murder</u> of their parents.　他们被控有预谋地残杀了自己的父母。

1.10 **Hot-blooded** emotions such as anger or love are strong and difficult to control.　情感强烈的，易激动的，热切的
汉语用**热血**比喻为正义事业英勇奋斗、不怕牺牲的献身精神和热情，如：**热血**青年。

<u>hot-blooded</u> passion　强烈的情感
Coppola is one of our more <u>hot-blooded</u> directors.　考珀拉是我们较易激动的董事之一。

Column 1.1

This column is adopted to help understand some metaphorical expressions of **blood** that are unique to Chinese.

腥风血雨	a foul wind and a rain of blood—reign of terror
血口喷人	make unfounded and malicious attacks upon someone
血气方刚	full of animal spirits
一针见血	hit the nail on the head
有血有肉	true to life

body

1.11 A **body** is the whole physical structure of a person or animal, including the head, arms, and legs.　身体，躯体

A particular **body** is a group of people who are connected in some way, often because they are involved in the same activity.　一群，一批（人）

There is a large <u>body</u> of people who would use public transport if fares were cut.　如果票价降低，有一大批人会乘坐公共交通工具。

1.12 You can refer to a group of people who are connected in some way, often because they are involved in the same activity, as a **body**.　团体；机构
比较汉语中的**团体、集体、欧共体**等。

The government has set up a new <u>body</u>　政府设立了一个新部门对中学进行检

to inspect secondary schools.
The Institute of Chartered Accountants is a recognized professional <u>body</u>.
皇家特许会计师协会是得到认可的专业机构。

1.13 A **body of** something such as knowledge, information, or work is a large amount or collection of them.
大量，大批（知识、信息等）

There is a growing <u>body of</u> evidence to support this theory.
有越来越多的证据支持这一理论。

These films represent a major <u>body of</u> work.
这些影片代表了主要的作品。

1.14 **Body** is also used metaphorically to refer to the main, central, or most important part of something.
主体，主要部分

The <u>body</u> of the church dates from the 15th century.
教堂的主体部分是于15世纪建成的。

He is not mentioned in the main <u>body</u> of the text.
正文中没有提到他。

The <u>body</u> of the aircraft remained intact after the crash.
飞机失事后机身保持完好无损。

Column 1.2

This column is adopted to help understand some metaphorical expressions of **body** & **gut** that are unique to Chinese.

撑腰	support; back up; bolster up
肝胆过人	far surpass others in daring
量体裁衣	cut the garment according to the figure—act according to actual circumstances
略知皮毛	scratch the surface
满腹经纶	be possessed of learning and ability
满腹牢骚	full of resentment
满腔热忱	filled with ardor and sincerity
芒刺在背	feel prickles down one's back—feel nervous and uneasy
脾胃相投	have similar tastes
皮之不存，毛将焉附	with the skin gone, what can the hair adhere to—a thing cannot exist without its basis

热心肠	a warm-hearted and helpful person
牵肠挂肚	feel deep anxiety
胸无点墨	unlearned
腹背受敌	between two fires

bone

1.15 **Bones** are the hard parts that form a frame inside the body of a human or animal.
If you say that something that someone says or writes is **close to the bone**, you mean that although it is unpleasant it is true, and so makes you feel upset or uncomfortable.
His comments about racism may be too close to the bone for some people.

1.16 If something is **cut, trimmed** or **pared to the bone**, it is reduced to the lowest possible level or amount.
We've had to cut our profit margins to the bone in order to survive.
Universities feel they have already been pared to the bone by government cuts.

1.17 If you **feel** or **know something in your bones**, you feel certain about it, although you cannot explain or prove it.
Something was wrong—she could feel it in her bones.

骨；骨头
汉语中，骨可用来比喻人的品德、气概，如：傲骨、风骨、软骨头等。

露骨的
汉语用赤裸裸比喻毫不掩饰的样子，如：赤裸裸的强盗行径。

他对种族歧视的评论对于有些人来说也许太露骨了。

把某物减少到最低限度；使某物最小化

为了生存我们得把利润率减到最低限度。

一些大学感到，由于政府的财政削减，它们的经费已经少得只能维持基本运作了。

凭直觉确信某事；从心底预感某事

出事了，她可以凭直觉确信。

Column 1.3

This column is adopted to help understand some metaphorical expressions of **bone** that are unique to Chinese.

| 贱骨头 | miserable (or contemptible) wretch |
| 露骨 | thinly veiled; undisguised; barefaced |

贫骨头	① a person keen on petty gain ② a stingy person; niggard ③ an idle chatterer; windbag
软骨头	a soft bone—a weak-kneed person; a spineless person; a coward
主心骨	a definite view; one's own judgment
硬骨头	hard bone—a dauntless, unyielding person
敲骨吸髓	break the bones and suck the marrow—suck the lifeblood; be a cruel, bloodsucking exploiter
傲骨	unbending backbone—lofty and unyielding character
戳脊梁骨	backbite
骨子里	in the bones—beneath the surface; in one's innermost nature; in substance
恨之入骨	hate someone to the marrow of one's bones
脱胎换骨	cast off one's old self

ear

1.18 You use your **ears** to listen to the sounds around you, such as speech and music.

耳；耳朵

If you have an **ear**, or have a **good ear** for the sounds of something such as music, a language, or ways of speaking, you are very sensitive to them and can interpret or reproduce them well.

对……敏感；对……有辨别能力

He has always had a good ear for a tune.

他对于曲调总是很敏感。

I'm proud of my extraordinarily good ear for accents and dialects.

我感到自豪的是，我对口音和方言有非凡的辨别能力。

1.19 If you **have something coming out of your ears**, you have a lot of it, or more of it than you need.

有过多的……

We have information coming out of our ears and we just need time to sift through it.

我们满脑子都是信息，我们只是需要时间来整理一下。

eye

1.20 You use your **eyes** to look at and judge real objects in the world around you.
If you **have an eye for** something, you have a natural ability for seeing or finding the thing.
Proofreaders need to have a good eye for detail.

1.21 If you see an event or situation **through** someone's **eyes**, you understand it in the way that that person would understand it.
The story is told through the eyes of a child.

1.22 If you say that something is the case **in** a particular person's **eyes**, or **in the eyes of** a particular person, you mean that this is the way he judges it or considers it, although other people may judge it or consider it in a different way.
In his mother's eyes, the boy can do no wrong.
In the eyes of the law, theft is a less serious crime than handling stolen goods.

1.23 If you do one thing **with an eye** to something or someone else, you consider the second person or thing when you do the first thing. If you do one thing **with an eye** to doing another thing, you do the first thing with the intention of doing the second thing as a result of it.
The selections have been made with an

眼睛
汉语的**眼光**用来指观察事物的能力，如：事实证明，你真有**眼光**。
对……有识别力

校对者需要对细节有很好的识别力。

通过某人的眼睛；以某人的视角
眼光还可用来指观点，如：不要用老**眼光**来看新事物。

故事是以一个小孩的视角来讲述的。

在某人的眼里；在某人看来

在他的母亲看来，她的孩子不会做坏事。
从法律的角度看，偷窃比买卖赃物罪行轻些。

考虑到；有……的企图；试图；期待

选择这些商品是考虑到偶然光顾的买

eye to the casual buyer.
He bought the cottage <u>with an eye to</u> retiring there.
The Foreign Office says it's agreed to pay it, but <u>with an eye to</u> claiming the money back at a later date.

主的需要。
他买下那所乡间小屋以备退休后住在那里。
外交部说它同意支付这笔费用，但仍准备在日后要回它。

1.24 If someone is **in the public eye**, he is receiving a lot of public attention, for example, in the newspapers or on television.

引起公众注意的；众所熟知的

It was not until his retirement that he began the work which has kept his name <u>in the public eye</u> ever since.

直到退休他才开始那项工作，从此他的名字一直为公众所注意。

Column 1.4

This column is adopted to help understand some metaphorical expressions of **ear** & **eye** that are unique to Chinese.

耳边风	a puff of wind past the ear—unheeded advice
耳聪目明	have good ears and eyes—have a clear understanding
耳目闭塞	ill-informed
耳目一新	find everything fresh and new
耳濡目染	be imperceptibly influenced by what one sees and hears
耳软心活	credulous and pliable
软耳朵	a soft ear—a credulous person
洗耳恭听	listen with respectful attention
迅雷不及掩耳	a sudden peal of thunder leaves no time to cover the ears—as sudden as a flash of lightening
掩人耳目	deceive the public
耳朵软	credulous; easily influenced; susceptible to flattery
耳目	one who spies for someone else

face

1.25 Your **face** is the front part of your head, where your eyes, nose and mouth are.

脸；面部
汉语的<u>脸</u>、面都可用来指情面、情分，如：丢<u>脸</u>、讲<u>面子</u>等。

Face is used to refer to the qualities that something such as an organization has, or wants people to think it has.
This is the new face of banking in America.
He may have difficulty persuading the security forces to adopt a more human face.

1.26 If someone **loses face**, he is embarrassed publicly, and feels upset and humiliated as a result of this.
We need to find a way to end the conflict without either side losing face.

1.27 If someone **saves face**, he avoids being embarrassed or losing his respect.
This is an attempt by politicians to save face at taxpayers' expense.

1.28 If someone **puts on a brave face**, or **puts a brave face on** a bad situation, he tries to behave in public as if he was not upset or unhappy about his problems or failures.
Patrick tried to put on a brave face but he was terribly worried.
He did his best to put a brave face on his failure.

1.29 If you are **in the face of** something such as problems, difficulties, or dangers, you are in a situation where you have to deal with them.
They won in the face of stiff competition from all over the country.

1.30 If you **face** someone **down**, you oppose or confront them and defeat them by appearing very confident and

形象；面貌；风貌
比较汉语中的门脸儿、门面等。

这是美国银行业的新面貌。

在说服保安部队采用一种更有人情味的公开形象时，他也许碰到了困难。

丢脸；失面子

我们需要找到一种办法来结束冲突又不使双方丢面子。

保全面子

政客们企图用纳税人的钱来保全自己的面子。

摆出勇敢的样子

帕特里克试图装出一副勇敢的样子，但实际上他却极度担忧。
他竭力装出对失败满不在乎的样子。

面对

虽然面临来自全国各地的激烈竞争，他们还是赢得了比赛的胜利。

坚强地面对；压倒

brave, even if you do not really feel very confident or brave.

They showed they could <u>face down</u> the opposition.
他们表示能够压倒反对意见。

He had spent a lifetime <u>facing down</u> lesser men, men who lacked his courage.
他用毕生的时间降服了一些次要人物，即那些缺乏他所具有的勇气的人。

1.31 If you **face** a problem or it **faces** you, it is likely or certain to happen and you have to deal with it.
面临

How to combine a career and children is a dilemma <u>facing</u> many women.
怎样兼顾事业和孩子，是许多女性面临的两难问题。

The country <u>is</u> now <u>faced with</u> the prospect of war.
这个国家目前正面临战争。

1.32 If you **face** or **face up to** a difficult fact or problem, you accept and deal with it.
面对；正视；对付

We have to <u>face</u> the reality that, so far, the treaty has had little effect.
我们必须正视该条约至今仍没有多少效力这一现实。

I decided I must <u>face up to</u> the truth.
我决心面对现实。

1.33 If you **cannot face** a problem or a situation, you feel as if you cannot deal with it because it seems so unpleasant, difficult, or frightening.
不想做某事；不愿处理某事

He <u>couldn't face</u> the washing-up, so he left it until the morning.
他不想洗碗，所以留到早上去做。

Column 1.5

This column is adopted to help understand some metaphorical expressions of **face** that are unique to Chinese.

碍面子	just to spare someone's feelings
本来面目	true colors; true features
变脸	suddenly turn hostile
驳面子	not spare someone's sensibilities; not show due respect for someone's feelings

1 The Human Body

打肿脸充胖子	slap one's face until it's swollen in an effort to look imposing—puff oneself up to one's own cost
翻脸无情	turn against a friend and show him no mercy
厚颜无耻	shameless
脸面	face; self-respect
露脸	become known (by doing something); be successful; shine
满面春风	beaming with satisfaction
面目全非	be changed beyond recognition
面目一新	take on an entirely new look
破脸	turn against (an acquaintance or associate); fall out
赏脸	honor me with your presence
铁面无私	impartial and incorruptible
洗心革面	turn over a new leaf
争脸	try to win credit or honor

guts

1.34 **Guts** are all the organs inside your body, especially the ones in the stomach area.

Guts is used metaphorically to refer to the quality of being brave and determined.

She had the guts to decide what she wanted and go for it.

It takes a lot of guts and hard work to get where he is.

1.35 **Guts** can also be used metaphorically to refer to the most important parts of a system, plan, or machine.

That's basically the guts of Darwin's theory.

1.36 If you **work**, **slog**, or **fight your guts out**, you put all your time and

内脏；（尤指）肠胃
汉语中，胆常被用来指勇气，如：胆大心细、胆量、胆识等。
勇气；胆量；意志；决心

她有勇气确定目标并为之奋斗。

胆识加上努力工作使他取得了今天的成绩。

（系统、计划或机器的）核心部分

那基本上就是达尔文理论的要义。

拼命工作；玩命干

energy into working for something.
I <u>worked my guts out</u> getting my degree.
1.37 If you **hate** someone's **guts**, you hate him very much.
He won't get a penny out of her. She <u>hates</u> his <u>guts</u>.
1.38 Your **hand** is the part of your body at the end of your arm, including your fingers and thumb, which you use to hold things.

If you **give** or **lend** someone **a hand**, you help him to do something. If you **like**, **want** or **need a hand** with something, you need help with it.
Can you <u>give me a hand</u> with these boxes?
Would you <u>like a hand</u> with the cleaning up?
Lydia <u>lent a hand</u> with the costumes.
1.39 If you **have a hand in** an event or project, you take part in its organization.
The President has accused these people of <u>having a hand in</u> the killing.
1.40 **Hands-on** experience or training involves you doing something rather than just reading about it or watching other people do it.
You'll be expected to have a degree, a teacher-training qualification and a few years of <u>hands-on</u> experience.
This stimulating book places great emphasis on an enjoyable <u>hands-on</u> approach to learning.
1.41 A **hands-off** way of organizing

我拼命学习，攻读学位。
对某人恨之入骨

他将不会从她那儿得到一分钱。她对他恨之入骨。
手
汉语用**手足**喻指兄弟，如：**手足**情深。用**左右手**和**膀臂**比喻得力的助手，如：他是我的<u>左右手</u>；你来得好，给我添了个<u>膀臂</u>。
帮助（某人）

需要（帮助）

你能帮我拿这些盒子吗？

需要帮你收拾打扫吗？

莉迪亚帮忙准备服装。
参加；参与；插手

总统控告这些人参与了屠杀。

实际操作的；亲身实践的

对你的期望将是有一个学位、一个教师培训资格和几年的实践经验。

这本富有启发性的书非常强调一种令人愉快的、直接参与的学习方法。

放手的；不干涉的；不插手的

something involves letting people do what they want and make their own decisions, without telling them what to do.
a *hands-off* style of management
The administration has opted for a *hands-off* approach to foreign exchange.

汉语中，**放手**还可用来比喻解除顾虑或限制，如：**放手**发动群众。

放手不干涉的管理方式
行政机关已经选择在外汇方面采取放手的方法。

Column 1.6

This column is adopted to help understand some metaphorical expressions of **limb** that are unique to Chinese.

碍手碍脚	be in the way
白手起家	start from scratch
膀臂	capable assistant; reliable helper; right-hand man
抱粗腿	latch on to the rich and powerful
缠手	(of a matter) be troublesome; be hard to deal with; (of an illness) be hard to cure
拔腿	leave (one's work); get away; free oneself
拔不出腿	be tied up
扯后腿	hold someone back (from action); be a drag on someone; be a hindrance to someone
赤膊上阵	go into the battle stripped to the waist—throw away all disguise
措手不及	be caught unprepared
大手大脚	wasteful
放手发动群众	go all out to mobilize the masses; fully arouse the masses
胳膊扭不过大腿	the arm is no match for the thigh—the weaker can't contend with the stronger
举手之劳	the effort of lifting the hand—a slight effort
失之交臂	just miss the person or opportunity
手忙脚乱	in a rush
手软	be irresolute when firmness is needed; be softhearted
甩手	refuse to do; wash one's hands of
缩手缩脚	shrink back in apprehension

（论点等）站不住脚；（对行为）无合理解释等	not have a leg to stand on; do not hold water
左膀右臂；左右手	a capable assistant
捉襟见肘	too many difficulties to cope with

head

1.42 Your **head** is the top part of your body that has your brain, eyes, mouth etc in it.

头；头部
汉语中类似的隐喻表达方式包括：头面人物、头目、头领、头头脑脑等。

Head is used metaphorically to refer to the leader or most important person in a group.

首领；领导人；头儿

The ceremony was attended by <u>heads</u> of government from eleven countries.

11个国家的政府首脑出席了这一典礼。

1.43 If someone **heads** or **heads up** a group or organization, he is in charge of it and is responsible for its actions.

担任（……的）主管；领导

Lord Justice Scott <u>will head</u> the inquiry.

法官斯科特大人将担任这个调查组的负责人。

You will work with the management team <u>headed up</u> by Miles Broughton.

你将与以迈尔斯·布劳顿为首的管理团队一起工作。

Column 1.7

This column is adopted to help understand some metaphorical expressions of **head** that are unique to Chinese.

出头露面	appear in the public/be in the limelight
初露头角	begin to show ability or talent
低首下心	bow and scrape
俯首贴耳	be servile
俯首听命	be at someone's beck and call
改头换面	change the appearance but not the essence; new deal
焦头烂额	in a sorry plight
老脑筋	put the clock back, old (or outmoded) way of thinking
没头没脑	without rhyme or reason
齐头并进	advance side by side

掐头去尾	break off both ends
千头万绪	thousands of strands and loose ends
头破血流	one's head covered with bumps and bruises—be badly battered
摇头摆尾	shake the head and wag the tail—assume an air of complacency or levity
摇头晃脑	sway one's head—look pleased with oneself
硬着头皮	toughen one's scalp—brace oneself
油头滑脑	smooth
晕头转向	confused and disoriented
崭露头角	begin to show one's brilliant talents

heart

1.44 Your **heart** is the organ in your chest that pumps blood around your body.
Heart is used to refer to your feelings and emotions considered as part of your character.

心；心脏
汉语中，心可用来指思想的器官和思想、感情等，如：用心、全心全意等。
感情；心底

My advice would be to follow your heart.
我给你的劝告是跟着感觉走。

Ted may not be rich but he's got a good heart.
特德可能不是很有钱，但他有一副好心肠。

She loved his brilliance and his generous heart.
她爱他的聪明和慷慨大度的秉性。

1.45 You can refer to the central part of something as its **heart**.

中心

a beautiful house deep in the heart of the English countryside
英格兰乡村深处的一座漂亮房屋

1.46 If someone **breaks** your **heart**, he makes you feel very sad and unhappy, usually because he ends a love affair or closes relationship with you.

使……心碎；使伤心

You broke my heart, Margaret, you wrecked my life.
玛格丽特，你让我伤透了心，你毁了我的生活。

1.47 If a bad situation or sad event **breaks** your **heart**, it makes you feel

使……感到痛苦；使……感到失望

extremely unhappy or disappointed.

It would <u>break</u> her <u>heart</u> to have to go away. 不得不离开会使她心碎。

living in a state of filth and disease that would <u>break</u> your <u>heart</u> 生活在会让你痛心不已的肮脏、疾病的境地之中

1.48 If your **heart goes out to** someone, you sympathize very deeply with his problems. 同情

My <u>heart goes out to</u> this compassionate man. How could anyone see him as a criminal? 我站在这个富有同情心的人一边。怎么能把他看成是罪犯呢?

Her sincerity and her unhappiness were clear and his <u>heart went out to</u> her. 她的诚意和痛苦都明明白白,他对她深表同情。

1.49 If someone has a **change of heart**, his feelings towards something change. (情感的)变化

汉语中,变心指改变原来对人或事业的爱或忠诚。

If a government or large organization has a **change of heart**, its policy towards something changes. (政策的)变化,调整

What has brought about this sudden <u>change of heart</u>? 是什么引起了这个突然的政策变化?

This is a massive <u>change of heart</u> by the German central bank which only recently put up German rates by 0.75%. 这是德国中央银行的大规模政策调整,这家银行只是在最近才增加了0.75%的德国利率。

1.50 There are several expressions using **heart** which refer to courage and determination. 勇气;决心

If you **take heart**, you become more courageous. 鼓起勇气;受到鼓舞

<u>Take heart</u>, for all is not lost. 勇敢些,并不是一切都失败了。

1.51 If you **lose heart**, you feel discouraged and lose the determination to continue what you were doing. 失去勇气;丧失信心

I think he <u>lost heart</u> after losing the first game. 我想他输了第一局后就泄气了。

1.52 If your **heart sinks**, or if you feel a **sinking** of your **heart**, something which you hear or see makes you feel very discouraged and depressed.

（某人的）心直往下沉（指突然感到担忧、苦恼或失望）

There was no sign of him, and her <u>heart sank</u>.

看不到他出现的迹象使她灰心丧气。

I felt a definite <u>sinking</u> of the <u>heart</u>.

我确实感到灰心丧气。

heart-breaking

1.53 If you describe an event or situation as **heart-breaking**, you mean that it makes you feel very sad.

使人悲伤的；令人心碎的

It's <u>heartbreaking</u> to lose a pet.

丢失宠物是件让人伤心的事。

They live in <u>heartbreaking</u> poverty.

他们生活贫困的程度令人心碎。

heart-broken

1.54 If someone is heart-broken, he is extremely sad and upset.

极度伤心的；心碎的

If anything happened to the baby you would be <u>heart-broken</u>.

要是那婴儿出了什么事，你会痛苦万分的。

There had been a row with her boyfriend, and she was <u>heart-broken</u>.

因为和男友吵了一架，她感到伤心透了。

heart-warming

1.55 Something that is **heart-warming** makes you feel happy, usually because other people are being kind.

暖人心扉的；温馨感人的

It's really <u>heart-warming</u> to see such generosity.

看到这样慷慨大方的行为真令人感动。

-hearted

1.56 **-hearted** is used with some adjectives to make adjectives describing someone's character or feeling.

（和某些形容词连用构成形容词）表示"有……性格的，有……感情的"

1.57 Someone who is **big-hearted** is kind and generous towards other people.

仁慈的；慷慨的；宽宏大量的

The <u>big-hearted</u> fighter forgave his opponent and reassured him he was not to blame for the injuries.

这位大度的斗士原谅了他的对手，他让对手放心，说自己受伤不是他的过错。

1.58 Someone who is **faint-hearted** is not brave or enthusiastic.
Our groups must be totally self-sufficient. This is not a journey for the <u>faint-hearted</u>.

怯懦的；胆怯的；冷漠的

我们的团队必须完全依靠自己。没有勇敢精神的人是无法参加这次旅行的。

1.59 If you describe an event as **half-hearted**, you mean that people are not trying their best to make it successful, or are not very interested in it.
a <u>half-hearted</u> attempt
The celebrations were rather <u>half-hearted</u>.

半心半意的；兴趣不大的；不热心的

汉语用三心二意形容犹豫不决，意志不坚定或用心不专一。

心不在焉的尝试

这些庆祝活动搞得很勉强。

1.60 If you give something **whole-hearted** support or agreement, you support or agree with it completely and enthusiastically.
We would like to express our <u>whole-hearted</u> support for the campaign.
It was a <u>whole-hearted</u> performance by an excellent team.

全心全意的

我们想表达我们对这次运动的全力支持。

这是一支优秀队伍全力以赴的表演。

Column 1.8

This column is adopted to help understand some metaphorical expressions of **heart** that are unique to Chinese.

不得人心	not enjoy popular support
粗心大意	careless
胆大心细	bold but cautious
得心应手	with facility
掉以轻心	lower one's guard
焦心	feel terribly worried
刻骨铭心	be engraved on one's bones and heart—be remembered with deep gratitude
利欲熏心	be blinded by greed

戮力同心	unite in a concerted effort
平心静气	calmly
收买人心	buy popular support
死心塌地	be dead set/be hell-bent
枉费心机	hatch plots in vain
推心置腹	repose full confidence in someone
心潮澎湃	feel an upsurge of emotion
心胆俱裂	be frightened out of one's wits
心腹之患	disease in one's vital organs—serious hidden trouble or danger
心花怒放	burst with joy
心怀鬼胎	have evil intentions
心心相印	have mutual affinity
心血来潮	be prompted by a sudden impulse
心直口快	frank and outspoken
心腹	trusted subordinate; reliable agent

lip

1.61 Your **lip** is one of the two edges that form the top and bottom parts of your mouth.

嘴唇
汉语用**唇舌**比喻言辞，如：徒费唇舌。用**唇**和**齿**的关系来比喻互相依存，如：唇齿相依、唇亡齿寒等。

You can refer to disrespectful and rude remarks that someone makes as **lip**.
Don't give me any more of your lip, Sara!

唐突无理的话

不要再这么无理地对我说话，萨拉。

nose

1.62 Your nose is the part of your face that you use for smelling and breathing.

鼻子
汉语用**被别人牵着鼻子走**比喻受制于人。用**仰人鼻息**比喻依赖别人。

If you **have a (good) nose for something**, you have the ability to find or recognize something.
He had a nose for a good news story.

善于发现某事物；对某事物很敏感

他善于发现好的新闻素材。

1.63 If something happens **under your**

就在你的面前；就在你眼皮底下

nose, it happens in a place or situation where you should notice it, but you do not.

They were dealing drugs right <u>under the noses</u> of the police. 他们就在警察的眼皮底下交易毒品。

shoulder

1.64 Your **shoulder** is one of the two parts of your body between your neck and the top of your arms.

肩；肩膀
汉语用**比肩**比喻相当、比美，如：他虽然是票友，水平却可与专业演员<u>比肩</u>。

If blame or a difficult job falls **on** someone's **shoulders**, he has to take responsibility for it.

承担重担；担当重任
比较汉语中的**挑担子**、**撂挑子**等。

She's an old, wise woman with a lot of responsibility resting <u>on her shoulders</u>.

她是位聪明的老人，肩上承担着很多责任。

The government's reforms place too great a burden <u>on the shoulders</u> of the ordinary people.

政府的改革措施在普通民众肩上压了太沉重的负担。

1.65 If you **shoulder** responsibilities, burdens etc., you deal with or accept them.

担负；承担

The government cannot ask the public to <u>shoulder</u> the extra cost.

政府不能让公众负担额外的费用。

Companies can't keep <u>shouldering</u> the burdens imposed by central government.

公司不能一直承担中央政府强加的重负。

skeleton

1.66 Your **skeleton** is the frame of your body, which supports the rest of it.

骨骼；骨架
参见 1.1, 1.15

Skeleton is used metaphorically to the basic parts of something such as a plan or organization without any details.

轮廓；梗概；提要

a <u>skeleton</u> argument

论证纲要

1.67 A **skeleton staff**, **crew**, **service** etc., is only enough workers or services to keep an operation or organization running.

最基本人员；最基本服务

We'll be operating with a <u>skeleton staff</u> until after the holidays.

我们在假期结束之前都将依靠基本员工来进行运作。

spine

1.68 Your **spine** is the row of bones down the middle of your back.
Spine is used to refer to courage.
He'll never do it —he's got no <u>spine</u>.

脊椎；脊柱
参见 1.1, 1.15
勇气；骨气
他决不会做的，他没骨气。

spineless

1.69 If you describe someone as **spineless**, you mean that you think that he lacks strength and courage, and is therefore weak and likely to be easily influenced by other people.
I feel a bit stupid and <u>spineless</u> for not having stood my ground.
<u>spineless</u> acceptance

没有勇气的；没有骨气的
参见 1.1, 1.15

我因为没有坚持自己的主张而感到有些愚蠢和怯懦。
怯懦的接受

stomach

1.70 Your **stomach** is the organ inside your body where food begins to be digested.
If you say someone **has a strong stomach**, you mean that he is able to do or eat unpleasant things without feeling ill.
You need to <u>have a strong stomach</u> to be an ambulance driver.
1.71 If you **have no stomach** for a fight, task etc., you have no desire to do it.
They <u>have no stomach</u> to fire on the demonstrators.
You've <u>never had</u> any <u>stomach for</u> fighting this man.
1.72 If you **cannot stomach** something, you cannot bear to do it or deal with it.

胃
汉语用胃口比喻对事物的兴趣或欲望，如：这工作很适合他的<u>胃口</u>。
有好胃口；有很强的承受能力
胃口还可用来比喻野心，如：侵略者的<u>胃口</u>总是很大的。

当救护车司机你一定要有很强的承受能力。
拒绝做某事；不愿做某事

他们不愿向示威者开火。

你从来不想与这个人争斗。

无法忍受；难以承受

She couldn't <u>stomach</u> the sight of him.
Losing to their rivals was difficult to <u>stomach</u>.

一看到他，她就受不了。
败给对手使他们难以承受。

tongue

1.73 Your **tongue** is the soft part inside your mouth that you can move about and use for eating and speaking.

舌头；舌
参见 1.61

Tongue is used to refer to a particular way of speaking or writing.

说话方式；写作风格

She has a rather sharp <u>tongue</u>.
I hope you've not allowed yourself to be persuaded by Laura's <u>silver tongue</u>.

她说话相当尖刻。
我希望你没被劳拉的三寸不烂之舌给说动。

1.74 You can refer to a particular language as a particular **tongue**.

语言

English was clearly not his native <u>tongue</u>.

英语显然不是他的母语。

1.75 If you **loosen someone's tongue**, you make him more willing to speak or give information.

使某人更愿意说话；使某人说出

Three-quarters of a bottle of wine had <u>loosened her tongue</u>.

喝了大半瓶酒后，她打开了话匣子。

tooth

1.76 Your **tooth** is any of the hard white objects inside your mouth that you use for biting and for chewing food. The plural form of tooth is **teeth**.

牙；牙齿
汉语用爪牙比喻坏人的党羽或帮凶，如：培植爪牙。

If a law or an organization has **teeth**, it has the power to force people to obey it.

必要的权力

The new regulations give the planning committees more <u>teeth</u>.
Since a big part of every employee's compensation is tied to achieving the standards, the system <u>has teeth</u>.

新规定赋予计划委员会更大的权力。
由于每个雇员的赔偿金的一大部分与所要达到的标准直接挂钩，因而这个制度很有效力。

Column 1.9

This column is adopted to help understand some metaphorical expressions of **lip, mouth, tongue** & **tooth** that are unique to Chinese.

不足挂齿	not worth mentioning
插嘴	interrupt; chip in
长舌	long tongue—a gossipy person; gossip-monger
费唇舌	take a lot of talking or explaining
口蜜腹剑	honey on one's lips and murder in one's heart
夸嘴（夸口）	boast; brag; talk big
快嘴	① one who readily voices his thoughts; one who is quick to articulate his ideas; a straight person ② one who has a loose tongue
伶牙俐齿	have a ready tongue
拾人牙慧	pick up phrases from someone and pass them off as one's own
耍嘴皮子	lip service
说走了嘴	a slip of the tongue
以牙还牙	an eye for an eye
油嘴滑舌	glib-tongued
爪牙	lackeys; underlings

Processes in your body

bite

1.77 If someone **bites**, he uses his teeth to cut, crush, or chew something.

咬；咬断
汉语中，咬有追赶进逼、紧跟不放的意思，如：比分<u>咬</u>得很紧。参见1.78

If something **bites**, it starts to have an unpleasant effect.
The figures show that the economic slowdown is beginning to <u>bite</u>.

产生不良影响；起坏的效果
数字表明经济发展速度放缓开始产生不良后果。

chew

1.78 If you **chew** or **chew on** particular food, you bite it several times before swallowing it.

嚼碎；咀嚼
比较汉语中的品评、品味、咬文嚼字等。

If you **chew on** something, you think about it carefully for a long time before

斟酌；仔细考虑

making a decision about it.
The investors have several economic reports to <u>chew on</u>.
1.79 If you **chew over** something, you think carefully about it for a period of time.
Officials meet regularly to <u>chew over</u> the future of the company.

投资者有几份经济报告需要仔细思考。
仔细考虑；商讨

官员们定期见面商讨公司的未来。

digest
1.80 When your stomach **digests** food, it changes it into the substances that your body needs.
If you say that you **digest** something such as news or information, you mean that after you have heard or read it, you think about it until you understand it.
He <u>will have digested</u> the news that there are to be no cash handouts.
The financial community here in Britain <u>has been digesting</u> the latest inflation figures.

消化（食物）
汉语用消化比喻理解、吸收学习的内容，如：帮助学生消化所学的东西。
理解；吸收
消化还可用来比喻自行安排解决财力、物力等，如：原料涨价后，原则上由企业消化，不许转嫁给消费者。
他将会仔细研究那条关于不准备发救济金的消息。
这里英国金融界的人士正在研究最新的通货膨胀数字。

spit
1.81 If you **spit**, you force a small amount of saliva out of your mouth.
If you **spit** or **spit out** something such as curses or insults, you say them quickly and angrily.
Politicians <u>spat</u> insults at each other during the debate.
She <u>spat out</u> threats at him.
Is that it—"money?" She <u>spat</u> the word <u>out</u>.

吐唾沫；吐痰
比较汉语中的吐口、酒后吐真言等。
快速而愤怒地说出；厉声说出

在辩论中政客们气冲冲地相互辱骂。

她大声威胁他。
说的是不是"钱"？她咬牙切齿地说出了这个字。

swallow
1.82 When you **swallow** something such as food or drink, you cause it to go from

吞下；咽下
汉语用吞吞吐吐形容说话有顾虑，不

your mouth down to your stomach.
If someone **swallows** a story or information, he seems to believe it, even though it seems to him that it is very unlikely to be true.
I found the film's ending a bit hard to swallow.
I swallowed his story because it gave me the chance to prove myself.
1.83 If someone has to **swallow** feelings he has, such as pride, anger etc., he does not show his feelings or allow them to affect the way he behaves.
He finally had to swallow his pride and ask for help.
1.84 If a company or country **is swallowed up** by a larger one, it becomes part of it and no longer exists on its own.
The company was swallowed up in a corporate merger.
1.85 If something **is swallowed up**, it disappears because something destroys, covers or hides it.
The whole building was swallowed up by flames.
Jane was soon swallowed up in the crowd.
1.86 If a lot of something such as money, time, or effort **is swallowed up**, they are used up completely.
Campaigning swallows up a lot of time without guaranteeing success.

痛快，想说又不敢说的样子。参见 1.83
相信（不太可能属实的事）

我发现这部影片的结尾有点令人难以置信。
我接受了他所说的话，因为它给了我一个证实自己的机会。
丢下（自尊）；抑制住（怒火）
比较汉语中的忍气吞声。

他最后不得不抛开面子求助。

吞并（较小的公司或国家）

这家公司在一次公司合并中被吞并了。
彻底摧毁；使消失；吞没

整幢楼被大火吞没了。

珍妮很快就消失在人群之中。
消耗，耗费（许多金钱、时间、努力等）

宣传活动消耗了许多时间，能否成功并没有保障。

2 Health and Illness

ailing
2.1 If someone is **ailing**, he is ill and weak.

生病的；体弱的
汉语用病入膏肓比喻事情到了无法挽救的程度。

An **ailing** organization or economy is not strong or successful.
The company is about to sell its <u>ailing</u> publishing division.

（组织）境况不佳的；（经济）不景气的
公司即将要出售其处境艰难的出版分公司。

anaemic
2.2 If you are **anaemic**, you are suffering from a condition called **anaemia**, which means that you do not have enough iron in your blood.

贫血的；患贫血症的

贫血（症）

Actions or processes that are **anaemic** seem weak or not effective.
Their decor was expensive but rather <u>anaemic</u>.

无力的；无效的

他们的装潢昂贵但了无生气。

The film is a competent but <u>anaemic</u> rehash of John Grisham's novel.

这部电影对约翰·格里沙姆的长篇小说的改编还算可以，但与小说相比已经大为逊色。

bruise
2.3 A **bruise** is a mark that you get on your body if you are hit or if you knock against something.

（人体受击打或碰撞后的）伤痕，青肿

If you **are bruised** by an unpleasant experience, it makes you feel unhappy or emotionally weakened.

（受到）打击；（受到）挫伤
比较汉语中的伤脑筋、伤神、造谣中伤、出口伤人等。

A spokesperson said the star <u>had been bruised</u> by the unfair reports in the

发言人说这位明星因上周媒体的不公正报道而名声受损。

press last week.
They *had been badly bruised* by the defeat.

bruising

2.4 If someone has **bruising** on his body, he has bruises on it.

Bruising is used to refer to damage to someone's reputation or confidence.

He took a *bruising* in the televised debate.

2.5 In a **bruising** battle or encounter, people fight or compete with each other in a very aggressive or determined way.

That is the crucial question in what looks set to turn into a *bruising* battle between the company and the union.

In some fundamental way, my trust in Alex had been impaired by that *bruising* interview.

cancer

2.6 **Cancer** is a serious disease in which cells in a person's body increase rapidly in an uncontrolled way, producing abnormal growths.

Cancer is used metaphorically to refer to an evil or dangerous thing that spreads quickly.

Violence is a *cancer* in our society.
the *cancer* of greed

contagion

2.7 **Contagion** is the spreading of a particular disease by someone touching another person who is already affected by the disease.

失败使他们的自信心大为受挫。

（身体的）伤痕，青肿
参见 2.3
（对名声或信心的）损伤，挫伤

他在电视辩论中被挫败。

极为费力的；十分激烈的

在这些看来肯定会转为公司和工会之间的一场两败俱伤的争斗的情况之中，这是个关键的问题。
我对阿列克斯的信任已被那次令人难堪的会面从根本上破坏了。

癌症

（危害大且难以阻止的）弊端，痼疾，社会恶习

暴力行为是我们社会的毒瘤。
贪婪的毒瘤

接触传染
汉语常用蔓延形容事物像草一样不断向周围扩展，而感染则被用来指通过语言或行为引起别人相同的思想感情。如：小说里的悲欢离合感染了读

者。参见 2.19, 2.32
（情绪或想法的）传播，蔓延

Contagion is used to refer to a situation in which feelings or ideas spread quickly from one person or place to another.

the *contagion* of ignorance that appeared to be spreading through the nation's young people

似乎在这个国家的年轻人之中蔓延的无知

the *contagion* of political extremism

政治极端主义的蔓延

contagious

2.8 A **contagious** disease spreads from one person to another through touch or through the air.

（疾病）接触传染的
参见 2.7, 2.32

A **contagious** feeling or idea spreads quickly from one person or place to another.

（情绪或想法）有感染力的

His laughter was *contagious*.

他的笑声很有感染力。

He has told me his plans and he's made a good impression on me; his enthusiasm is *contagious*.

他把他的计划告诉了我，给我留下了很好的印象，他的热情富有感染力。

cripple

2.9 **Cripple** is an offensive word for someone who is physically disabled, especially unable to walk.

残疾人；（尤指）跛子，瘸子
比较汉语中的"残存"、"残品"、"残破"等。

If you describe someone as an **emotional cripple**, you mean that he has a particular psychological or emotional problem which prevents him from living a normal life.

感情有缺陷的人

If, from my letter, you have judged me to be an *emotional cripple* who is incapable of forming normal relationships, you are wrong.

如果你根据我的信判断我是个没有能力建立正常关系而且情感不健全的人，那你错了。

2.10 If someone **is emotionally crippled** by something unpleasant that happens

（心理或情感上）受到伤害

to him, he suffers so much as a result of this that he becomes psychologically damaged in a way that stops him from understanding and expressing his emotions normally.
The horrific costs can leave couples financially devastated and <u>emotionally crippled</u>.

2.11 To **cripple** a machine, organization, or a system means to damage it severely or prevent it from working properly.
The war <u>had crippled</u> the country's economy.

这些吓人的代价可以让夫妇们经济破产，心理受到严重创伤。

严重损坏（或毁坏）

战争使该国经济陷于瘫痪。

crippling

2.12 A **crippling** illness or disability is one that severely damages your health or your body.

If you say that an action, policy, or situation has a **crippling** effect on something, you mean it has a very serious, harmful effect.
Leeds were near the bottom of Division Two and facing <u>crippling</u> debts.
In the 1950s movie theatres suffered a <u>crippling blow</u> as television sets made their way into more homes, offering entertainment at no charge.

使残疾的；（尤指）使跛的
参见 2.9

造成严重损害的；引起严重问题的

利兹联队的位置接近乙级队的垫底，它面对着将使它一蹶不振的债务。
20 世纪 50 年代，由于电视机进入越来越多的家庭，给人提供免费娱乐，电影院的业务遭受了致命的打击。

cure

2.13 A **cure** is a medicine or treatment that makes someone who is ill become healthy.

Cure is used metaphorically to refer to a solution to a problem.
It's the only possible <u>cure</u> for our chronic trade deficit.

（有效的）药，疗法
汉语用**灵丹妙药**比喻能解决一切问题的办法。
对策；解决方案

这是解决我们长期贸易赤字唯一可行的对策。

Tax cuts are not the <u>miracle cure</u> the Right seems to think.

2.14 If doctors or medical treatments **cure** an illness or injury, they cause it to end or disappear.

If someone or something **cures** a problem, he brings it to an end.

Better quality control might <u>cure</u> our production problems.

2.15 If an action or event **cures** someone of a habit or an attitude, it makes him stop having it.

Nothing seemed to <u>cure</u> him of his nervousness.

减税并非如右翼人士认为的那样是灵丹妙药。

治愈

汉语用**对症下药**比喻针对具体情况采取解决问题的相应措施。

解决

更好的质量管理可能会解决我们的生产问题。

控制，消除（不良的习惯、情感或态度）

好像什么都没法消除他的紧张。

deadly

2.16 If something is **deadly**, it is likely or able to cause someone's death, or has already caused someone's death.

Deadly is used metaphorically to emphasize an unpleasant or undesirable quality.

A <u>deadly</u> silence followed her announcement.

It started as a joke, but soon they were fighting in <u>deadly</u> earnest.

The broadcast was accurate and reliable but <u>deadly</u> dull.

致死的；致命的

汉语用**致命**来形容后果极其严重，如：酗酒是司机的**致命**弱点。

彻底的；十足的

汉语中，**死**也可表示达到极点，如：高兴**死**了、笑**死**人了。

她宣布之后一片死寂。

这开始时是个玩笑，但很快他们就真的打起架来。

广播新闻是准确可靠的，但是它没有任何趣味。

disease

2.17 A **disease** is an illness that affects people or animal.

You may refer to a serious problem in society or someone's attitude as a **disease**.

Greed is a <u>disease</u> of modern society.

I have yet to meet a single American

病；疾病

汉语中，**病**可用来比喻痛苦或不幸，如：同**病**相怜。

（社会的）弊病；（人的态度的）不健康

贪婪是现代社会的恶疾。

我至今还没有见过一个想当然地认为

who automatically thinks any foreign product must be better than his own. The *disease* seems to be uniquely British.

外国货要比本国货好的美国人。这个毛病似乎是英国人特有的。

dissect

2.18 If someone **dissects** the body of a dead person or animal, he carefully cuts it up in order to examine it scientifically.
If someone **dissects** something such as a theory, a situation, or a piece of writing, he considers and talks about each detail of it.
Her latest novel *was dissected* by the critics.

解剖
比较汉语中的剖析、鞭辟入里、入木三分、细致入微。
仔细研究；详细评论；剖析

评论家对她最近出版的一部小说作了详细剖析。

epidemic

2.19 An **epidemic** is a situation in which a disease spreads very quickly and infects many people.
Epidemic is used metaphorically to refer to a sudden increase in something bad or unpleasant that affects many people.
An *epidemic* of petty crime has hit the area.

（疾病的）传播，流行
汉语用泛滥比喻某种有害事物的广泛传播。
（坏事的突然）盛行，泛滥
参见2.7

该地区的小案件已经泛滥成灾。

fatal

2.20 A **fatal** accident or illness causes someone's death.
A **fatal** action has very undesirable effects.
The recession has proved *fatal* to many businesses.
The sudden resignations dealt a *fatal* blow to the government.
Yesterday's report highlighted *fatal* flaws in the system.

致命的；致死的
参见2.16
毁灭性的；灾难性的

经济萧条对许多企业来说是灾难性的。
这些人突然辞职给了政府致命的一击。
昨天的报告强调指出了这个系统的致命缺陷。

I made the <u>fatal</u> mistake of falling in love with her.

我犯了个严重的错误，就是爱上了她。

fester

2.21 If an injury or sore place on your body **festers**, it becomes infected.

化脓；溃烂
参见 2.1

If a problem or unpleasant feeling **festers**, it becomes worse because no one has dealt with it.

（问题）恶化；（怨恨）郁积

This <u>festering</u> hatred could tear the community apart.

这种不断郁积的怨恨能够使社会分裂。

fever

2.22 If you have a **fever**, the temperature of your body is very high and you feel ill.

发烧；发热
比较汉语中的**疯狂、狂热**。
参见 17.6

Fever is used metaphorically to refer to strong excitement and enthusiasm that affects a lot of people.

激动不安；高度兴奋；狂热

The whole country was in the grip of election <u>fever</u>.

全国掀起了选举热潮。

feverish

2.23 If you are **feverish**, you are suffering from a fever.

发烧的；发热的
参见 2.22, 17.6

Feverish is used metaphorically to describe something such as an activity or emotion that is extremely excited.

特别激动的；极度兴奋的；狂热的

There was a lot of <u>feverish</u> activity backstage.

有许多秘密进行的狂热活动。

headache

2.24 A **headache** is a pain in your head.

头痛
汉语用**头痛**比喻感到为难或厌恶。

You may refer to something that causes you a lot of problems as a **headache**.

麻烦事；令人头痛的事

Parking is a major <u>headache</u> in this part of town.

在镇里的这个地区停放车辆是件麻烦事。

Financial problems have been a

财政问题一直是令中心主任们头痛的

constant <u>headache</u> for the Centre's directors.

health

2.25 **Health** is the condition of your body, especially whether or not you are ill.

The **health** of something such as an organization or a system is its success and the fact that it is working well.

A corporation's annual report supposedly presents a clear, precise picture of the financial status or <u>health</u> of the company.

healthy

2.26 Someone who is **healthy** is well and is not suffering from any illness.

If you describe something as **healthy**, you mean that it works well and is likely to continue to be successful.

The country still has a <u>healthy</u> rural economy.

The car industry isn't looking very <u>healthy</u> at the moment.

2.27 A **healthy** amount of money is a large amount of it.

Last year the company made a <u>healthy</u> profit of over five million pounds.

2.28 A **healthy** attitude is good and sensible.

The children had been brought up with a <u>healthy</u> respect for books.

hurt

2.29 If something **hurts** you, it causes you pain. If a part of your body **hurts**, you feel pain there.

问题。

健康（状况）
比较汉语中的平稳、稳健。

发达；兴旺

一家公司的年度报告应该是展示这家公司财务状况的一幅清楚、精确的图画。

健康的；健壮的
参见2.25
兴旺发达的

这个国家的农村经济依旧繁荣。

目前的汽车业似乎不是非常兴旺。

（资金）相当多的，数额大的

去年该公司实现了500多万英镑的可观利润。

（态度）健康的，有益身心的

孩子们从小就养成了尊重书本的健康态度。

（使）疼痛；（使）受伤；感到疼痛
参见2.3

You can say that something **hurts** someone or something when it has a bad effect on him or prevents him from succeeding.
The weakness of the dollar has <u>hurt</u> car sales.

危害；损害

ill

2.30 Someone who is **ill** is suffering from a disease or a health problem.

不健康的；有病的
参见 2.1

You can use **ill** in front of some nouns to indicate that you are referring to something harmful or unpleasant.

坏的；有害的；糟糕的

Their defeat was mainly due to their <u>ill-discipline</u>.

他们的失败主要归咎于他们纪律不严。

The fish didn't taste fresh, but we suffered no <u>ill</u> effects.

那鱼尝起来不新鲜，但我们没有不良反应。

Bouts of <u>ill</u> temper punctuated the match.

一次次的发脾气使比赛不时中断。

ills

2.31 Difficulties and problems are sometimes referred to as **ills**.

问题；困难
参见 2.1

A change of government is regarded as the cure for all the nation's <u>ills</u>.

更换政府被认为是解决该国所有难题的良方。

infectious

2.32 An **infectious** disease is one that can spread from one person to another.

（疾病）传染性的
参见 2.7, 2.19

Feelings or ways of behaving that are **infectious** make other people feel the same or behave in the same way.

（心情、行动）有感染力的，有影响力的

His enthusiasm was <u>infectious</u>.

他的热情很有感染力。

inject

2.33 To **inject** someone with a substance such as a medicine, or to inject it into him, means to use a needle and a syringe to put it into his body.

注射
比较汉语中的**倾注**，如：毕生精力倾注于教育事业。

If you **inject** a new, exciting, or interesting quality into a situation, you add it.
Young designers are injecting new life into the fashion scene.
She tried to inject confidence into her voice.
2.34 If you **inject** money or resources into a business or organization, you provide more money or resources for it.
They may sell the property to inject cash into the business.

jaundiced

2.35 **Jaundice** is an illness which makes your skin and eyes turn yellow.
Someone who has a **jaundiced** view of something is unenthusiastic about it, often because he is tired or has had discouraging experiences.
She took a rather jaundiced view of Christmas shopping.

lame

2.36 A **lame** animal cannot walk very well because its leg or foot is damaged.

A **lame** excuse, explanation etc. is difficult to believe because it seems so unlikely.
It sounds a lame excuse, but I never seem to have time to visit.
2.37 **Lame** can also be used metaphorically to talk about something that is boring or not very good.
Saturday's game was rather a lame performance.

注入；增添

年轻的设计师们为时装界注入了新的活力。

她努力想使自己说起话来自信些。

注入（资金）

他们可能会变卖财产来为企业注入现金。

黄疸（病）

不满的；厌恶的；有偏见的

她对圣诞购物带有相当大的偏见。

（动物）跛的，瘸的
汉语用蹩脚来形容质量不好、本领不强、水平不高，如：文章写得很蹩脚。
（借口、辩解等）站不住脚的，理由不充分的，无说服力的

这个借口听起来好像很牵强，但看起来我压根就没有时间去。
差劲的；拙劣的

周六的比赛简直就是一场拙劣的表演。

limp

2.38 If someone **limps**, he walks in a slow and awkward way because he has hurt or injured one or both of his legs.
If you say that something such as an activity or a process **limps along**, or **limps**, you mean that it continues to exist or function, but with obvious difficulty.
The yacht is limping towards the island.
The council will have to limp along until fresh elections can be organized.

一瘸一拐地走；跛行
比较汉语中的挣扎。

艰难地移动；艰难地继续生存
游艇挣扎着驶向岛屿。
在新的选举进行之前该委员会将不得不艰难地支撑下去。

pain

2.39 **Pain** is the feeling that you have in a part of your body when you are hurt or become ill.
You can refer to feelings of great unhappiness as **pain**.
Dealing with the subject sensitively can help prevent a lot of pain.
The incident must have caused my parents great pain.

痛；疼痛
汉语用痛痒比喻紧要的事情，如：不关痛痒。参见2.60
痛苦；悲痛
谨慎对待这个话题有助于防止许多痛苦。
这个事件一定已经给我的父母带来了巨大的痛苦。

2.40 If you **take pains** to do something or **go to great pains** to do something, you try hard to do it, because you think it is important to do it.
I had taken great pains to make the evening perfect.
She always takes great pains with her lectures.

煞费苦心；非常努力
汉语中，痛有尽情、彻底之意，如：痛饮、痛歼等。比较汉语中的痛改前非、痛下决心。
为了使这个晚会尽善尽美，我已经是竭尽全力。
她总是煞费苦心地仔细备课。

2.41 If something **pains** you, it makes you feel very upset or unhappy.
It was clear the subject pained him.
It pains her to think that they would never talk to each other again.

使痛苦；使苦恼
显然这个问题使他感到很苦恼。
一想到他们将再也不能交谈，她感到十分痛苦。

2 Health and Illness

painful
2.42 If part of your body is **painful**, you feel pain there.
Situation, memories, or experiences that are **painful** are difficult and unpleasant to deal with.
He sobbed as he relived the painful memory.
His autobiography recounts the unique and painful experience of imprisonment.
2.43 If a performance or interview is **painful**, it is so bad that it makes you feel embarrassed for the people taking part in it.
His performance was painful to watch.

疼痛的
参见 2.39, 2.40
痛苦的；羞愧的

当再度体验那痛苦的回忆时，他啜泣不止。

他的自传记述了在狱中那段绝无仅有的痛苦经历。

令人难堪的

他的表演简直惨不忍睹。

paralyse
2.44 If someone **is paralysed** by an accident or an illness, he loses the ability to move his body or part of it.
If a person, place, or organization **is paralysed** by something, he/it becomes unable to act or function.
A railway strike would have paralysed the country.

使瘫痪；使麻痹

汉语用**瘫痪**比喻机构失灵，不能正常运转，处于停顿状态，如：交通瘫痪。
使陷入瘫痪；使无法正常运转

一次铁路工人大罢工会使整个国家陷入瘫痪。

paralysis
2.45 **Paralysis** is the loss of the ability to move your body or part of it, usually because of an injury or illness.
You may refer to the state of being completely unable to operate normally or effectively as **paralysis**.
the paralysis currently affecting the government

（通常因受伤或疾病而引起的）瘫痪（症）
参见 2.44
瘫痪状态；停顿

当前影响政府的瘫痪状态

rash
2.46 A **rash** is an area of small red spots

皮疹

on your skin, caused by an illness or an allergic reaction to something you have touched, eaten etc.

You can refer to a number of similar things that happen around the same time as **a rash of** those things.

Local police are investigating *a rash of burglaries* in the area.

（短时出现的）大量同类事物（尤指令人不快的事物）

当地警察正在调查发生在该地区的多起入室盗窃案。

scar

2.47 A **scar** is a permanent mark on your skin where you have been injured.

Scar is used metaphorically to refer to a permanent effect on someone's mind, caused by an unpleasant experience he has had.

She bore the <u>scars</u> of an unhappy childhood.

2.48 If an unpleasant experience **scars** someone, it has a permanent effect on the way he thinks and lives.

emotionally <u>scarred</u>

Their lives <u>were scarred</u> by poverty and illness.

伤疤；疤痕；伤痕
参见 2.39, 2.60
（精神）创伤

汉语用**烙印**比喻不易磨灭的痕迹或深刻地留下印象，如时代烙印；这些生动的艺术形象，将烙印在广大观众的心头。

她承受着不幸童年所造成的创伤。

在（精神上）留下创伤

感情上受伤的
他们的生活饱受贫穷和疾病的磨难。

sick

2.49 If you are **sick**, you do not feel well.

If you say you are **sick of** something, you are emphasizing that you are very annoyed by it and want it to stop.

I'm <u>sick of</u> the way you've treated me.
We're <u>sick of</u> waiting around like this.

2.50 If something that someone does or says is **sick**, it is so unpleasant that it would upset some people.

（感觉）不适的，生病的

（对……）厌倦的，厌烦的，厌恶的
比较汉语中的腻味。

你对待我的那一套我都烦了。
这么等来等去，我们感到很腻味。

令人恶心的；令人作呕的

sick humour
令人恶心的幽默

2.51 A **sick** organization, company, or economy has a lot of serious problems, especially financial problems.
有问题的；遇到困难的

In 1920 the country was one of the world's biggest debtors and had a sick economy, without relief it cured itself, repaid the debts and can now raise foreign capital.
1920年这个国家曾是世界上最大的债务国之一，经济问题不少；在没有援助的情况下它后来自己解决了问题，还清了债务。现在它已能筹集外资了。

The fact is that sick companies can't afford to do this.
事实是问题百出的公司没有做这件事的实力。

sickness

2.52 The noun **sickness** can be used with the same meanings as sick.
问题；疾患
参见2.1

He has been at the centre of politics for too long to escape responsibility for the state's deeper sickness.
他在政治中处身得太久了，因此他逃脱不了对这个国家更深层次的问题所应该担负的责任。

He told her that her belief was part of a general sickness of the modern mind, a sickness that was also producing fascism.
他对她说，她的信念是现代思维的普遍疾患中的一个部分，这个疾患也正在导致法西斯主义的产生。

symptom

2.53 A **symptom** of an illness is something wrong with your body or mind that is a sign of the illness.
症状
参见2.14

A **symptom** of a bad situation is something that happens which is considered to be a sign of this situation.
迹象，征兆，征候
比较汉语中的征兆、兆头、苗头等。

The fighting is a symptom of growing insecurity in the region.
这次争斗是该地区越来越缺乏安全保障的征兆。

symptomatic

2.54 If something is **symptomatic** of an illness, it is a physical sign that someone has that illness.
显露症状的；症状性的
参见2.14

If you say that something is
表明（有问题或不好的情况）的；作

symptomatic of a problem or a bad situation, you mean that it is a sign that that bad problem or bad situation exists.
The dispute is <u>symptomatic</u> of tensions that exist within the union.

syndrome
2.55 A **syndrome** is a medical condition that has a particular set of effects on your body or mind.
You can refer to an undesirable condition that is characterized by a particular type of activity or behaviour as a **syndrome**.
Many parents face "empty nest <u>syndrome</u>" when their children leave home.
If we look at history, what has happened at NATO is not unusual; I call it the rearview mirror <u>syndrome</u>.

unhealthy
2.56 An **unhealthy** person is ill or not physically fit.
If you describe a situation as **unhealthy**, you think that it is not normal or desirable and that it is likely to have bad effects.
There are many who feel that it is <u>unhealthy</u> for a nation to carry on constantly electing the same party.
2.57 An **unhealthy** business or economy does not make a lot of money.
The enforced reduction of skilled and experienced workers is a clear sign of an <u>unhealthy</u> economy.

为……征兆的

这次争论表明了联合会内部的紧张关系。

综合症状；综合征
参见2.14

（在某种情况下的）一系列情绪（或举动）

许多父母亲在自己的孩子离开家门后体验到人去楼空的失落情绪。

如果我们回顾一下历史，北大西洋公约组织所发生的事情就不是反常的了；我把它称为后视镜综合征。

有病的；不健康的
参见2.1
不正常的，有害的

有许多人感到，老是选举同一个政党执政，这样下去对一个国家没有好处。

（企业或经济）不景气的

对有经验的技术工人的强制性裁减是一种不良经济的明显的征兆。

wound

2.58 A **wound** is an injury in which your skin or flesh is damaged, usually seriously.

伤；伤口
参见 2.3, 2.39, 2.40

Wound is used metaphorically to talk about emotional damage caused by something bad that happens.

（感情上的）创伤，伤害

The party had never healed the <u>wounds</u> left by the crisis.

该政党一直都没能治愈危机留下的创伤。

2.59 If someone **licks** his **wounds**, he tries to recover from a hurtful or damage experience, usually by going somewhere quiet by himself.

治愈创伤；恢复；舔舐伤口

She would go home for the weekend: she would retreat and <u>lick</u> her <u>wounds</u> a little.

她将回家去度周末：她要退避几天，让心灵的创伤能够有所恢复。

2.60 To **reopen** or **open (old) wounds** means to make someone remember something bad that happened in the past.

揭旧伤疤

汉语用**好了伤疤忘了痛**来比喻境遇好了，就忘了过去的苦楚。

To condemn him publicly would <u>reopen</u> <u>wounds</u> within the party.

公开指责他将会重揭党内的旧伤疤。

2.61 **Wound** is also used metaphorically to talk about hurting someone's feelings by doing or saying something unpleasant.

（在感情上）使受创伤，伤害

It was a remark that <u>had</u> deeply <u>wounded</u> him.

那是一句深深刺伤了他的话。

A string of rejections <u>had</u> really <u>wounded</u> his pride.

一连串的拒绝确实伤害了他的自尊。

Column 2

This column is adopted to help understand some metaphorical expressions of **health & medicine** that are unique to Chinese.

| 边患 | trouble on the frontier (as caused by foreign invasion) |
| 好了伤疤忘了疼 | forget the pain once the wound is healed—forget the bitter past when released from one's suffering |

换汤不换药	the same medicine with a different name—the same old stuff with a different label; a change in form but not in content (or essence)
祸患	disaster; calamity
急性病	impetuosity
旧病复发	relapse into one's old bad habits; slip back into one's bad old ways
输血	give aid and support; bolster up; give someone a shot in the arm
痛痒	① sufferings; difficulties ② (usu. used in negative sense) importance; consequence
头痛医头，脚痛医脚	treat the head when the head aches, treat the foot when the foot hurts—treat the symptoms but not the disease; take stopgap measures; apply palliative remedies
无病呻吟	adopt a sentimental pose (in writing or speech)
心腹之患	disease in one's vital organs—danger from within; serious hidden trouble or danger
包治百病	be guaranteed to cure all ills
病急乱投医	try anything or consult anybody when in a desperate plight
病入膏肓	beyond cure
不可救药	hopeless
不治之症	incurable disease
对症下药	prescribe the right remedy for an illness
旧病复发	have a relapse
灵丹妙药	panacea
手到病除	illness departs at a touch of the hand
药石之言	unpalatable but salutary advice
治标	effect a temporary cure; merely alleviate the symptoms of an illness
治本	effect a permanent cure; tackle a problem etc. at its root
治病救人	cure the sickness to save the patient; help someone mend his or her ways

3 Animals

General words for animals

General words for animals

3.1 Words such as **animal**, **beast**, and **brute** are often used as metaphors to talk about the way people behave, by suggesting that their behavior is more like that of an animal than a person. These words are often, but not always, used in this way showing disapproval.

禽兽，畜生
汉语中，用<u>禽兽</u>、<u>畜生</u>来比喻行为卑鄙恶劣的人。如：衣冠<u>禽兽</u>、<u>禽兽</u>行为、人面<u>兽</u>心。

animal

3.2 If you say that someone is an **animal**, you mean the person behaves in a very violent, cruel, or rude way.

动物
汉语中，与 animal 相对应的词是**动物**，用作中性词，泛指生物的一大类，不带有褒贬义。
那人是畜生。

That man is an <u>animal</u>.

乐于从事某项活动的人

3.3 If you refer to someone as a particular kind of **animal**, you mean that he enjoys that kind of activity and that he is very naturally very good at it.

I know how to deal with James, but Michael is a different <u>animal</u>.
a political/social <u>animal</u>

我知道怎样对付詹姆斯，但迈克尔是不同类型的人。
政治/社会人物

3.4 **Animal passions** or **animal instincts** are very strong feelings or instincts, such as strong sexual feelings, that are associated with your senses and instincts rather than with your

非常强烈的感觉或本能

personality or intelligence.
Newman lay back on the bed. It had been sheer <u>animal passion</u>.
Like all great discoveries, I locate it by pure <u>animal instinct</u>.

纽曼又躺到床上。这已经纯粹是动物的本能了。
就像所有伟大的发现一样，我也是靠了纯粹的动物本能找到它的。

beast

3.5 **Beast** is an animal, especially a dangerous or strong one.
Beast can be used metaphorically to talk about a cruel or immoral person, especially one who behaves in a violent or sexual way.
They hate that <u>beast</u> of a foreman.

动物，兽
汉语中，兽比喻野蛮，如：兽行。
粗野凶残的人；道德败坏的人；淫荡的人

他们恨那畜生般的工头。

3.6 **Beast** can also be used to refer to something with a particular quality.
The music business is an unpredictable <u>beast</u>.
The US cinema audience is a very different <u>beast</u>.

有（某种特性）的东西

音乐界的发展真是不可预测。

美国的电影观众欣赏口味很不一样。

3.7 **Beast** can also be used as a friendly, affectionate way of referring to someone, usually a man or boy, who you know very well, if he has been a little silly or bad.
I know he was a grumpy little <u>beast</u>, but I loved him.

（以友好亲热的方式称呼对方）小鬼，家伙

我知道他是个脾气坏的小家伙，但我爱他。

beastly

3.8 In expressing disapproval, **beastly** can be a very strong word, which means "of, like, or characteristic of a beast."
the <u>beastly</u> behavior of the aggressors

野兽般的；野蛮的；贪欲的

侵略者的残暴行为

3.9 **Beastly** means very unpleasantly. This is an old-fashioned word, used in informal spoken English.
"The main reason why I'm not married

令人不快的；讨厌的

"我不结婚的主要原因是因为男人对

is because men are in general so utterly *beastly* to women," she said.

女人一般都极为粗鲁，"她说。

brute

3.10 A **brute** is a big strong animal.

（大而强壮的）兽

Brute can be used metaphorically to talk about a strong man who acts in a cruel or violent way.

残暴的人，粗野的人

That is why society must be protected from brutes like him.

这就是为什么必须保护社会使之免受他那样的禽兽侵扰的原因。

3.11 **Brute force** or **brute strength** refers to strength that is purely physical, rather than power that comes from intelligence or skill.

蛮力

He stresses that his sport is very much a test of skill and technique rather than brute strength.

他强调说自己的运动项目更注重技巧和技术，单靠蛮力是不行的。

Pets

pet

3.12 A **pet** is an animal or bird that you keep in your home for pleasure. **Pet** is used metaphorically to refer to someone you give special treatment to because you like him more than others.

宠物

汉语用宠儿比喻受到宠爱的人，如：时代的宠儿。

宠儿；得宠的人

She's the teacher's pet.

她是那老师的得意门生。

3.13 A **pet theory** or **project** is one which someone strongly believes in and supports.

特别钟爱、倾心的理论或工程

Getting kids to do more sport is one of his pet projects.

让孩子们多做些运动是他最喜爱的事情之一。

a chance to expound her pet theory about men

一个阐述她关于男人的一贯主张的机会

cat

3.14 If a woman is said to be a **cat**, she

心地恶毒的女人；爱说人坏话的女人

makes spiteful remarks.
Mrs. Smith is a perfect <u>cat</u>.　　史密斯太太是个地地道道的长舌妇。

3.15 Cat is used metaphorically in the expression **fat cat** to talk about people who are lazy or greedy. If someone refers to successful business people as fat cats, he disapproves of them because he thinks that they are making too much profit for themselves, and not giving enough money to their workers or to the government.　　懒惰而且贪婪的人

foreign exchange <u>fat cats</u> making a fortune at the expense of others　　损人而发财的做外汇生意的大亨们

3.16 "**Has the cat got your tongue?**"　　猫把你的舌头叼去了？你为什么不吭声？

3.17 If you **let the cat out of the bag**, you tell someone something that was intended to be secret.　　泄露秘密

He has <u>let the cat out of the bag</u> about the government's true intentions.　　他已经把政府的真实意图泄露出去了。

3.18 If someone is **like a cat on hot bricks**, the person is unable to stay still or concentrate for being nervous or worried.　　局促不安
汉语中类似意义的隐喻可用**热锅上的蚂蚁、如坐针毡**等来表达。

You are like <u>a cat on hot bricks</u> today. What's wrong?　　看你今天一副局促不安的样子，出了什么事了？

3.19 If someone is **like the cat that got the cream**, the person is very pleased about something achieved.　　（对取得的成就）心满意足，得意洋洋；沾沾自喜

3.20 If you **look like something the cat dragged**, you have a very dirty or untidy appearance.　　不修边幅；十分邋遢

3.21 If you **put** or **set the cat among the pigeon**s, you cause trouble by doing or saying something.　　（言行）引起麻烦，惹出乱子

3.22 Still there are several other expressions associated with **cat** widely used in English, including both metaphors and metonymies as listed below.

(1) be the **cat's** whiskers/pajamas
(2) by a **whisker**
(3) a **cat-and-dog** life
(4) a **cat** in hell's chance (of doing something)
(5) no room to swing a **cat**
(6) **play cat and mouse** or **play a cat-and-mouse game with someone**
(7) wait for the **cat** to jump/to see which way the **cat** jumps
(9) **cat** burglar

(10) **cat's** paw
(11) bell the **cat**
(12) have a **catnap**
(13) a **copycat**
(14) When the **cat** is away, the mice will play.

关于猫的其他隐喻表达方式举例

了不起的东西、人、主意等
以细微之差
（在一起居住者）经常吵架的生活
一点儿机会也没有

没有生活、工作等的足够空间
欲擒故纵；对某人时好时坏、忽冷忽热
待情况明朗后再采取行动或做出决定
（沿墙壁或水管潜入屋内的）小偷，飞贼
被人利用做冒险或厌恶事情的人
系铃猫颈；为大家的利益承担风险
打盹
模仿者，仿效者
山中无老虎，猴子称霸王

catty

3.23 If you say that someone, especially a woman, is **catty**, you mean that she enjoys saying cruel or unpleasant things about other people.

a *catty* remark
a *catty* women

恶毒的；恶意的；刁钻刻薄的

尖酸刻薄的话
尖嘴毒舌搬弄是非的女人

kitten

3.24 A **kitten** is a young cat. **Kitten** is used metaphorically to talk about women who are considered to be very sexually attractive and who flirt a lot.

小猫
汉语中，往往以**狐狸**喻指妖媚迷人的女子，含贬义，如：狐狸精、狐媚等。

Sharon Stone admits she has to fight against being typecast as a blonde sex <u>kitten</u>.

3.25 If you **have kittens**, you get to be very nervous, worried, or upset.

She was <u>having kittens</u> because it was very late and her daughter wasn't home yet.

莎伦·斯通承认，她不得不尽力摆脱性感金发女郎的固定形象。

心慌意乱；焦虑不安

她心中非常焦急不安，因为时间已经很晚了而她女儿还没回家。

kittenish

3.26 If you say that a woman's behavior is **kittenish**, you mean that she flirts with men in a playful and youthful way.

She was over forty, but still <u>kittenish</u>.

（忸怩或卖弄风情地）嬉耍的

她已年过四十，却还是忸怩作态，搔首弄姿。

pussy

3.27 A **pussy** is a cat, used especially by children.

Pussy can be metaphorically used as an insulting word for a man who is not strong, brave or determined.

猫咪（尤为儿语）

（指男子）脓包

pussyfoot

3.28 You are said to **pussyfoot** when you move with stealth or caution, like a cat. **Pussyfoot** is used metaphorically to describe a person who is shy from a definite commitment or from taking a firm stand.

Put that story into words and don't <u>pussyfoot around</u> with it.

蹑手蹑脚

抱骑墙态度；持暧昧态度；观望；缩手缩脚

把那事写出来，不要犹豫不决。

Column 3.1

This column is adopted to help understand some metaphorical expressions of **cat** that are unique to Chinese.

阿猫阿狗	people of small importance; Tom, Dick and Harry
猫哭老鼠	the cat weeping over the dead mouse—shed crocodile tears
夜猫子	a person who goes to bed late; night owl
醉猫儿	drunken cat—a person acting oddly under the influence of liquor

dog

3.29 **Dogs** are very common pets in Britain and the United States and are generally considered to be friendly, affectionate, and loyal animals. However, when **dog** is used as a metaphor, it is nearly always used for negative things.
Nobody but a <u>dog</u> would evict his own mother.

3.30 Some people use **dog** to refer to something that is of bad quality or very unsuccessful.
He said the car was an absolute <u>dog</u> to drive.
I invested in an Internet start-up but it turned out to be a real <u>dog</u>.

3.31 If you say that a situation is **dog eat dog**, you mean that people involved compete very hard and will do anything to be successful.
We all have to make a living and there's no point in having a <u>dog-eat-dog</u> attitude.

3.32 **A dog in the manager** is someone who does not want or need something, but will not let other people have it.
He is <u>a real dog in the manager</u>—even though he doesn't have a car he won't let anyone else use his garage.

狗
狗，汉语中又做犬，用来比喻忠于主子的奴才或帮助作恶的人，如：<u>犬</u>马之劳、走<u>狗</u>等等。
不好的（人或事物）

只有禽兽一般的人才会把亲生母亲逐出家门。
劣质的东西；蹩脚货；失败

他说那辆汽车开起来绝对是蹩脚货。

我曾投资开了一家小型因特网公司，但最后血本无归。
残酷无情的竞争

汉语用<u>狗咬狗</u>比喻坏人之间互相倾轧、斗争。

我们大家都得谋生，采取互相攻击的态度是没有意义的。

占马槽的狗；占着茅坑不拉屎的人

他真是占着茅坑不拉屎的人：自己没有汽车，却又不让别人用他的车库。

3.33 If you say something is **a dog's dinner**, you mean it is very untidy or badly done. 一团糟

3.34 **Every dog has its day** is used for saying that everyone will have a time during their life when they are important, lucky, or successful. 人人皆有得意时；风水轮流转

3.35 **Give a dog a bad name** is used for saying that once someone has a bad reputation, people will blame him for everything. 人言可畏；坏名声洗刷不掉

3.36 If a place or organization is **going to the dogs**, it is not as good as it was in the past. （指组织、机构等）一蹶不振，不复往日之盛，大不如前

According to some pessimists, the country is going to the dogs. 按照某些悲观者的看法，那个国家正在衰亡。

3.37 If you **help a lame dog over a stile**, you do someone a great favor. 帮助某人渡过难关；雪中送炭

3.38 A **top dog** is the best, most important or most powerful person, often the winner in a competition. 最佳者；要人；当权者；（常指竞赛的）优胜者

3.39 An **underdog** is a person, team, or group that seems least likely to win a game, competition, election etc. However, **underdog** is used metaphorically to talk about a person or group that has very little money, or social status. （比赛或选举等中）处于劣势的人（或一方），可能失败的人（或一方）

弱者，弱势群体

3.40 **A dog's life** is not fair and is full of troubles. 悲惨的生活；猪狗不如的日子

3.41 **You can't teach an old dog new tricks** is used when it is very difficult to make someone who is conservative do something in a new way. 很难让因循守旧的人接受新事物

3.42 Still there are several other expressions associated with **dog** widely 关于狗的其他隐喻表达方式举例

used in English, including both metaphors and metonymies as listed below.

(1) **dog**-eared	（指书）翻旧而页角折卷的
(2) **dog**-trot	（从容的）小跑
(3) take a hair of the **dog** that bit you	以毒攻毒；以酒解酒
(4) **dog's** life	悲惨境况；痛苦的日子
(5) wake a sleeping **dog**	惹是生非；惹麻烦
(6) **dog**-tired	累极，疲惫之至
(7) hang-**dog** look	卑鄙的模样
(8) not have a **dog's** chance	毫无机会；绝无可能
(9) put on the **dog**	炫耀；摆阔
(10) a gay **dog**	喜欢玩乐的人
(11) a surly **dog**	性情乖戾的人
(12) a dumb **dog**	沉默不语的人
(13) a dirty **dog**	坏蛋
(14) die a **dog's** death	死得可鄙或可悲
(15) A living **dog** is better than a dead lion.	好死不如赖活着
(16) **Dog** does not eat **dog**.	同类不相残，同室不操戈，虎毒不食子
(17) Better be the head of **dog** than the tail of lion/better be a bird's beak than a cow's rump.	宁为鸡口，毋为牛后
(18) Love me, love my **dog**.	爱屋及乌
(19) straw **dogs**	替罪羊
(20) work like a **dog**	拼命工作；苦干

3.43 If someone **is dogged** by something unpleasant, or if it dogs him, the unpleasant thing affects him for a long period of time. （被）困扰，（被）折磨

He has been dogged by persistent back problems. 他一直以来都被背痛所困扰。

3.44 As a verb, **dog** is also used metaphorically to talk about following 跟踪，尾随

closely, usually in an annoying way.
*Photographers **dogged** the princess all her adult life.*

公主成年后一直有摄影记者追踪拍摄。

dogged

3.45 If you describe people's character or action as **dogged**, you mean that they are determined to achieve something and continuing to try despite difficulties.
*Their success was due to the **dogged** determination of their coach.*

坚持不懈的；顽强的

他们的成功要归功于他们教练的顽强决心。

Column 3.2

This column is added to help understand some metaphorical expressions of **dog** that are unique to Chinese.

白云苍狗	white clouds change into grey dogs—the changes in human affairs often take freakish forms
打落水狗	beat a drowning dog—completely crush a defeated enemy
落水狗	dog in the water—a bad person who is drown
狗胆包天	monstrously audacious
狗拿耗子，多管闲事	a dog trying to catch mice—poke one's nose into other people's business
狗皮膏药	dog skin plaster—quack medicine
狗屁不通	unreadable rubbish
狗头军师	inept adviser
狗尾续貂	a dog's tail joined to sable—a wretched sequel to a fine work
狗血喷头	let loose a stream of abuse against sb.
狗眼看人低	be a bloody snob
关门打狗	bolt the door and beat the dog—block the enemy's retreat and then destroy him
看家狗	watchdog—a person who takes care of the affairs and property of a landlord, high official, etc.
丧家之犬	a stray cur

bitch

3.46 A **bitch** is a female dog. Bitch is an

（侮辱性用语）坏女人；淫妇；狗婆

insulting word when it is used metaphorically to talk about a rude or cruel woman.
娘

You are putting the men down and they don't like it, they think you are a <u>bitch</u>.
你是在当众羞辱那些男人，他们不喜欢你这样做，认为你是个泼妇。

3.47 Bitch can be used metaphorically to talk about something difficult or unpleasant.
非常难办的事；令人极不愉快的事

That last shell was a <u>bitch</u> to locate.
找到那最后一颗子弹壳可真不容易。

These milk cartons are a real <u>bitch</u> to open.
这些牛奶盒可真不好开。

3.48 Bitch can be used metaphorically to talk about a conversation in which people complain or say unkind or cruel things about someone else.
（对某人的）怨言，坏话

We had a good <u>bitch</u> about Steve while he was out.
史蒂夫不在的时候我们说了他一通坏话。

3.49 If one **bitches** about another person, the first person says unpleasant things about the second when he is not present. People use **bitch** in this way to show that they disapprove of this behavior.
（尤指背着某人)抱怨，发牢骚

Everyone was talking about property or inside deals between <u>bitching</u> about colleagues.
人人都在对同事说三道四的同时谈论有关财产或者内部交易的事情。

He was quite talkative about his wife, mostly he <u>bitched</u> her.
他爱谈论他的妻子，多数情况下是抱怨她。

hound

3.50 A hound is a type of dog used for hunting for other animals or for racing.
猎狗

If one person **hounds** another, the first person follows the second in a determined way in order to get something from him.
紧追，烦扰（以获得某物）

The policeman hounded the thief until he caught him. 警察对小偷穷追不舍，直到把他抓住。

She was sick of being hounded by the press. 媒体的追踪让她烦透了。

3.51 If people **hound** someone **out of** a position or place, they force that one to leave the position or place by always being unpleasant to him. （通过不断地烦扰）迫使离开

He claims the media hounded him out of office. 他声称是媒体迫使他离职的。

Poultry

chick

3.52 A **chick** is a baby bird. 雏鸟

Chick can be used metaphorically as a way of referring to a young woman. This is an informal use which is usually considered offensive. （冒犯语）少女；少妇；小妞儿

3.53 A **chick flick** is a film intended especially for women, often about a romantic relationship. （尤指针对女性观众的）爱情电影

chicken

3.54 If you say that some one is a **chicken**, you mean the person is not brave enough to do something. Similar meanings can be expressed with **chicken-heart** or **chicken-hearted**. 懦夫；胆小鬼

汉语用鼠来比喻胆小的人，如：胆小如鼠。

You are a chicken; that's why you won't climb the tree. 你是个胆小鬼，所以你不肯爬树。

I was terrified, but I didn't want the others to think I was chicken. 我吓坏了，但我不想让别人以为我胆小。

3.55 If people **chicken out**, they decide not to do something because they are too frightened. （因胆怯而）临阵退缩

I was going to tell her how much it really cost, but I <u>chickened out</u>.
我本来要告诉她实际的花费，但最后还是没敢。

3.56 If you say an amount of money is **chicken feed**, you mean it is too small to be satisfactory.

微不足道的

Your salary is <u>chicken-feed</u> compared to what you could earn in America.
你的薪水和在美国时的相比太少了。

3.57 If you **play chicken**, you are involved in a game in which the winner is the person who continues something dangerous the longest.

（尤指儿童玩的）比试胆量的游戏

The kids were <u>playing chicken</u> on the railway track when the accident happened.
事故发生的时候孩子们正在铁路上比试胆量。

3.58 If you say that a woman is **no spring chicken**, you mean she is old.

（尤指女子）年龄不小了

She needs lots of make-up to hide the fact that she's <u>no spring chicken</u>.
她必须浓妆艳抹才能掩饰她已经年龄不小了。

3.59 If you say people **run around like a headless chicken**, you mean that they are very busy and active trying to do something, but not very organized.

无头绪地瞎忙一通

3.60 **A chicken-and-egg situation or problem** is one in which it is difficult to tell which one of two things was the cause of the other.

先有鸡还是先有蛋的问题；因果难定的问题

3.61 **Don't count your chickens (before they are hatched)** is used for telling someone not be too confident that something will be successful, because something may still go wrong.

蛋未孵出不要先数小鸡；别忙打如意算盘

3.62 **Chickens come home to roost** is used for saying that the bad results of something someone has done are starting to happen or to become clear.

开始自作自受；开始遭到报应
参见 5.54

cock

3.63 A **cock** is an adult male chicken. If you say someone is a **cock of the walk**, you mean the person is one who thinks he is stronger, cleverer, or more successful than the rest of his group.

公鸡
（人群中）称王称霸的人

cocky

3.64 If you say someone is **cocky**, you mean the person is very confident in an annoying way.

For a young man on his first day at work he's remarkably <u>cocky</u>.

趾高气扬的；过分自信的

这年轻人头一天上班，也显得太自信了。

hen

3.65 A **hen** is a female chicken.

If you say something is **as scarce as hen's teeth**, you mean its number is extremely small.

母鸡
凤毛麟角
汉语用**凤毛麟角**比喻稀少而可贵的人或物。

duck

3.66 A **duck** is a water bird with short legs, webbed feet and a large flat break.

Duck or **ducks** are informally used for talking to someone you like.

How are you, <u>duck</u>?
Be a <u>duck</u> and help me with this.

3.67 Still there are several other expressions associated with **duck** widely used in English, including both metaphors and metonymies as listed below.

(1) a lame **duck**

(2) a dead **duck**

(3) like water off a **duck's** back

鸭；鸭子

（表示友好的称呼）乖乖；宝贝儿

你好吗，亲爱的？
乖一点，帮我做做这件事。
关于鸭的其他隐喻表达方式举例

处于困境无法自理的人、组织或事物；（任期将满的）官员；损坏的飞机、轮船、车辆等

被放弃的或将失败的计划等

（尤指批评对某人）不起作用，有如耳边风

3 Animals

(4) a sitting **duck** — 容易攻击或容易击中的人或事物
(5) look like a dying **duck** in a thunderstorm — 惊惶失措
(6) ugly **duck** — 丑小鸭
(7) play **ducks** and drakes — 玩打水漂游戏

goose

3.68 A **goose** is a bird like a large duck with a long neck. — 鹅

Goose can be metaphorically used to talk about a silly person. — 傻瓜；笨蛋

Don't be such a silly goose. — 不要做这样的傻瓜。

3.69 A **wild-goose chase** is an attempt to find something that does not exist or that you are very unlikely to discover. — 白费力气的追逐；徒劳之举

Sideshows and wild-goose chases cropped up occasionally during the investigation. — 调查过程中难免会出现一些枝节问题和劳而无功的事。

3.70 **The goose that lays the golden eggs** is a person or thing that provides money. — 摇钱树

Column 3.3

This column is adopted to help understand some metaphorical expressions of **poultry** that are unique to Chinese.

赶鸭子上架	drive a duck onto a perch—try to make somebody do something beyond him
鸡飞蛋打	the hen has flown away and the eggs in the coop are broken—all is lost
鸡犬不宁	even fowls and dogs are not left in peace—general turmoil

Farm animals

bull

3.71 A **bull** is an adult male of the cattle family. — 牛；公牛

Bulls are big and fierce, and are associated with strength, confidence, and aggression.

3.72 In economics, **bulls** are investors who expect the prices of shares rise and may buy them so they can sell them later at a profit.

A **bull market** is a situation in which a lot of people are buying shares and values are going up.

The *bulls* are dejected. Tokyo's stock market never did what they hoped.

See also **bearish**: 3.108

3.73 If you say that a person is **like a bull in a china shop**, you mean the person is careless or acts in a rough way.

3.74 A person who **takes the bull by the horns** is one who deals with a problem in a very direct and confident way, even though there is some risk in doing this.

bull-headed

3.75 If you say that someone is **bull-headed,** you mean the person is rather stubborn.

bullish

3.76 A **bullish** market is one in which the prices of shares are expected to rise.

The latest survey of manufactures shows the biggest increase in optimism for ten years. It is particularly *bullish* about exports.

3.77 If someone is **bullish** about something, he is cheerful and optimistic

汉语中，牛用来比喻骄傲、固执或狂妄。如：牛气、牛脾气等。

多头；买进股票投机图利者

牛市

证券投资者们灰心丧气。东京的证券市场从来不做他们所希望的事。

笨拙莽撞的人；冒失鬼

勇敢地对付困难或危险；知难而进

汉语中，执牛耳用来指在某一方面居领导地位。

固执的

（金融市场价格）看涨的

对制造商的最新调查显示，现在是近十年来人们对未来的信心增幅最大的时候。人们对出口尤其抱乐观态度。

抱有希望的；乐观的

about it.
The team was in a <u>bullish</u> mood before the start of the game.
See also **bearish**: 3.109

cow

3.78 A **cow** is an adult female of the cattle family.
Cow is an insulting word for a woman, especially one who is stupid or unkind.

母牛

蠢婆娘；泼妇；母老虎

donkey

3.79 A **donkey** is a grey or brown animal similar to a horse, but smaller and with long ears. **Donkey** can be used metaphorically to talk about either a stupid or a stubborn person.

驴

笨蛋；蠢驴
犟驴；固执的人

3.80 In some countries, donkeys are used for riding and for pulling or carrying heavy loads. Thus, **donkey's years** can be metaphorically used to talk about an extremely long time.
The dish of apple must be <u>donkey's years</u>.
I haven't been swimming in <u>donkey's years</u>.

很久；多年
汉语用**驴年马月**喻指不可知的年月（就事情遥遥无期，不能实现说）。如：照你这么磨磨蹭蹭，驴年马月也干不成。也说**猴年马月**。
这苹果菜肴肯定是历史久远了。
我已经很久没游泳了。

3.81 **Donkey work** is the hard boring part of a job or task.
Why do I have to do all the <u>donkey work</u>?

单调、乏味的苦差事

我为什么得做这些乏味的苦差事呢？

goat

3.82 A **goat** is an animal similar to a sheep but with long legs and a thinner coat.
Goat, sometimes **old goat**, is an insulting word for an old man, especially one who shows a great sexual

山羊

老色鬼；色狼

interest in woman.

3.83 If a person **gets another person's goat**, the former annoys the latter very much.

The fellow gets my goat with his constant boasting of his own achievements.

使某人异常恼怒

那家伙老是吹嘘自己的成就，使我极为恼火。

hog

3.84 A **hog** is a male pig whose sex organs have been removed.

Hog is used metaphorically to talk about someone who eats rudely or takes too much of something that other people might eat.

3.85 If someone **hogs** something, he takes or uses it in a way that prevents other people from having it.

He had to be reminded, at times, not to hog the conversation.

3.86 A **road hog** is someone who drives in a dangerous way, often making it difficult for other cars to pass.

A road hog terrorized a woman driver

阉公猪

贪吃的人；自私的人

贪心攫取；独占

必须不时提醒他，谈话时不要凭自己高兴从头说到尾，不让别人插话。

横冲直撞的汽车驾驶员；危险驾车者

一名玩命的司机将一位驾车的女士吓坏了

lamb

3.87 A **lamb** is a young sheep.

Lamb is metaphorically used to talk to or about someone in a kind way, especially a small child. Some people use **lamb** to refer to people who they feel sorry for.

Poor little lamb.

I'll stay with the poor little lamb just as long as he needs me.

God tempers the wind to the shorn lamb.

羔羊；小羊

（用于善意地称呼或提及某人，尤指小孩）小乖乖；小宝贝

可怜的小宝贝！

只要这个可怜的小东西需要我，我就会一直和他在一起。

天怜受难人。

3.88 You may say that people are **(like) a lamb or lambs to the slaughter**, when they are going to do something dangerous without realizing it.
He was *like a lamb* in the hands of swindlers.

温顺的；怯懦的（如同）羔羊被牵往屠宰场（指将遇危险而不自觉的人）

在骗子手中他极易上当受骗。

sheep

3.89 A **sheep** is an animal kept by farmers for its wool or meat.
Sheep can be metaphorically used to talk about someone who does the same as everyone else without thinking about it.
follow like sheep
We're not political sheep.

羊；绵羊

盲目从众的人；没有主见的人

盲从
我们不是政治上的小绵羊（没有主见的人）。

3.90 A **black sheep** refers to someone who is not approved of by the other members of his family or the group he belongs to because he is thought to behave badly.
the black sheep of the family
separate the sheep from the goats

败类；害群之马
汉语用**害群之马**比喻危害集体的人。如：除掉害群之马，大家才能团结一致。

家族败类
区别好人与坏人

sheepish

3.91 You can say that someone looks **sheepish** if he is ashamed or embarrassed about something you have done.
He gave them a sheepish grin and left without further explanation.
John nodded sheepishly in agreement.

羞愧的；不好意思的；困窘的

他有些胆怯地向他们露齿一笑，没作更多的解释就离开了。
约翰羞怯地点头同意。

horse

3.92 A **horse** is a large animal that people ride.
If you **back** or **pick the wrong horse**, you choose the wrong thing or person

马
汉语用**千里马**比喻有才干的人。

挑错了东西或人

for a particular purpose.

3.93 If you **beat** or **flog a dead horse**, you waste time on something you know is not going to happen.　　徒劳；做无用功

3.94 If you **change horses in midstream**, you change your mind about something in the middle of doing it.　　在做某事的中途改变主意

3.95 Information **from the horse's mouth** means the information that comes from someone who is directly involved.　　（情报）来自直接参与者的；第一手的

3.96 If someone **horses around**, he plays in a very lively or rough way.　　胡闹；哄闹

This is a research site. Not the best place for a couple of boys to be <u>horsing around</u>.　　这是做研究的地方。不是让一些孩子哄闹的最佳场所。

pig

3.97 A **pig** is an animal with no fur and a curly tail kept by farmers for its meat.　　猪

If you call someone a **pig**, you think he is very unpleasant, for example, because he has been greedy, rude, or unkind.　　（侮辱性用语）猪猡;贪婪（或肮脏）的人；令人不快的人

He'd been a <u>pig</u> of money.　　他对钱贪得无厌。

He is a complete <u>pig</u> to the women in his life.　　对于卷入他生活中的女人们来说，他是个不折不扣的猪猡。

3.98 **Pig** can be used metaphorically to talk about something that is very difficult or unpleasant.　　难办的事情；不愉快的事情

We had a <u>pig</u> of game.　　我们的游戏玩得很不愉快。

3.99 If you say a person **makes a pig of himself or herself**, you mean he or she eats too much at a time.　　吃得过多；狼吞虎咽

She <u>made a pig of herself</u> with the ice-cream.　　她大吃了一通冰淇淋。

3.100 **A pig in a poke** is something that you have bought without seeing it.
When they bought that house, they bought <u>a pig in a poke</u>.
（未曾过目便）乱买的东西
那所房子是在他们未曾过目的情况下随便买下的。

3.101 If you **make a pig's ear (out) of something**, you make a mess of it.
把事情弄糟

3.102 You may say "**Pigs might fly.**" to show that you do not believe something will ever happen.
"With a bit of luck, we'll be finished by the end of the year." "Yes, and <u>pigs might fly!</u>"
（表示不相信某事会发生）太阳从西边出来；无稽之谈
"运气不错的话，我们年底就能完成"。"是啊，太阳能打西边出嘛！"

3.103 If people eat an extremely amount of food or indulge themselves in a certain kind of activity for amusement, you can say that they are **pigging themselves** or that they are **pigging out**.
Don't give me cakes—I'll just <u>pig myself</u>.
kids <u>pigging out</u> on junk food and soda
It was time to <u>pig out</u> on rock and roll.
狼吞虎咽地大吃；过渡沉溺
可别给我拿蛋糕，那我会吃个没够的。
大吃垃圾食品、大喝汽水的孩子
该是尽情享受摇滚乐的时候了。

3.104 **Pig-headed** persons are those who refuse to change their mind about something, even when it is obvious that they are wrong.
the <u>pig-headed</u> politicians who run this country
顽固的；固执的
治理这个国家的顽固的政客们

swine

3.105 As an old word meaning a "pig", **swine** can be used metaphorically to talk about an extremely unpleasant or cruel man.
He and his young family were terrified of the kidnapper. He said, "I won't feel safe until the <u>swine</u> is behind bars."
猪猡；下流坯
他和他年轻的家庭成员对那个劫持者很恐惧。他说："这个暴徒不蹲监狱我就不会感到安全。"

"Tell me what you did with the money, you swine." "告诉我你拿这些钱干什么去了，你这个坏蛋。"

Column 3.4

This column is adopted to help understand some metaphorical expressions of **farm animals** that are unique to Chinese.

千里驹	thousand-li colt—a son who is showing great promise
孺子牛	a herd boy's willing ox—a servant of the people
顺手牵羊	lead off a goat in passing—pick up something on the sly
羊质虎皮	a sheep in a tiger's skin—outwardly strong, inwardly weak
一言既出，驷马难追	an honest man's word is as good as his bond

Wild animals

ape

3.106 **Apes** are chimpanzees, gorillas, and other animals in the same family. 猿；类人猿

If someone **goes ape**, he becomes very excited, enthusiastic, or angry about something. 发狂；变得狂热；变得恼怒

He *is sure as hell going to ape* that you didn't see Rocky yesterday. 你昨天没看见落基，他肯定会为这件事气得发疯。

3.107 If someone **apes** something or someone, he tries to behave like them. 举止上模仿；学……的样

He *apes* their walk and mannerisms behind their backs with hilarious results. 他在他们背后模仿他们的步态和怪癖，样子很滑稽。

bear

3.108 A **bear** is a large wild animal with thick fur. 熊

In economics, bears are investors who expect the prices of shares to fall, so they sell them. 预期股市看跌的投资者

In a **bear market**, prices are falling because a lot of people are uncertain 熊市

about the future, so are more likely to sell than to buy.

Even the <u>bears</u> on Wall Street agree that the company's operating profits will improve.

甚至华尔街的股票投资看空者也同意，这家公司的运营利润将会改善。

Wait two or three years for the next <u>bear market</u>, and buy into the company.

等上两三年，到下一个熊市时买进这家公司的股票。

See also **bull: 3.72**

bearish

3.109 A **bearish** market is one in which the prices of shares are falling.

（股市）行情下跌的

Japanese banks and life insurers remain <u>bearish</u>.

日本的银行和人寿保险机构的业务依然呈熊市走势。

a <u>bearish</u> outlook on the US economy

认为美国经济会下滑的估计

See also **bullish: 3.76**

dinosaur

3.110 A **dinosaur** is a large frightening animal that lived a very long time ago but is now extinct.

恐龙

Dinosaur is used to refer to someone or something that is very old-fashioned and no longer useful or effective.

汉语用**古董**比喻过时的东西或顽固守旧的人。

迂腐落伍的人；过时无用的东西

"You are a <u>dinosaur</u>," Michael said. "The world has moved on and you don't even know it."

"你是个老古董，"迈克说。"世界已经进步了，而你竟然连这也不知道。"

As an international venue it's a bit of a <u>dinosaur</u>.

作为一个国际会议场所，它是有点陈旧了。

ferret

3.111 A **ferret** is a small thin fury animal with a long tail that people use for hunting rabbits and rats.

（猎兔或猎鼠用的）白鼬，雪貂

If you **ferret** somewhere for something, you search for that thing, in an enthusiastic but not very organized way.

搜索

She was <u>ferreting</u> around in a drawer

她在抽屉里翻找钥匙。

for her keys.

3.112 If someone **ferrets out** something, especially information, he finds it by searching very thoroughly for it.

Several top American columnists <u>ferret out</u> information that others would prefer to keep confidential.

查明

一些最知名的美国专栏作家通过彻底搜索，获得了别人更愿意保密的情报。

fox

3.113 A **fox** is a wild animal similar to a small dog, with red-brown fur, a pointed face, and a thick tail.

狐狸

汉语用狐朋狗友比喻品行不端的朋友，用狐群狗党比喻勾结在一起的坏人。参见 3.24

Fox is used metaphorically to refer to someone who is clever at tricking people.

Enrico was too good, an old <u>fox</u>, cunning. He was giving nothing away.

狡猾的人；奸诈

恩利克太好了，这只老狐狸，够狡猾的。他什么都没透漏。

3.114 **Fox** is also used to refer to someone who is very sexually attractive, especially a woman.

特别性感的人；（尤指）妩媚的女子
参见 3.24

3.115 If something **foxes** you, it confuses you and is impossible for you to understand or solve.

This is the sort of proposal that <u>foxes</u> the opposition.

Our accident investigation experts are going to <u>be</u> completely <u>foxed</u> by this one.

使……迷惑；使猜不透；把……难住
比较汉语中的狐疑。

这是那种迷惑反对党的建议。

我们的事故调查专家将会被这件事故完全弄糊涂。

foxy

3.116 If you describe someone as **foxy**, you mean that he is good at tricking or cheating people.

a quick, cunning, foxy child

3.117 A **foxy** woman is sexually attractive.

I saw you on TV. I said to my agent, that

狡猾的；奸诈的；精明的

一个脑子快、狡猾、精明的孩子

性感的
参见 3.24

我在电视上看到了你。我对我的代理

is one _foxy_ lady.

hare

3.118 A **hare** is an animal like a larger rabbit with very long ears.
If you say that someone **hares** off somewhere or **hares** there, you mean that he goes there as quickly as possible, in a great hurry.

He hares off towards the main gate, shouting wildly to the guard house to raise the alarm.
He went haring round to her flat.

3.119 A **hare-brained** idea or plan is foolish and not likely to succeed.

I've had enough of your hare-brained scheme.

lion

3.120 A **lion** is a large African wild animal with golden fur.

Lion is used metaphorically to refer to someone who is powerful, impressive, or brave.

3.121 You can refer to the largest part of something as **the lion's share**.

The lion's share of his money went to his grandchildren.

monkey

3.122 A **monkey** is an animal with a long tail that climbs trees and uses its hands in the same way that people do.

Monkey is used to refer to someone, especially a child, who behaves badly but in a funny way rather than in an

人说，那是一位性感女郎。

野兔
汉语中，**兔脱**用来比喻很快地逃走。
飞跑；飞奔

他匆匆忙忙地奔向正门，对着警卫室狂喊，以向人们发出警报。

他匆忙向她的公寓跑去。
愚蠢的；不可能成功的

我受够了你那些愚蠢的计划！

狮子
汉语用**狮子大开口**比喻要大价钱或提出很高的物质要求。
勇敢的人；威严的人
汉语用**虎**比喻勇猛威武，如：虎将、虎虎有生气。
（某事物的）最大的一分

他的孙辈们得到了他最大的一份财产。

猴子
汉语用**猴儿精**比喻机灵或顽皮的人，也用来形容人很精明，如：这小子猴儿精的。
猴子似的人；淘气鬼；捣蛋鬼

annoying way.
Ooh, you little <u>monkey</u>! What have you done now?

3.123 If someone **monkeys around**, or **monkeys with** something, he plays with it or interferes with it in an irresponsible way.

Generic engineering must stop short of <u>monkeying around</u> irresponsibly with the species.

Not a day goes by without him getting and <u>monkeying with</u> something.

mouse

3.124 A **mouse** is a small furry animal with a long tail.

You can refer to someone who is quiet and prefers not to be noticed as a **mouse**.

I didn't know how to act. I didn't want to be too aggressive but I didn't want to be a <u>mouse</u> either.

mousy

3.125 A **mousy** person is quiet and prefers not to be noticed.

A short, <u>mousy</u> woman, this was her first teaching job and she wasn't enjoying it.

rat

3.126 A **rat** is an animal like a large mouse with a long tail.

Rat is used metaphorically to refer to someone who is not loyal or who tricks you.

He saved three people from a burning house in the blitz, but was a thieving <u>rat</u>

嗬，你这个小淘气鬼！你又干什么了？

胡闹；捣蛋

基因工程必须停止对那些物种不负责的胡闹行为。

他没有一天不进去捣乱的。

鼠；老鼠
参见 3.54

安静、害羞的人

我不知道该怎么做。我不想咄咄逼人，但我也不想显得胆小如鼠。

安静、害羞的

她是一个胆怯的矮小女人，这是她的第一个教学工作，她没有感到她有什么乐趣。

老鼠
比较汉语中的鼠辈、鼠窜、鼠目寸光等。参见 3.54

背信弃义的人；卑鄙小人

他在空袭时从一所燃烧的房子里救出了三个人，但除此之外他是个窃贼。

otherwise.
But you promised to help us, you **rat**.
3.127 If someone **rats on** you, he tells someone in authority about something wrong that you have done.
They'll kill you if they find out you've ratted on them!

你是答应过要帮我们的，你这个骗子。
告密；告发

如果发现是你告的密，他们会要了你的命。

3.128 If someone **rats on** promise, settlement etc., he does not do what he promised to do.
I can't back someone who rats on his promise.

背信弃义

我不会支持背信弃义的人。

snake

3.129 A **snake** is a long thin animal with no legs and a smooth skin.
You can refer to someone who cannot be trusted as a **snake in the grass**.
Some snake in the grass told the teacher our plans.

蛇
汉语用**蛇蝎**比喻狠毒的人。
不可信赖的人；口蜜腹剑的人

有个奸细把我们的打算告诉了老师。

vermin

3.130 **Vermin** are small animals, birds, and insects that are harmful because they destroy crops, spoil food, and spread disease.
Vermin is used metaphorically to refer to unpleasant people who cause problems for society.
The vermin are the people who rob old women in the street and break into houses.
The multi-cultural society is working quite well and we must not let a minority of racist vermin to make trouble.

（引起破坏或疾病的）害兽，害虫，寄生虫
汉语将害人的人比喻为**害人虫**。

害人虫；歹徒

歹徒是那些在街上抢劫老年妇女和破门闯入民房的人。

多元文化的社会正运作得相当不错，我们绝不能让少数种族主义的害虫继续制造麻烦。

weasel

3.131 A **weasel** is a small thin animal with brown fur, short legs, and a long tail that hunts its food.

鼬；黄鼠狼

If someone **weasels out** of a duty or promise, he manages to avoid doing his part of it by using clever or dishonest excuses.

逃避责任

A buyer will not usually be able to <u>weasel out</u> of these promises later.

以后在通常情况下买主将无法违背诺言。

wolf

3.132 A **wolf** is a wild animal similar to a large dog that lives in group.

狼
汉语用**狼心狗肺**比喻心肠狠毒或忘恩负义，用**狼子野心**比喻凶暴的人用心狠毒，用**狼奔豕突**比喻成群的坏人乱窜乱撞。

The big bad wolf is used to refer to someone or something that is bad and causes all the problems in a situation.

惹是生非的坏蛋；惹麻烦的坏东西

I get tired of being portrayed as <u>the big bad wolf</u>.

我对被描绘成一个惹是生非的坏蛋感到厌烦。

3.133 You can refer someone who seems friendly but is in fact unpleasant or cruel as **a wolf in sheep's clothing**.

披着羊皮的狼；假装友好的敌人

3.134 If someone **wolfs** his food, or **wolfs** it **down**, he eats extremely quickly, so that he does not have time to chew or taste his food properly.

狼吞虎咽地吃

The girls <u>wolfed down</u> the pizza in minutes.

女孩子们几分钟之内就把比萨饼狼吞虎咽地吃下去了。

wolfish

3.135 If you describe a man or his behavior as **wolfish**, you mean that he behaves in a way that seems sinister or threatening.

凶残的；狡诈的
汉语用**虎视眈眈**形容贪婪而凶狠地注视。

a wolfish smile 　　　　　　　狞笑

Column 3.5

This column is adopted to help understand some metaphorical expressions of **wild animals** that are unique to Chinese.

豺狼当道	jackals and wolves hold sway
过街老鼠	a rat crossing the street—a person or a thing that provokes a hue and cry
狐群狗党	a pack of rogues; a gang of scoundrels
虎视眈眈	glare like a tiger eyeing its prey
虎头蛇尾	a fine start and a poor finish; in like a lion, out like a lamb
狼狈为奸	act in collusion with each other
狼子野心	wolfish nature
龙争虎斗	a fierce struggle between will-matched opponents
骑虎难下	He who has a tiger by the tail dare not let go.
蛇蝎心肠	as venomous as snakes and scorpions
鼠肚鸡肠	narrow-minded
鼠目寸光	see only what is under one's nose; be short-sighted
投鼠忌器	hesitate to pelt a rat for fear of smashing the dishes—hold back from taking action against an evil-doer for fear of involving or harming good people
兔死狐悲	the fox mourns the death of the hare—like feels for the like
獐头鼠目	with the head of a buck and the eyes of a rat—repulsively ugly and sly-looking

4 Plants

Plants

cabbage

4.1 A **cabbage** is a hard round vegetable with green or purple leaves that can be eaten raw in salads or cooked.

卷心菜；甘蓝

Cabbage is used as an offensive word for someone who is completely unable to move or speak due to brain damage.

（因脑部受重伤而完全不能移动或说话的）废人；植物人（该词具冒犯义）

Now he cannot speak to us and though it hurts to say this, he is little more than a <u>cabbage</u>.

现在他已无法和我们说话。虽然这样说是令人难过的，但他差不多是个植物人了。

carrot

4.2 A **carrot** is a long hard organ vegetable that grows under the ground and has green leaves on it.

胡萝卜

Carrot is used to refer to something that someone promises you as a way of encouraging you to do something.

（为鼓励某人做某事而作出的）诱人的承诺

the electoral <u>carrot</u> of early tax cuts

早期减免税的选举承诺

They are holding out a <u>carrot</u> of $120 million in economic aid.

他们许诺给予1.2亿美元的经济援助。

4.3 If you use the **carrot and stick (approach)**, you persuade someone to try harder by offering him a reward if he does, or a punishment if he does not.

胡萝卜加大棒；威逼利诱；软硬兼施

the government's <u>carrot and stick approach</u> in getting young people to

政府为解决青年人就业问题而采取的软硬兼施的手段

find jobs

grass

4.4 **Grass** is a very common wild plant with thin green leaves and stems that are eaten by cows, horses, sheep etc.

If you say that **the grass is (always) greener on the other side**, you mean life seems better somewhere else, or other people's situations seem better than your own.

4.5 You can use the **grass roots** to refer to the ordinary people in a community, country, society, or organization rather than its leader.

We must insist our policemen go back to grass roots to restore our faith in them.

4.6 **Grass-roots** campaigns or **grass-roots** support are campaigns or support organized by ordinary people rather than by the leaders.

We need to win support at grass-roots level.

laurel

4.7 A **laurel** is a small tree with shiny dark green leaves that do not fall off in winter.

You can refer to honours that you receive for something you have achieved as **laurels**.

She won laurels for her first novel.

4.8 If you **look to your laurels**, you work hard in order not to lose the success that you have achieved.

With so many good new actors around, the older ones are having to look to

草
参见 4.5, 4.6

草是那边绿；这山望着那山高；别处的月亮（总是）比这里圆

基层民众；平民百姓
比较汉语中的草民、草莽英雄。

我们必须坚持要我们的警察回到草根阶层去，使其恢复对我们的信任。

基层的
汉语用草芥比喻轻贱、微末的东西，如：视同草芥。

我们需要得到基层的支持。

月桂树

荣誉；赞誉；荣耀

她因第一部小说而赢得荣誉。
努力保持自己的桂冠；努力保住自己的成功

由于新演员中人才辈出，老演员不得不时时小心保持自己的荣誉。

their laurels.

4.9 If you **rest** or **sit on your laurels**, you feel satisfied with what you have already achieved that you do not try to do any more.

满足于既得成就；不思进取

The liberals sat on their laurels after their victory.

自由党人获胜后满足于现状。

lily

4.10 A **lily** is a large flower in the shape of a bell that is often white but can be many other colours.

百合花

Gild the lily is used for saying that someone has spoiled a good thing by trying to improve it.

画蛇添足；多此一举

mushroom

4.11 **Mushrooms** are a type of fungi with round flat heads and short stems.

蘑菇
汉语用**雨后春笋**比喻新事物大量出现。

If something **mushrooms**, it increases or develops very quickly.

迅速增加；快速发展

Trade between the two countries has mushroomed.

两国之间的贸易迅速发展。

We expect the market to **mushroom** in the next two years.

我们期望未来两年内市场会迅速发展。

nettle

4.12 A **nettle** is a tall plant with pointed leaves and small hairs that sting if you touch them.

荨麻
汉语用**荆棘**比喻困难、障碍、纷乱，如：**荆棘**载途。**荆棘**也可用来比喻坏人，如：剪除荆棘。

If you **grasp the nettle**, you deal with an unpleasant situation firmly and without delay.

迎难而上；大胆抓棘手问题
比较汉语中的**披荆斩棘**。

We've got to grasp the nettle of prison reform.

我们得抓一抓监狱改革这个棘手的问题。

4.13 If someone or something **nettles**

使烦恼；使恼火；惹怒

you, he/it annoys you.
The noise of car alarms <u>nettled</u> him. 汽车的警报声使他很恼火。

vegetable

4.14 Vegetables are plants such as carrots, potatoes, and onions, which you can cook and eat. 蔬菜

Vegetable is used to refer to people who have suffered brain damage and are unable to think or move. 植物人

Severe brain damage turned him into a <u>vegetable</u>. 严重的脑损伤使他变成了植物人。

Parts of plants

bloom

4.15 A **bloom** is a flower on a plant. 花

You can use **bloom** to refer to the time or the condition of being young, healthy, and attractive. 青春焕发的时期；风华正茂

She had lost a good deal of her <u>bloom</u> and bounce. 她大量的青春年华已逝去。

a young man still in the bloom of youth 正值豆蔻年华的年轻人

4.16 You can refer to the healthy look of someone's skin as **bloom**. （皮肤的）红润

She had a healthy <u>bloom</u> in her cheeks. 她面颊红润健康。

4.17 If someone **blooms**, he becomes happier, healthier, or more successful in a way that is very noticeable. 变得健康（或快活、自信）

The children <u>had bloomed</u> during their stay on the farm. 孩子们留在农场期间健康活泼有生气。

Some women seem to <u>bloom</u> during pregnancy. 有些女人在怀孕期间似乎变得容光焕发。

blossom

4.18 A **blossom** is a flower or a mass of flowers, especially on a fruit or bush. （尤指果树或灌木的）花朵，花簇

If someone or something **blossoms**, he/it becomes more healthy, confident or successful.
She has visibly <u>blossomed</u> over the last few months.
The town <u>has blossomed into</u> the country's most popular beach resort.

变得更加健康（或自信、成功）；发展；繁荣；兴旺

她几个月以来身体明显好多了。

这个城镇已经发展成为该国最受欢迎的海滨度假胜地。

branch

4.19 A **branch** is a part of a tree that grows out of its trunk with leaves, flowers, or fruit growing on it.

树枝

汉语用**枝节**比喻相关的次要的事情，如：枝节问题。枝节还可用来比喻在处理一件事情的过程中遇到的意外问题，如：另生枝节。

A **branch** of an organization is one of its offices or parts, usually working under the authority of the central office or part.
The store has <u>branches</u> in over 40 cities.
4.20 You can refer to one part of a large subject of study or knowledge as a **branch**.
Mechanics is a <u>branch</u> of physics.
4.21 If someone **branches out (into something)**, he starts doing something new or different.
Designers have <u>branched out</u> from clothes to cosmetics and toiletries.
In the longer term, the company wants to <u>branch out into</u> providing investment advice.

分店；分支机构

这家商店在40多个城市有分店。
（研究或知识领域的）分科；分支

力学是物理学的分支。
开拓新业务；扩大活动范围

设计者已经把业务范围从服装扩大到化妆品和梳妆用具。
从更长远看，公司想开拓投资咨询的新业务。

bud

4.22 A **bud** is a tightly curled up part of a plant that will open to form a leaf or flower.
If someone **nip something in the bud**, you

芽；花蕾

汉语用**萌芽**比喻新生的、稚嫩的事物，如：这是新事物的<u>萌芽</u>。

把某事物消灭于萌芽状态；防某事物

stop it from becoming worse by taking action at an early stage of its development.
It is important to recognize jealousy as soon as possible and to nip it in the bud before it gets out of control.

于未然

尽早识别嫉妒心，在其失控前就将其解决在萌芽状态，这很重要。

budding
4.23 A **budding** artist, writer etc. is one who is at the beginning of his or her career and is likely to be successful at it.
A **budding** thing is just beginning or developing.
a short story competition designed to encourage budding authors
our budding romance

开始发展的；崭露头角的；刚开始的
参见 4.22

旨在鼓励崭露头角的作家的短篇小说竞赛
我们刚刚发展起来的恋爱关系

flower
4.24 A **flower** is the coloured part of a plant from which the plant's fruit develops.
The flower of something is the best part or best example of it.
They remembered her as she'd been in the flower of their friendship.
I feel I can still do it even though I am no longer in the full flower of youth.

花；花卉

某物最好的部分；某物中的精华

他们记得她，记得昔日友情最深厚的她。
我觉得我仍能做这件事，虽然我青春的最好时光已逝去。

flowering
4.25 The **flowering** of something is a period when it is very strong, popular, or successful.
the flowering of modern democracy

兴盛时期；成熟期

现代民主的兴盛时期

fruit
4.26 A **fruit** is the part of a plant that consists of a stone or seeds and flesh that can be eaten as food and usually tastes sweet.

水果；果实

The fruit of or **the fruits of** something are the good results of an activity or a situation.
成果；成效；结果

The book is the fruit of years of research.
这本书是多年研究的成果。

Retirement is a time to relax and enjoy the fruits of your labour.
退休是休息和享受自己劳动成果的时期。

4.27 If something that you have worked hard on **bears fruit**, you are finally able to see good results from your efforts.
取得成果

Our policies must be given time to bear fruit.
我们的政策必须假以时日才能取得成果。

fruitful

4.28 **Fruitful** fields or trees produce a lot of crops.
果实结得多的；多产的

Fruitful is used metaphorically to talk about something being successful or having good results.
富有成果的

This area of enquiry did finally prove fruitful.
这个调查领域最后证明的确是富有成果的。

We have had a friendly and very fruitful discussion.
我们进行了友好而富有成果的讨论。

fruition

4.29 If things such as plans or ideas **reach** or **come to fruition**, they start to produce the results that were planned, usually after a long wait or a lot of work.
（计划或想法的）实现；完成；取得成果

Nobody was sure whether the deal would ever come to fruition.
谁也不敢肯定这次交易是否能够成功。

fruitless

4.30 An action, plan, or idea that is **fruitless** does not produce any useful results.
无结果的；无收益的；徒劳的

All their efforts to find her proved
他们为寻找她而付出的所有努力都是

fruitless.
root

4.31 A **root** is the part of a plant that grows under the ground, through which the plant gets water and food.
You can refer to the origins or background of something as **roots**.
What are the historical roots of the region's problems?
The Association has its roots in the early 1940s.

4.32 You can refer to the place, culture, or family that you come from originally as **your roots**.
I'm proud of my Italian roots.
After 20 years in America, I still feel my roots are in England.

4.33 If you **put down roots** somewhere, you start to feel that a place is your home and to have relationships with the people there.
After ten years' travelling the world, she felt it was time to put down roots somewhere.

4.34 If you do something **root and branch**, you do it thoroughly and completely.
The government set out to destroy the organization root and branch.

4.35 If an idea, belief, or system **takes root**, it becomes established and accepted.
Compromise is essential if peace is to take root in this troubled area.

4.36 If one thing **is rooted in** another, it

徒劳的。

（植物的）根；根茎
根在汉语中可用来指事物的本源，如：
祸根、刨根问底等。

根源；背景

该地区问题的历史根源是什么？

这个协会源于20世纪40年代初期。

祖籍；背景；根
根在汉语中也可用来比喻子孙，如：
这孩子就是李家的根儿。
我为我的意大利血统感到骄傲。
尽管在美国生活了20年，我还是觉得我的根在英国。

定居
汉语的扎根可用来比喻人深入某处，扎扎实实地学习和工作，如：扎根基层。
游历世界十年之后，她觉得该是找个地方定居的时候了。

彻底地；完全地
比较汉语中的根除、斩草除根。

政府着手完全彻底地摧毁这个组织。

（思想、信仰或体制）被接受；深入人心

要在这个动荡的地区实现和平，就必须妥协。

根源的；起源的

is based on it, has developed from it, or is influenced by it.
The conflict in the area <u>was rooted in</u> history and religion.
这个地区冲突的根源在于历史和宗教。

seed

4.37 A **seed** is a small hard part produced by a plant that can grow into a new plant of the same type.
种子；籽
参见 4.32

The seeds of something is something that makes a new situation start to grow and develop.
起源；起因；萌芽；开端

He considered that there were, in these developments, <u>the seeds of</u> a new moral order.
他认为在这些进展中存在着产生一个新道德秩序的因素。

the seeds of conflict
冲突的起因

4.38 You can refer to a player or team in a competition as number one, two, three etc. **seed** according to how likely they are to win.
种子选手；种子队

The top <u>seed</u> won comfortably.
头号种子选手轻松获胜。

4.39 If someone or something **goes** or **runs to seed**, he/it becomes less attractive or good, especially because he/it is getting old and has not been properly looked after.
（尤指因对自己照顾不够而）显老；颓废

After his divorce, he let himself <u>go to seed</u>.
离婚后，他自暴自弃。

He was not yet fifty, but he <u>was</u> already <u>going to seed</u>.
他还不到 50 岁，但已经开始显老。

4.40 If you **sow** or **plant the seeds of** a particular situation or result, you start the process that leads to it.
成为……的肇端；播下……的种子

In this way he <u>sowed the seeds of</u> his own success.
就这样，他奠定了自己成功的基础。

The seeds of doubt were already planted
怀疑的种子已经埋在他的头脑中。

in his mind.

shoot

4.41 A **shoot** is a very young plant, or a new part growing on a plant.
You can refer to the first sign that a situation is improving, especially an economic situation, as **green shoots (of recovery)**.
Typically the first <u>green shoots of recovery</u> herald an increase in bankruptcy.

嫩芽；秧苗；新枝
参见 4.22
（尤指经济）复苏的迹象

经济复苏的先兆预示着破产的增加，这是一种典型现象。

stem

4.42 The **stem** of a plant is the long thin central part from which the leaves and flowers grow.
If one thing **stems from** another, the first thing is a result of the second.
His popularity <u>stemmed from</u> the fact that he was born in the area.
Many of her problems <u>stem from</u> her family.

（植物的）茎；柄；梗

源于；是……的缘故

他受到欢迎是因为他出生于该地区。

她的很多问题都源于她的家庭。

thorn

4.43 A **thorn** is a sharp point that sticks out from the stem of a plant.

A thorn in your **side** is someone or something that annoys you or causes problems for a long period of time.
His mother-in-law is <u>a thorn in his flesh</u>.

刺

汉语中，刺可喻指尖刻的话，如：他说话常常带刺儿。

某人的肉中刺；令人烦恼的人；使人苦恼的事

他的岳母让他不得安生。

thorny

4.44 Something that is **thorny** is covered with thorns.
A **thorny** issue, problem, subject etc. is one that is difficult to deal with.
Now we come to the <u>thorny</u> question of

带刺的；多刺的

棘手的；难处理的

现在我们来讨论成本这个棘手的问

cost.

题。

Cultivating plants

crop

4.45 A **crop** is the amount of grain, fruit, etc. that is grown in one season.
A crop of things refers to several things that happen or are produced at the same time. **A crop of people** is several people who achieve something or become known for something at the same time.
This summer's crop of Hollywood films will be reviewed on Saturday.
this year's crop of rookie politicians
4.46 If something **crops up**, it happens or appears suddenly and in an unexpected way.
His name just cropped up in conversation.
While the construction work progressed, another difficulty cropped up.

收成；产量

（同时发生或生产的）一批；一系列

今年夏天的这批好莱坞影片将于星期六审查。
今年涌现的一群政治家
（突然）发生；显现

交谈时无意中就提到了他的名字。
当建筑工作有了进展时，另一个困难突然出现了。

cultivate

4.47 To **cultivate** land or crops means to prepare the land and grow crops in it.
Cultivate is used metaphorically to talk about the action of developing something such as an attitude, ability, or skill.
He's trying to cultivate a more caring image.
She tried to cultivate an air of sophistication.
4.48 If you **cultivate** a relationship with a person or organization, or if you cultivate a person, you try to get his

开垦；耕作；栽培；种植

培养；养成（某种态度、谈话或举止方式等）

他正在努力树立自己更为体贴的形象。
她竭力养成一种老于世故的气派。

结交（朋友）；培植（关系）
汉语用**栽培**比喻培养、造就人才，如：感谢老师的栽培；也比喻官场中的照

friendship or support, usually in order to get an advantage from him.
He purposely tried to cultivate good relations with the press.
It helps if you go out of your way to cultivate the local people.

cultivated

4.49 **Cultivated** land is used for growing crops or plants.
A **cultivated** person is well educated and knows how to behave politely.
a cultivated young woman
His voice was pleasant and cultivated.

harvest

4.50 A **harvest** is the activity of collecting a crop.
Harvest is used metaphorically to talk about the result of something that was done in the past.
The grim harvest of these cuts was an increase in preventable diseases.

4.51 If you **reap the harvest** of your actions, you see the results of them.
He began to reap the harvest of his sound training.

4.52 If you say that people **harvest** useful things, you mean that they collect them and bring them together to use.
We have thousands of ideas to harvest.
The harvesting of knowledge from space will be one of the great scientific endeavours of the next century.

prune

4.53 To **prune** a plant means to cut off some of its branches to make it grow

顾、提拔。类似的表达方式还有**扶植**，如：**扶植**新生力量。
他特意设法与新闻界搞好关系。

主动结交当地人大有好处。

（土地）耕种的；耕作的

有修养的；有教养的；文雅的

温文尔雅的年轻女士
他说话的声音悦耳文雅。

收割；收获；收成

结果；后果；成果

开支的削减所带来的严重后果是本可预防的疾病在增多。

享受成果

他开始收获他的优质训练所带来的成果。

获得；得到

我们有成千上万的主意要收集。
从空间获取知识将是下个世纪伟大的科学努力之一。

修剪；修整（树木）

better.
If you **prune** something, you make it smaller by removing parts that you do not need or want.
Companies must continually *prune* costs to stay competitive.
Prune out any unnecessary details.
The government forced it to *prune* back its promises.

削减；裁减
比较汉语中的**裁减**、**剔除**。
公司必须不断削减成本以保持竞争力。
把无关紧要的细节统统删掉。
政府迫使它删改它承诺的内容。

plant

4.54 To **plant** a seed, plant, or young tree means to put it in the ground so that it will grow.
If you **plant** someone or something or yourself in a particular place, you firmly put him/it/yourself there.
Toby's aunt *planted* a big, wet kiss on his cheek.
Henry *planted* himself in the car next to me.

种；植；栽种
参见 4.48

站稳；坐稳；安置

托比的姑妈在他的脸颊上印了一个大大的、湿漉漉的吻。
亨利稳稳地坐在了我旁边的位子上。

4.55 If you **plant** something illegal or stolen, you put it on someone secretly, or hide it in his possessions, so that he appears guilty when it is found.
Three officers were accused of *planting* evidence in the suspect's room.

栽赃

有 3 名官员被指控在嫌疑人的房间里放置证物栽赃陷害。

4.56 If you **plant** someone in a group or organization, you put him in it so that he can find out information secretly.
The police had *planted* an officer in the club to catch the drug dealers.

安插（眼线、密探等）

警方在该俱乐部安插了一名警官，准备抓捕毒贩。

4.57 If someone **plants** a bomb, he hides it where he wants it to explode.
A call warned police that a two-hundred-pound bomb *had been planted* in a car

安放（炸弹）

一个电话警告警方说，一枚二百磅炸弹已经放在了镇中心的一辆汽车

in the centre of the town.

4.58 If you **plant** an idea in someone's mind, you introduce it so that he begins to think about it.

灌输（思想）

Both candidates will make promises and plant ideas, trying to earn trust.

两位候选人都将作出种种承诺并向人们灌输各自的主张，以期赢得信任。

sow

4.59 To **sow** means to plant seeds in the ground.

播（种）

If you **sow fear, doubt, confusion etc.**, you make people feel afraid, confused etc.

使产生恐惧、怀疑、迷惑等

These people are terrorists who want to sow fear and panic among our people.

这些人是恐怖分子，他们想在我们的人民中间散播恐惧和惊慌。

reap

4.60 To **reap** crops means to cut and gather them.

收割（庄稼）

If you **reap** something such as benefit, reward, profit etc., you get it as a result of what you have done.

收获；获得

We will all reap the benefits of this important research.

我们都将从这项重要研究中获益。

4.61 If you **reap what you sow**, you have to deal with the bad effects or results of something that you originally started.

自食其果；种瓜得瓜，种豆得豆

weed

4.62 Weeds are wild plants that grow in places such as gardens or fields where crops are being grown and so prevent the cultivated plants from growing properly.

野草
参见 4.5, 4.6

To **weed** a garden or a field means to remove the weeds from it.

（为……）除去杂草

If you **weed out** a person or thing from

清除；剔除；淘汰

a group or collection, you remove him/it because he/it is not suitable or good enough.

We need a process that <u>weeds out</u> corrupt police officers.

我们需要一种剔除腐败警官的程序。

Growth

flourish

4.63 If a plant **flourishes**, it grows well and is healthy.

茂盛；兴盛；茁壮成长

If something such as a business, country, or idea **flourishes**, it develops well and is successful.

成功；繁荣；兴盛
比较汉语中的**繁荣**、**繁盛**等。

Few businesses <u>are flourishing</u> in the present economic climate.

在目前的经济气候下，很少有企业兴旺发达。

The congregation continued to grow and <u>flourish</u>.

教堂会众不断增加，更加兴盛。

flourishing

4.64 **Flourishing** can be used before a noun to mean "obviously successful."

繁盛的；欣欣向荣的；蒸蒸日上的
汉语用**欣欣向荣**比喻事业蓬勃发展。

There is now a <u>flourishing</u> black market in software there.

那里现在有个非常繁荣的软件黑市。

germinate

4.65 If a seed **germinates**, or if it is germinated, it begins to grow.

（使）发芽
参见 4.22

If an idea, feeling etc. **germinates**, it begins to develop.

（思想等）萌发

A sense of unease began to <u>germinate</u> in the group.

一种忧虑感开始在那个群体中萌发。

shrivel

4.66 If something such as a plant **shrivels** or **shrivels up**, it becomes smaller and thinner than usual and it does not look fresh and healthy.

（植物）枯萎；皱缩
汉语用**枯木逢春**比喻重新获得生机。
参见 4.70

4 Plants

Shrivel is used metaphorically to talk about the action of becoming weaker or smaller in amount.
Funding for the project eventually shrivelled up.
Her angry tone had shrivelled any confidence he had left.

减少；变弱；(使)消减；(使)降低
比较汉语中的**枯竭**。

项目的资金最终减少了。

她生气的口吻使他剩下的那点信心也丧失殆尽。

sprout

4.67 If vegetables, seeds, or plants **sprout**, they start to grow, producing shoots, buds or leaves.

If things **sprout** or **sprout up** somewhere, they appear there or increase in number suddenly and quickly.
Anti-government posters are sprouting up on nearby walls.
New businesses began to sprout up across the country.

发芽；萌芽；抽条
参见 4.22

突然出现；突然增加

反政府的海报突然之间贴满了附近的墙。
新公司开始在全国各地涌现。

wilt

4.68 If a plant **wilts**, it gradually bends towards the ground because it needs water or is dying.

If a person **wilts**, he has less energy, confidence, or enthusiasm.
The spectators were wilting visibly in the hot sun.
He was wilting under the pressure of work.

(植物)枯萎；凋谢
参见 4.66

(人)变得萎靡不振

看得出观众在炎热的阳光下快支撑不住了。

他被工作压得喘不过气来。

wither

4.69 If a plant **withers** or something **withers** it, it dries up and dies.

If something **withers** or **withers away**, it becomes weaker or smaller and then disappears.
They worry that honoured traditions

(使)枯萎；凋谢
参见 4.66, 4.70

萎缩；消失

他们担心许多优良传统将会逐渐消

will <u>wither</u>.
Their love was <u>withering away</u>.

withered

4.70 A **withered** plant has become dry and is dying.

A **withered** person looks old, thin, and weak, and has a lot of wrinkles on his skin.

withering

4.71 A **withering** look, expression, or remark deliberately makes you feel silly or embarrassed.

She lowered her eyes, unable to face his <u>withering</u> scorn.

失。
他们的爱情正在凋零。

（植物）枯萎的；干枯的
汉语用蔫形容人情绪低落、精神不振。
（人）枯槁的；多皱纹的

使人感到愚蠢的；使人难堪的

她双目低垂，无法面对他那种令人难堪的嘲笑。

Column 4

This column is adopted to help understand some metaphorical expressions of **plants** that are unique to Chinese.

陈谷子，烂芝麻	stale topics of conversation
节外生枝	side issues or new problems crop up unexpectedly; raise obstacles deliberately; complicate an issue
金枝玉叶	golden branches and jade leaves—people of imperial lineage; royalty
连理枝	two trees with branches interlocked—a loving couple
攀高枝儿	make friends or claim ties of kinship with someone of a higher social position
添枝加叶	add color and emphasis to (a narration); add highly colored details to (a story); embellish (a story)
细枝末节	minor details; nonessential
粗枝大叶	crude and careless; sloppy; slapdash
百花齐放	a hundred flowers in blossom—free development of different forms and styles in the arts
铁树开花	the iron tree in blossom—something seldom seen or hardly possible

4 Plants

残花败柳	faded flowers and withered willows—fallen women
昙花一现	flash in the pan
花枝招展	(of women) be gorgeously dressed
火树银花	dazzling displays of fireworks and lanterns
移花接木	graft one twig on another—stealthily substitute one thing for another
墙头草，随风倒	grass atop a wall swaying in the wind—a person who follows the crowd
斩草除根	cut the weeds and dig up the roots—stamp out the source of trouble
披荆斩棘	hack one's way through difficulties
疾风知劲草	the force of the wind tests the strength of the grass—strength of character is tested in crisis
枯木逢春	spring comes to the withered tree—get a new lease of life
泡蘑菇	play for time
瓜熟蒂落	when a melon is ripe it falls off its stem—things are easily settled once conditions are ripe
姜还是老的辣	old ginger is hotter than new—veterans are abler than recruits
藕断丝连	the lotus root snaps but its fibres stay joined—(of lovers, etc.) still in contact though apparently separated; separated but still in each other's thoughts
桃李满天下	have pupils everywhere (usu. said in praise of a teacher)

5 Cooking and Food

acid
5.1 An **acid** fruit or drink has a sour or sharp taste, often in a way that many people find unpleasant.

酸的；酸味的
酸在汉语中可用来指迂腐，如：酸秀才。酸也可用来形容妒忌的心情，如：心里酸溜溜的。

An **acid** remark or **acid** humour shows criticism in a way that is very clever but cruel.

尖酸的；刻薄的；辛辣的

an <u>acid</u> comment

尖刻的评论

She has an <u>acid</u> tongue. She can raise laughs at other people's expense.

她说话尖刻，能借奚落他人引人发笑。

acidly
5.2 You can also say that someone speaks **acidly** if it sounds unfriendly or critical or if he says cruel things.

尖刻地

"If you mean Simon, as I assume you do," said Jeanne <u>acidly</u>, "he hasn't mentioned it."

"如果你是指西蒙，而我想你确实是指他，"珍妮愤愤地说，"那么他并没有提到过这件事。"

bake
5.3 When a cake or bread **bakes**, or when you **bake** it, it cooks in an oven without any extra liquid or fat.

烘，烤，焙（面包、蛋糕等）
汉语用成熟来比喻事物发展到完善地步，如：我的意见还不够成熟。

A **half-baked** idea or plan is not practical because it has not been thought about carefully.

（想法或计划等）考虑不周的，草率的

The vast majority of ordinary people do not want or need these <u>half-baked</u> ideas about the world.

绝大多数普通百姓不要或不需要这些不成熟的关于世界的想法。

bitter

5.4 Something that is **bitter** has a strong sharp taste that is not sweet.

有苦味的；苦的
汉语中用苦尽甘来比喻苦难的遭遇结束，顺心的局面到来。参见 5.57

If someone is **bitter** about a disappointment or a bad experience, he feels unhappy and angry about it, and continues to feel like this for a long time afterwards.

（尤指受到不公正对待时）愤怒的，苦恼的

I'm still bitter about the whole affair.
She knew from bitter experience it wasn't worth complaining.

我对整件事仍然愤愤不平。
惨痛的经历使她认识到这没什么好抱怨的。

5.5 You can describe an experience which is extremely disappointing as **a bitter blow** or **a bitter disappointment**.

令人非常不愉快的经历；令人痛苦的打击

It was a bitter blow when they decided not to offer him the contract.

他们决定不和他签合同，这对他是个沉重打击。

5.6 A **bitter** argument or fight is one in which the people involved feel extremely angry and unhappy with each other.

（敌人或对手）势不两立的，怀恨的

Jill wanted to keep separate bank accounts, which was the cause of many a bitter argument between us.

吉尔想要单独开银行户头，这就是引发我们之间许多激烈争吵的原因。

one of the President's more bitter critics

对总统态度较激烈的批评者之一

5.7 You can say that a bad experience **leaves a bitter taste** in your mouth if you continue to feel angry or annoyed after it, and if it causes you to have a bad opinion of the people involved.

留下不好的印象

This affair is going to leave a bitter taste for many governments.

这件事将给许多政府留下长期的阴影。

bitterly

5.8 If you complain **bitterly**, you do it in a way that shows you are extremely angry or disappointed.

愤怒地；苦恼地；失望地

He complained <u>bitterly</u> that no one had bothered to ask his opinion.
他满腹牢骚地抱怨没有人征求他的意见。

5.9 If you do something **bitterly**, you do it in a determined and angry way.
坚定不移地；愤怒地

Many people are <u>bitterly</u> opposed to the idea.
许多人坚决反对这个主意。

Parliament is <u>bitterly</u> divided on this issue.
议会在这个问题上有很严重的分歧。

bitter-sweet

5.10 Food that has a **bitter-sweet** taste seems to taste bitter and sweet at the same time.
又苦又甜的

Bitter-sweet is used metaphorically to describe events or situations that have both happy and sad qualities.
有苦有乐的；苦乐参半的

There is something for everyone in this <u>bitter-sweet</u> tale.
在这个喜乐参半的故事里，每个人都能得到他想要的东西。

bland

5.11 Food or drink that tastes **bland** has very little flavour.
清淡的，无味的

Bland is used metaphorically to describe people or things that seem dull or boring and have nothing special or exciting about them.
平淡的；枯燥无味的

She had pleasant but rather <u>bland</u> features.
她很可爱但长相平平。

They are hoping to add spice to a <u>bland</u> contest.
他们希望给一场平淡的比赛增加一点刺激。

5.12 **Bland** comments or remarks are pleasant and intended not to make anyone upset or angry, but they may not be sincere.
（评论或话语）温和的，无关痛痒的

He gave the usual <u>bland</u> assurances about their commitment to peace.
他照例为他们的和平承诺作些无关痛痒的保证。

boil

5.13 If a liquid **boils**, or if you **boil** it, it
沸腾；烧开；煮沸

becomes so hot that there are bubbles in it and it starts to become a gas.

汉语常用火比喻暴躁或发怒，如：你先别*火儿*。类似的表达方式还有**发火**、**火暴脾气**等等。

If you say that you **are boiling with rage** or with another strong negative emotion, you mean that you are so angry or feel so strongly that you find it difficult to control your behaviour.

激动；发怒

James felt the fury <u>boiling</u> within him.
<u>*Boiling with rage*</u>, *Kate slammed the car door and drove off.*

詹姆斯感到怒火中烧。
凯特怒火中烧，砰地关上车门，开车走了。

5.14 If something **makes your blood boil**, it makes you feel very angry.

使人怒火中烧

Her patronizing sarcasm <u>made my blood boil</u>.

她那傲慢的嘲笑使我怒火中烧。

5.15 If a liquid **boils over**, it rises so much when it boils that it flows over the top of the container that it is in.

沸溢；煮溢

If a situation or feeling **boils over**, people cannot control their anger and start to fight or argue.

（局势）失去控制；发怒

The dispute finally <u>boiled over</u> into a series of violent protests.

争论最终失去控制，发展成一系列强烈抗议。

5.16 To **boil up** a liquid means to heat it until it boils.

烧热；煮滚

If a situation or feeling **boils up**, people start to feel angry.

（形势）发展到危险程度；（怒火）升腾

Anger <u>was boiling up</u> inside me.

我怒火中烧。

5.17 If you say that a problem or a complicated situation **boils down to** a particular thing, you mean that that is the most important or basic aspect of it.

归结为；是……的主要原因；是……的最基本部分

It's difficult to choose which appliance to buy, but in the end it usually <u>boils down to</u> cost.

很难决定买哪种工具，但最终通常取决于价钱。

boiling point

5.18 **Boiling point** is the temperature at which a liquid boils.

If you say that someone's feelings have reached **boiling point**, you mean that his feelings have become so strong that he is about to take some dramatic action.

Their impatience is clearly bubbling up toward the boiling point.

With tempers and emotions almost at boiling point, it's important to take one step at a time.

5.19 **Boiling point** is also used metaphorically to refer to the moment when a situation becomes more serious or dangerous because people start to feel very angry.

Tension between the two groups has almost reached boiling point.

Racial tension has reached boiling point.

burner

5.20 A **burner** is an object used for heating or burning something.

If you **put something on the back burner**, you decide not to deal with it until later.

Obviously this means you're going to have to put one project on the back burner.

For ten years she has looked after three children, with her career very much on the back burner.

5.21 If an issue, a plan, etc. is **on the**

沸点

（激烈情绪的）爆发点

显然他们的不耐烦难以抑制，快要爆发了。

在愤怒情绪几乎快要爆发的情况下，重要的是每次只采取一个步骤。

危急关头

汉语用**火烧眉毛**比喻情势十分急迫。比较汉语中的**一触即发**。

两个集团间的紧张关系几乎已经达到白热化的程度。

种族间的紧张状态已达到一触即发的程度。

燃烧器；炉子

汉语用**出炉**比喻新产生出来，如：年度最佳运动员昨日出炉。

暂时搁置某事

显然这意味着你将不得不把一个项目搁置在一边了。

十年来她一直照顾三个孩子，而她的事业则在很大程度上搁在一边了。

（问题、计划等）处于重要地位；受

5 Cooking and Food

front burner, it is considered to be very important and urgent.
Anything that keeps education <u>on the front burner</u> is good.

到重视；为当务之急

任何重视教育的事都是好事。

cook

5.22 To **cook** food means to prepare it and heat it so that it is ready to eat.

烹调；煮；烧

If someone **cooks up** an excuse, reason, plan etc., he invents it, especially one that is slightly dishonest or unlikely to work.
Between them they <u>cooked up</u> a story to tell their parents.

捏造；编造；策划
汉语用<u>炮制</u>泛指编造、制定之意（含贬义），如：经过一番精心<u>炮制</u>，满篇谎言的文章出笼了。
他们私下里编了个故事来哄父母。

diet

5.23 **Diet** is the food that a person or animal usually eats.

食物；饮食

A diet of something is too much of an activity that you think is boring or has bad effects.
We are fed <u>a diet of</u> game shows and soap operas.

（尤指劣质的）经常大量接触的东西

我们被灌输大量的游戏节目和肥皂剧。

dilute

5.24 To **dilute** a liquid means to make it less strong by adding water or another liquid.

稀释；冲淡
比较汉语中的<u>淡化</u>，如：<u>淡化</u>行政干预，强化竞争机制。

If someone or something **dilutes** a belief, quality, or value, he/it makes it weaker and less effective.
Large classes <u>dilute</u> the quality of education that children receive.
Nervousness <u>diluted</u> her excitement slightly.

削弱；降低

大班上课会降低孩子所受教育的质量。
紧张有点使她兴奋不起来。

drily

5.25 If someone speaks **drily**, he sounds unfriendly and unemotional, although

枯燥地；干巴巴地；冷冰冰地

he may be making a joke or being ironic.
"Do you know anybody who doesn't cheat?" I asked drily.

"你知道有谁会不作弊吗？"我机械地问道。

dry

5.26 **Dry** food contains little or no liquid, such as fat or juice.

脱水的；没有脂肪的；没有汁的；干的

Dry is used metaphorically to describe information that is presented in a way that makes it seem uninteresting.
The style was too pompous and <u>dry</u> for a children's book.
They will give brief, practical and interesting information, not just <u>dry</u> scientific facts.

生硬的；枯燥无味的
汉语中，干瘪可用来指（文辞等）内容贫乏，枯燥无味，如：语言干瘪。
这种风格对于儿童书籍来说有点儿过于浮华、生硬。
他们将提供简短、实际和有趣的信息，不光是干巴巴的科学事实。

5.27 **Dry** humour involves saying funny things in a serious way.
Even when he might appear to be depressed, his <u>dry</u> sense of humour never deserted him.

（讲笑话时）故作严肃的，一本正经的
即使他有可能显得抑郁，但机智的幽默感从来不曾从他身上消失。

flavour

5.28 The **flavour** of food or drink is the particular taste of it.

味道；滋味
汉语中，滋味可用来比喻意味或感受，如：别有一番滋味在心头。

A **flavour of** something is something that you experience, which is just enough to give you a good idea of what that thing is like.
The music gives some <u>flavour of</u> the traditional ways of singing.

风格；风味；风韵

这种音乐具有传统演唱方式的某些风格。

5.29 **Flavour** is also used metaphorically to refer to a particular quality that is typically of something.
The foreign visitors added an international <u>flavour</u> to the occasion.

特色；特点

外宾们给这次活动增添了国际特色。

His paintings really catch the mood and *flavour* of the country.　　他的绘画真正抓住了这个国家的情调和特色。

5.30 If you refer to a person or thing as **flavour of the month**, you mean that he/it is very popular at the moment, but you are suggesting that this will not continue for long.

红极一时的人物

She is very much *flavour of the month* in Hollywood.　　她目前是好莱坞红极一时的人物。

grill

5.31 If you **grill** something, or if it **grills**, you cook it by putting it on a flat metal frame with bars across it, above or below strong direct heat.

（在烤架上）炙烤

汉语用**炙手可热**比喻气焰很盛，权势很大。

If someone **grills** you, or gives you a **grilling**, he asks you a lot of detailed questions in a way which you find unpleasant or frightening.

盘问；拷问

The committee spent weeks *grilling* witnesses.　　委员会花了几个星期盘问证人。

He now faces a tough *grilling* and a report will be sent to the Crown Prosecution Service which will decide whether to press charges.　　他现在面对着一次难以应付的审问，随后报告会送往英国政府检察部门，由它决定是否起诉。

ingredient

5.32 An **ingredient** is one of the foods or liquids that you use in making a particular meal.

（烹调用的）原料，配料

Ingredient is used metaphorically to refer to one of the things that give something its character or make it effective.

因素；要素

Good communication is an essential *ingredient* of good management.　　良好的沟通是成功管理的基本要素。

He also knows that the most important *ingredient* in any team is confidence.　　他也知道，在任何球队中，信心是最重要的因素。

The meeting had all the <u>ingredients</u> of high political drama.

这个会议具有高级政治戏剧的全部特征。

juicy

5.33 **Juicy** food tastes good because it contains a lot of liquid.

（食物）多汁的

Juicy stories are slightly shocking but interesting or fun to listen to.

（故事）生动有趣的，绘声绘色的

a <u>juicy</u> bit of gossip

绘声绘色的流言蜚语

The whole world will be watching, anxious for all the <u>juicy</u> details.

全世界都将观看，人们急欲了解所有有趣的细节。

5.34 A **juicy** job or activity is interesting and enjoyable.

（工作或活动）有乐趣的

He gets all the <u>juicy</u> jobs.

他干的全是有趣的活儿。

5.35 You can also use **juicy** to describe something that is very profitable.

值很多钱的；价值很高的

a <u>juicy</u> contract

数额巨大的合同

The fees to the bankers that arrange the issues are <u>juicy</u>.

为安排这些事情而支付给银行家们的费用，数目很可观。

peppery

5.36 **Peppery** food tastes spicy because there is a lot of pepper in it.

胡椒味的；似胡椒的
比较**泼辣**、**老辣**、**辛辣**等。

Peppery is used to describe people, especially elderly people, who are grumpy or who seem to get irritated easily.

急躁的；易怒的
汉语中辣子可用来比喻泼辣的人（多指妇女）。如：《红楼梦》里的凤姐叫凤<u>辣</u>子。

He was a <u>peppery</u> old man who was a good deal kinder than he looked.

他是个脾气坏的老人，但他其实远比从外表看来要和蔼可亲。

The President was in a particular <u>peppery</u> mood this morning.

今天早上总统特别容易动怒。

pressure cooker

5.37 A **pressure cooker** is a deep cooking pan with a tight lid that allows the pressure of steam to cook food quickly.

压力锅；高压锅

Pressure cooker is sometimes used

困境

metaphorically to refer to stressful situations.

the <u>pressure cooker</u> atmosphere of the bank's currency dealing office

银行货币交易办公室凝重的氛围

recipe

5.38 A **recipe** is a set of instructions for cooking or preparing a particular food.

食谱；烹饪法

Recipe is used metaphorically to refer to a method or an idea that seems likely to have a particular result.

方法；秘诀；诀窍

When asked for his <u>recipe</u> for happiness, he gave a very short but sensible answer: work and love.

当人们向他讨教幸福的处方时，他的回答简单而合乎情理：工作和爱。

Giving your kids too much choice can be a <u>recipe</u> for disaster.

给孩子太多的选择很可能是导致灾难的根源。

Clubs are relying more and more on fitness and strength as <u>recipes</u> for success, at the expense of skill.

俱乐部正愈来愈多地依赖体能和力量，它们将这两个因素作为成功的处方，而把技术抛在一边。

roast

5.39 To **roast** meat or other food means to cook it in an oven or over a fire.

烤；烘
参见5.31

If you say that one person **roasts** another, or **gives** him a **roasting**, you mean that the first person shouts at or severely criticizes the second person.

严厉批评；非难

If it had been Mattie's class at the training centre, Mattie would have <u>roasted</u> him in front of all the others.

如果这发生在训练中心马蒂的班上，马蒂将会当着所有人的面狠狠教训他。

There was no way Bobby should have done what he did. I have given him the biggest <u>roasting</u> of his life.

无论有什么理由，鲍比都不应做出这种事。我已狠狠教训了他。这是他一生中所受到的最严厉的批评。

salty

5.40 **Salty** food or drink tastes of salt.

含盐的；咸的

Salty is used metaphorically to describe language that is honest and interesting

尖锐的；辛辣的；粗鲁的

but occasionally includes swearing or offensive language.

His work is dense and sharp, with <u>salty</u> language.
他的工作紧张而热烈，常常伴随着一些有趣而粗鲁的对话。

She was the <u>salty</u> commentator on everything that happened in the ward.
她对病房里发生的一切都用有趣、尖刻的语言加以评论。

simmer

5.41 When you **simmer** food or when it simmers, you cook it by keeping it at boiling point or just below boiling point.
煨；用文火炖

If you say that disagreements or unpleasant feelings **simmer**, you mean that they continue to exist over a period of time, often growing more intense, so that they sometimes result in a serious row or unpleasant situation.
激化（状态），即将爆发（状态）

The dispute, which <u>has been simmering</u> for years, came to the boil in April.
已经憋了好几年的争论在4月份爆发出来了。

The authorities have managed to keep the lid on any <u>simmering</u> discontent.
当局已经设法防止任何正在滋长的不满情绪的爆发。

5.42 If you say that someone **is simmering down**, you mean that he becomes calmer after being excited or angry.
平静下来；冷静下来

Now, <u>simmer down</u> and let's talk this over quietly.
且别激动，咱们心平气和地来好好谈谈这件事情。

After things were beginning to <u>simmer down</u> a little, the talks resumed.
情况开始平静一些之后，会谈继续进行。

slice

5.43 A **slice** of bread, meat, cake, or other food is a thin piece of it that has been cut from a larger piece.
（切下的食物）薄片，片

You can refer to a part or share of something as a **slice of** it.
部分；份

We're working hard to get a bigger <u>slice</u>
我们正在争取旅游业的更大份额。

of the tourist trade.
Universities depend less on government grants today; a significant slice of their income is from the private sector.

5.44 **A slice of cake** is used metaphorically to refer to a part of money or help that is being shared between people.
Mental health organizations should receive a bigger slice of the cake.

5.45 You can refer to a period of time as a **slice of** time.
We each need privacy: a slice of time apart and alone.

5.46 You can use a **slice of** luck or a **slice of** fortune to refer to an unexpected event which is lucky for someone.
Even at their best, the team might need a slice of luck.

5.47 **A slice of life** is a description or image of ordinary life.
Independent travel, when it lives up to its promise, gives you a slice of life as others live it.

5.48 If you say that someone wants **a slice of the action**, you mean that he wants to join in with an activity that is successful.
The US banks are now likely to want a slice of the action.
Everyone it seems wants to know what is going on down there and how he can get a slice of the action.

sour

5.49 Food that is **sour** has a sharp taste

大学对政府拨款的依靠更少了；它们的收入中有一大部分来自私人捐赠。

分享的一份利益（指钱或帮助）

心理健康机构应该得到更大的资助。

一段（时间）

我们每个人都需要私人生活：一段时间的分离和独处。

一些（运气）

即便在他们处于最佳状态的情况下，这个队仍可能需要有点运气。

现实生活的描写；日常生活的写照

如果独立的旅行能达到预期的效果，那么它就能让你体验一下别人所过的生活。

一项活动

美国的银行现在可能想要参与这项活动了。

人人都好像想知道那里发生了什么事，他们怎样才能参与这项活动。

酸的

like the taste of a lemon or an unripe apple. 参见 5.1

If someone is **sour**, he is bad-tempered and unhappy, often because he has had some unpleasant experiences. You can also use **sour** to describe people's expressions if they look angry and unhappy.
脾气坏的；不友善的；乖戾的

He was a <u>sour</u> and cruel man.
他曾是个脾气很坏、恶毒的男人。

When I said hello, he gave me a really <u>sour</u> look.
我对他打招呼时，他朝我狠狠地瞪了一眼。

5.50 If something **goes sour** or **turns sour**, it is unsuccessful or does not develop in a satisfactory way.
失败；变糟；出毛病

The relationship <u>turned sour</u> over a financial dispute.
因为财务纠纷关系变僵了。

Their investments had begun to <u>go sour</u>.
他们的投资开始出问题了。

5.51 If a relationship or situation **sours** or something **sours** it, it stops being successful or satisfactory.
（使）（关系、情况）变糟，变坏

Mutual accusations <u>soured</u> the peace talks.
相互指责导致和谈破裂。

Relations between them <u>have soured</u>.
他们之间的关系变糟了。

sourly

5.52 If someone does something in a way that shows that he is feeling bad-tempered or unhappy, you can say that he does that thing **sourly**.
气愤地

A tall thin woman, whose mouth turned down <u>sourly</u> at the corners, stood up to greet her.
一个瘦高个的妇女生气地撇着嘴角站起身来迎接她。

sourness

5.53 **Sourness** is anger and unhappiness, which have usually been caused by bad experiences, and which
愤怒，痛苦
参见 5.52

make people behave unpleasantly towards others.
His face carried an habitual expression of sourness.
You will find a great deal of resentment and sourness among the workers.

他的脸上习惯地带着一种痛苦的表情。
你将在工人中发现许多不满和愤怒的情绪。

stew

5.54 To **stew** food such as meat or fruit means to cook it slowly in liquid.

炖；煨；焖

If you **let someone stew (in his own juice)**, you deliberately leave him to worry about something he has done wrong.

让某人自作自受
汉语用**搬起石头砸自己的脚**比喻存心损害别人，结果反而害了自己。

That was weak of me, for I should have let Marcus stew in his own juice.
I thought I'd leave him to stew in his own juice until Tuesday afternoon.

那是我软弱的表现，因为我应该让马库斯自作自受。
我想我要让他自作自受到星期二下午。

5.55 A **stew** is a meal which you make by cooking vegetables and meat in liquid for a long time.

炖煮的菜肴

If you think that a plan or situation is not successful because it has been made by putting together several things without considering them carefully, you can refer to it as a **stew**.

拼凑之物；杂烩
汉语用**大杂烩**比喻把各种不同的人或物胡乱拼在一起的混合体。

The budget is a dreadful stew of federal subsidies and tax breaks.

这项预算不过是将联邦政府的补助及税收削减的因素拙劣地拼凑起来而已。

taking all they can remember of early 90's culture and throwing it all together into one undignified stew

将他们关于 90 年代早期文化的全部记忆拾起来，胡乱凑成一个不成样子的杂烩

5.56 If someone is **in a stew**, he is very worried or upset about something.

焦虑的；紧张的；困惑的

He's been in a stew since this morning and now you arrive late for this

他今天早上一直忧心忡忡，而这个他认为如此重要的讨论，你却迟到。

discussion he considers so important.

sweet

5.57 **Sweet** food or drink tastes like sugar.

甜（味）的
汉语用**甘苦**比喻美好的处境和艰苦的处境，如：同甘苦，共患难。

Someone who is **sweet** is pleasant, good-tempered, and kind.
Caroline was the *sweetest* little girl I have ever looked after.
It was so *sweet* of you to do this.

和蔼可亲的；温柔的；体贴的
卡罗琳是我照看过的最温顺的小女孩。
你这么做实在是太体贴了。

5.58 A **sweet** voice is pleasant and smooth, and usually high-pitched.
Her voice was as soft and *sweet* as a young girl's.

（声音）甜美的，悦耳的
她的嗓音和年轻女孩的一样温柔甜美。

sweetly

5.59 You can say that people behave **sweetly** if they are pleasant, good-tempered, and kind.
Kate nodded and smiled *sweetly*.

可爱地；亲切地；温柔地

凯特点点头，甜甜地笑着。

unsavoury

5.60 Food that is **unsavoury** smells and looks bad.

（食品）难闻的，看起来很糟糕的

If you describe a person, place, or thing as **unsavoury**, you mean that you find him/it unpleasant or morally unacceptable.
an *unsavoury* reputation
Matthew is suddenly very alone without his brother and drifts around town with a group of faintly *unsavoury* characters.

令人不快的；令人讨厌的；不诚实的

坏名声
没有兄弟在身边，马修突然感到非常孤独，他于是同一伙稍有些违法行为的人一起在镇里游荡。

water down

5.61 To **water down** a liquid means to add water to it in order to make it less strong.
If something such as a statement or newspaper article **is watered down**, it is

掺水冲淡；加水稀释

淡化，削弱（陈述或报纸文章等的攻击力、冲击性或细节）

5 Cooking and Food

less offensive, powerful, or detailed. 参见 5.24
Some of the more forthright sections 一些更直接的部分被编辑淡化了。
<u>were watered down</u> by editors.

Column 5

This column is adopted to help understand some metaphorical expressions of **cooking & food** that are unique to Chinese.

饱尝辛酸	taste to the full the bitterness of life
备尝艰苦	suffer untold hardships
柴米油盐	fuel, rice, oil and salt—chief daily necessities
柴米夫妻	a couple who live from hand to mouth
炒冷饭	stir-fry leftover rice—say or do the same old thing; dish up the same old stuff; rehash
炒鱿鱼	give someone the sack; sack; fire
陈谷子，烂芝麻	old millet and stale sesame—stale topics of conversation
吃白饭，吃白食	not earn an honest living; live off others
吃不了兜着走	land oneself in serious trouble
吃醋	be jealous (usu. of a rival in love)
吃大锅饭	eat from the same big pot—get the same reward or pay as everyone else regardless of one's performance in work
吃太平饭	enjoy a peaceful life
吃闲饭	lead an idle life; be a loafer or sponger
吃现成饭	eat what is already prepared—enjoy the fruits of others' work
重起炉灶	begin all over again; make a fresh start
分一杯羹	take a share of the spoils or profits
灌迷魂汤	try to ensnare sb. with honeyed words
火候	level of attainment
夹生饭	a job not thoroughly done
家常便饭	common occurrence; routine; all in the day's work
捡了芝麻，丢了西瓜	pick up the sesame seeds but overlook the watermelons—concentrate on minor matters to the neglect of major ones

敬酒不吃吃罚酒	refuse a toast only to drink a forfeit—submit to someone's pressure after first turning down his request; be constrained to do what one at first refused to
旧瓶装新酒	new wine in old bottles—new content in old form
咀嚼	mull over; ruminate; chew the cud
啃书本	delve into books
捞油水	make a side profit; get a squeeze
连锅端	take all the pots and pans—take or get rid of the whole lot
露馅儿	let the cat out of the bag; give the game away; spill the beans
生米煮成熟饭	The rice is cooked—what's done can't be undone.
食而不化	eat without digesting—read without understanding
酸甜苦辣	sour, sweet, bitter, hot—joys and sorrows of life
贪多嚼不烂	bite off more than one can chew
甜水	sugar water—happiness; comfort
尝到甜头	become aware of the benefits of; come to know the good of
铁饭碗	iron rice bowl—a secure job
味同嚼蜡	like chewing wax—insipid
对胃口	to one's liking
香饽饽	a person who is liked best; favorite
一锅粥	a pot of porridge—a complete mess; all in a muddle
一锅煮	cook all things in one pot—treat different persons or things alike (or indiscriminately)
油水	pickings; profit
余味	pleasant impression
自食其果	eat one's own bitter fruit—reap what one has sown

6 Construction

access

6.1 If you have **access** to a building or other place, you are able or allowed to go into it.
If you have **access** to something such as information or equipment, you have the opportunity or right to see it or use it.
Access to up-to-date financial information is important to our success.
Some groups still have difficulty <u>gaining access</u> to social service.
She's one of a handful of aides with direct <u>access</u> to the president.

通道；入口
汉语用**敲门砖**比喻借以求得名利的初步手段。
享用权；享用机会

获得即时更新的金融信息对我们的成功至关重要。
一些群体要获得享用社会服务的权利还有困难。
她是少数几个可以直接面见总统的助手之一。

back door

6.2 A **back door** is a door at the back or side of a building.
If you say that someone is doing something **through** or **by the backdoor**, you disapprove of him because he is doing it in a secret, indirect, or dishonest way.
They managed to sneak the legislation in <u>through the back door</u>.

后门；旁门

秘密地；不正当地；走后门
参见 10.24

他们设法偷偷地设立了这项法规。

backyard

6.3 A **backyard** is an area behind a house covered with a hard brick or stone surface.
Something that is **in your (own) backyard** is in a place close to you or in

后院
汉语中，**后院**用以比喻后方或内部，如：后院起火。
在附近；在身边

a situation that you are directly involved in.
It's not the kind of thing you expect to happen <u>in your own backyard</u>.
The party leader is facing opposition <u>in his own backyard</u>.

这并非是你期望发生在你身边的那种事情。
该党领导面临着党内人士的反对。

bridge
6.4 A **bridge** is a road, railway, or path that goes over a river, over another road etc., and the structure that supports it.
Bridge is used metaphorically to refer to something that forms a connection between one group and another or between one situation and another.

桥；桥梁
汉语用**桥梁**比喻能起沟通作用的人或事物，如：桥梁作用。
（集团或情况之间的）纽带，联系，桥梁
汉语用**纽带**比喻能够起联系作用的人或事物，如：批评和自我批评是团结的**纽带**，是进步的保证。

Her job, basically, is to create a <u>bridge</u> between the business community and the world of education.
The new assembly is seen by many as a <u>bridge</u> to full independence.
6.5 To **bridge** disagreements, differences, or difficulties means to get rid of them so that to make something possible.
Both parties seem implacably opposed to <u>bridging</u> their differences.
a fund that bridges the gap between students' needs and their incomes

她的工作本质上说是在商界和教育界之间建立联系。

新议会被许多人看作是通向完全独立的桥梁。

弥合（差距）；消除（分歧）
汉语用**搭桥**、**穿线**比喻从中撮合、介绍、联系，如：牵线搭桥。
双方似乎极力反对消除他们之间的分歧。
缩短学生需要和学生收入之间差距的基金

build
6.6 To **build** something such as a house or a wall means to make it by joining things together.
Build or **build up** is used metaphorically to talk about creating and developing things.
He set out to <u>build</u> a business empire

建筑；建造

发展；建立

他开始着手建立一个企业王国并且获

and succeeded.
Many popular writers <u>built up</u> their reputations during the war.

6.7 To **build (up) a picture of** someone or something means to gradually develop an idea of what he/it is like.
We need to <u>build up a picture of</u> the community's needs.

6.8 **Build** or **build up** is also used to talk about increasing or making something increase.
The food industry needs to <u>build</u> consumer confidence again.
Don't allow resentment to <u>build up</u> between you and your partner.

6.9 To **build bridges** means to help two people, groups, or countries who have disagreed to have a more friendly relationship.

He played a key role in <u>building bridges</u> between managements and the unions.

6.10 To **build** someone **up** means to make him bigger, healthier, and stronger, especially by making him eat more.
You need a lot of fresh fruit to help <u>build you up</u>.

ceiling

6.11 A **ceiling** is the surface that is above you in a room.

You may refer to an upper limit set on the number or amount of something as a **ceiling**.
They imposed a <u>ceiling</u> on agricultural

得了成功。
许多受人欢迎的作家是在战争期间声名鹊起的。

构想；设想
汉语常用**蓝图**比喻建设计划，如：描绘国家建设的**蓝图**。
我们需要逐步构想出社区的需求。

（使）增长；加强；增强

食品业需要重新树立消费者的信心。

别让你与合伙人之间的怨恨越积越深。

沟通
汉语中，**疏通**可用来指沟通双方的意思，调节双方的争执，如：这件事还得你从中**疏通**。
参见 6.4, 6.5
他对管理层和工会之间的沟通起着重要作用。

使……更强壮；增进……的健康；增强……的体力

你需要吃许多新鲜水果来增进你的健康。

天花板；顶棚
汉语用**封顶**来指限定最高数额，如：奖金不**封顶**。
上限

他们为农产品的进口规定了上限。

imports.
A <u>ceiling</u> of £100 was put on all donations. 所有捐款的上限规定为 100 英镑。

cement

6.12 **Cement** is a grey powder used in building that becomes very hard when you mix it with sand and water. 水泥

Cement is used to refer to something that helps to make a relationship, idea etc. stronger. （对关系、看法等起巩固作用的）纽带

A belief in freedom is often seen as the <u>cement</u> of our nation. 对自由的信仰常常被看作是联系我们民族的纽带。

6.13 To **cement** a relationship, idea etc. means to make it stronger or more certain. 加强，巩固（关系、看法等）

The aim of the president's visit was to <u>cement</u> relations between the two countries. 总统来访的目的是要巩固两国之间的关系。

construct

6.14 To **construct** something such as a building means to make it by joining things together. 建造；修筑

If someone **constructs** something such as an idea, a scientific theory, or a system, he develops it by making various things fit together. 组成；形成

He could now <u>construct</u> short sentences in Spanish. 他现在能用西班牙语说出简短的句子了。

Police have called in an expert to <u>construct</u> a psychological profile of the murderer. 警方请来一名专家对该杀人犯进行心理特征分析。

cornerstone

6.15 A **cornerstone** is the stone at one of the bottom corners of a new building, often put there during a special 基石；奠基石

汉语中，**基石**用来比喻基础或中坚力量；**柱石**比喻起支撑作用的力量和担

ceremony.
Cornerstone is used metaphorically to refer to the basic part of something, on which everything depends.
Trust is the <u>cornerstone</u> of their marriage.
This study is the <u>cornerstone</u> of the whole research programme.

负重任的人。
基础；根本；基石；柱石

信任是他们婚姻的基础。
此项研究是整个研究计划的基础。

corridor
6.16 A **corridor** is a long passage inside a building with doors on each side.

走廊；通道
汉语用**走廊**比喻连接两个较大地区的狭长地带，如：河西走廊。

You may use **the corridors (of power)** to refer to the places where people use their political influence and major political decisions are made.
the lobbyists who inhabit <u>the corridors of power</u> in Washington

权力走廊（高层决策机构）

聚集在华盛顿权力走廊上的说客们

demolish
6.17 To **demolish** a building means to destroy it completely.

拆毁

Demolish is used metaphorically to talk about having a bad effect on someone's feelings or spoiling his plans.
It was an experience that completely <u>demolished</u> her confidence.

伤害（感情）；破坏（计划）

这是一次彻底摧毁她信心的经历。

6.18 To **demolish** an idea or theory means to show that it is completely wrong.
A recent book <u>has demolished</u> this theory.

推翻，驳倒（观点或理论）

最近出版的一本书推翻了这种理论。

6.19 If you **demolish** an opponent, rival etc., you defeat him easily and completely.
They <u>demolished</u> New Zealand 22-6 in the final.

轻易而彻底地打败

他们在决赛中以 22 比 6 大败新西兰队。

6.20 If you **demolish** something such as food, you eat it very quickly.

狼吞虎咽地吃；贪婪地吃

The children <u>demolished</u> their burgers and chips.　　孩子们狼吞虎咽地吃汉堡包和炸薯条。

demolition

6.21 **Demolition** is the deliberate destruction of a building.　　拆毁，毁坏

You may use **demolition** or **demolition job** to refer to an easy defeat in a game or competition.　　（在比赛或竞赛中的）轻松打败，完胜

Arsenal showed their worth in the <u>demolition</u> of their North London rivals.　　通过击败北部伦敦的对手，阿森纳队表现出了自身的价值。

Australia's 5-0 <u>demolition job</u> on England　　澳大利亚以 5 比 0 轻取英格兰

6.22 A **demolition job** is an occasion when someone or something is criticized severely.　　抨击

His speech did a very effective <u>demolition job</u> on the government's proposals.　　他的发言非常成功地驳倒了政府的提案。

door

6.23 A **door** is a large flat object you open when you want to enter or leave a building, room or vehicle.　　门

汉语用门槛比喻标准或条件，如：名牌大学门槛高，多数考生望而生畏。

You may refer to an opportunity to do something or a possibility that something will happen as a **door**.　　机会；可能；途径；通道

For these young men, a sports career can be a <u>door</u> to fame and fortune.　　对这些年轻人来说，运动生涯可以为他们提供获取名利的机会。

This new job has really opened a lot of <u>doors</u> for her.　　这份新工作确实为她创造了许多机会。

This decision could open the <u>door</u> to higher costs.　　这项决定可能会使费用更高。

edifice

6.24 An **edifice** is a large impressive building.　　（雄伟的）大厦

You may refer to a complicated system or policy as an **edifice**.　　庞大的体系；复杂的政策

The whole <u>edifice</u> of EC environment　　欧共体的整个环境政策体系都受到了

policy is threatened by this bill.
这个法案的威胁。

foundation

6.25 A **foundation** is the part of a structure of a building that is below the ground and supports the rest of it.

地基；地脚

Foundation is used to refer to the most basic part of something from which the rest of it develops.

汉语中，基础指事物发展的根本或起点，如：基础知识。

基础

He believes that religion is the foundation of a civilized society.
他相信宗教是文明社会的基础。

The first two years of study provide a solid foundation in computing.
前两年的学习为计算机操作打下坚实的基础。

Their current economic prosperity rests on rather weak foundation.
他们当前的经济繁荣根基相当薄弱。

gateway

6.26 A **gateway** is an entrance that is opened and closed with a gate.

出入口；门口
参见 6.1

You may refer to something that allows you to do or achieve something as a **gateway**.

手段；途径；方法

A good education is the gateway to success.
良好的教育是通往成功之路。

labyrinth

6.27 A **labyrinth** is a place where there are a lot of paths or passages and you can easily become lost.

迷宫；曲径
比较汉语中的繁文缛节。

You may refer to a system or process that has a lot of very complicated details as a **labyrinth**.

繁琐的制度（或程序）

a labyrinth of rules and regulations
错综复杂的规章制度

lock

6.28 If you **lock** something such as a door, a room, or a container that has a lock, you close it securely using a key.

锁；锁住

If you **are locked in** or **into** something
陷入，卷入（困境、争论、争执等）

such as a difficult situation, an argument, a disagreement etc., you are involved in it.

The two sides <u>were locked in</u> fierce debate over the proposed merger deal.
针对提出的合并协议，双方陷入了长时间激烈的争论之中。

So many people remain <u>locked in</u> the past by continually reliving the events that caused them pain.
如此多的人们仍然不断地回顾曾给他们带来痛苦的往事，并由此沉湎于过去的岁月而不能自拔。

One Christmas he spent the entire dinner with his back to me, <u>locked in</u> conversation with an attractive friend of his sister.
有一个圣诞节他整个晚餐时间都背对着我，一刻不停地在和他妹妹的一位漂亮朋友交谈。

pave

6.29 If a road or an area of ground **has been paved**, it has been covered with blocks of stone or concrete, so that it is suitable for walking or driving on.
（用砖、石块、水泥等）铺，铺砌
汉语用**铺路**来比喻为做某件事创造条件。

If one thing **paves the way** for another, it creates a situation in which it is possible or more likely that the other thing will happen.
作为某事的铺垫；为某事作准备

The agreement <u>will pave the way for</u> restoring economic ties.
该协议将为恢复经济联系铺平道路。

roof

6.30 A **roof** is the outer part of a building.
屋顶；房顶
参见6.11

If a level of something such as the price of a product or the rate of inflation **goes through the roof**, it suddenly increases very rapidly indeed.
迅速增加到很高的水平

Share prices <u>have gone through the roof</u> in the past six months.
股票价格已经涨到了六个月以来的最高值。

6.31 If you **hit the roof** or **go through the roof**, you suddenly become extremely angry.
大发雷霆；怒不可遏

It's a good job he never found out. He'd have <u>hit the roof</u>.
幸亏他一直未发现，要不然他会大发脾气的。

When he hears about this, my old man is going to <u>go right through the roof</u>.
一听到这件事，我老爸就要大发雷霆。

ruin

6.32 The **ruins** are the parts of a building that remain after it has been severely damaged.
废墟；遗迹

If something is **in ruins** or **falls into ruin**, it is completely spoiled.
毁灭；毁坏

Last month saw his dreams shattered and his business <u>in ruins</u>.
上个月他的梦想彻底破灭，他的生意破产了。

After the war many monasteries <u>fell into ruin</u>.
战争过后，许多修道院都逐渐破败了。

tower

6.33 A **tower** is a tall narrow structure or building that stands alone.
塔

If you refer to someone as **a tower of strength**, you appreciate him because he gives you a lot of help, support, and encouragement when you have problems or are in a difficult situation.
（在困境下）可依靠的人，可信赖的人，靠山

汉语用**靠山**比喻可以依靠的有力量的人或集体；用**后台**比喻背后操纵、支持的人或集团。

Lucy was <u>a tower of strength</u> after my husband died.
在我丈夫死后，露西成了我可以依靠的人。

You've been <u>a tower of strength</u> to me.
你一直是我的支柱。

towering

6.34 A **towering** building, tree, etc. is very tall and therefore rather impressive or frightening.
高耸的；参天的；屹立的

You may use **towering** to describe something that is extremely impressive, important or successful.
令人难忘的；极为重要的；非常成功的

Picasso is a <u>towering</u> figure in the history of 20th-century art.
毕加索是 20 世纪艺术史上一位极为重要的人物。

wall

6.35 A **wall** is one of the vertical sides of a building or room.

Wall is used metaphorically to refer to emotions or behaviour that prevents people from feeling close to each other.

The years had built a <u>wall</u> between the two families.

A <u>wall</u> of silence had grown up between them.

6.36 If you say that you, or your plans, have **met** or **come up against a brick wall**, you mean that other people disagree with you or are refusing to listen to your requests, so that you cannot continue with your plans.

The latest talks about Northern Ireland <u>have come up against a brick wall</u>.

6.37 If you say that you **are talking to a brick wall**, you mean that the people you are talking to refuse to listen to you or to take notice of you.

He was absolutely right. Unfortunately, he <u>was talking to a brick wall</u>.

I've tried to tell her, but it's like <u>talking to a brick wall</u>.

window

6.38 A **window** is a space or an area of glass in the wall of a building or vehicle that lets in light.

Window is used as a metaphor to talk about something that helps you to understand a particular situation or subject.

墙，墙壁

（感情或行为的）障碍，隔阂

这些年两家已经有了隔阂。

他们谁也不理谁了。

碰壁；遇到难以逾越的障碍

汉语中，**碰壁**用来比喻遇到严重阻碍或受到拒绝，事情行不通，如：到处**碰壁**。

最近举行的关于北爱尔兰问题的谈判没有取得任何进展。

像对墙说话；白费唇舌
比较汉语中的**对牛弹琴**。

他绝对是正确的。遗憾的是，他是对牛弹琴。

我试过告诉她，但那是白费口舌。

窗；窗户
汉语中，**窗口**用来比喻反映或展示精神上、物质上各种现象或状况的地方，如：**窗口**行业。

展示某物真实一面的事物

Is the play an accurate <u>window</u> on the world? 这个剧本是这个世界的准确写照吗?

This traditional art form provides a fascinating <u>window</u> into another culture. 这种传统的艺术形式提供了了解另一种文化的迷人窗口。

unlock

6.39 To **unlock** something such as a door, a room, or a container that has a lock means to open it. 打开

汉语中,**开后门**用来比喻利用职权给予不应有的方便和利益。

If you **unlock** something that is not available, you make it available. 开启;提供

This scheme <u>is unlocking</u> housing opportunities in rural areas. 这一计划提供了乡村地区的住房机会。

6.40 If you **unlock** the secret or mystery of something, you find out about it. 揭开(秘密)

So we have an opportunity now to really <u>unlock</u> the secrets of the universe in ways that have not been available to us before. 所以我们现在有机会用以前所不具备的方法,真正揭开宇宙的秘密。

Column 6

This column is adopted to help understand some metaphorical expressions of **construction** that are unique to Chinese.

拆东墙,补西墙	tear down the east wall to repair the west wall—reinforce one place at the expense of another; rob Peter to pay Paul
城府	a mind hard to fathom; subtle thinking
搭桥	act as a matchmaker
登堂入室	pass through the hall into the inner chamber—reach a higher level in one's studies or become more proficient in one's profession
顶梁柱	backbone
独木桥	difficult path
更上一层楼	climb one storey higher—attain a yet higher goal; scale new heights

过河拆桥	kick down the ladder
开后门	open the "backdoor"—give someone special advantage or privilege
空中楼阁	castles in the air
落井下石；墙倒众人推	kick somebody when he is down
上梁不正下梁歪	If the upper beam is not straight, the lower ones will go aslant—when those above behave unworthily, those below will do the same.
添砖加瓦	do what little one can to help
铜墙铁壁	a bastion of iron—an impregnable fortress
偷梁换柱	steal the beams and change the pillars—perpetrate a fraud
挖墙角	undermine the foundation; cut the ground from under somebody's feet
屋上架屋	build one house on top of another—needless duplication

7 Machines and Tools

Machines & parts of machines

chain
7.1 A **chain** is a series of metal rings connected to each other, used for fastening, pulling, or lifting things.

链子；链条；铁链
汉语用<u>锁链</u>、<u>枷锁</u>喻指束缚, 如: 打断了封建的<u>锁链</u>。<u>链</u>也用来喻指链状结构, 如: 产业<u>链</u>。

A **chain of** people or things is a series of them of the same type that form a connected line.
In 1910 there was a proposal for a <u>chain of</u> telegraph stations to link up the empire.
The region includes Sumatra, Java, and a <u>chain of</u> smaller islands extending eastwards.

一系列

1910 年有人提议成立一系列电报局把帝国连接起来。

这个地区包括苏门答腊、爪哇以及向东延伸的一群小岛。

7.2 A **chain of** events, facts, or ideas is a long series of them that are all related to each other.
a <u>chain of</u> events that eventually led to murder
The virus becomes weaker as it passes down the <u>chain of</u> infection.

一系列；一连串

最终导致谋杀案的一系列事件

经过一连串的感染, 病毒变弱了。

7.3 A **chain** of shops, hotels, or restaurants is a number of them that all belong to the same person or company.
a <u>chain</u> of electrical goods shops

连锁店；联号企业
比较汉语中的**分支机构**。

家用电器连锁店。

7.4 If one event starts off a **chain**

连锁反应

reaction, it causes a large number of other similar events to happen in an uncontrolled way.

We are witnessing an unstoppable chain reaction of job losses.

7.5 The **chain of command** is a system in which each person in an organization has a particular status and gives orders to the person immediately junior to him.

With the chains of command breaking down and supplies no longer reaching their destinations, the republics and regions have begun to put their own interests first.

7.6 You may use **chains** to refer to the conditions that limit your freedom, especially unpleasant responsibilities or bad conditions that you live in.

This offers the country the chance to break the chains of dependency and pursue a path of development.

It would release me from the chains of an office-based job and give me the freedom to pursue other projects, or even to travel.

7.7 If you **are chained to** something, you are forced to stay in an unpleasant situation.

With a major deadline to meet, Hannah had been chained to her desk all weekend.

clockwork

7.8 **Clockwork** is a set of springs inside a toy or other object that make it work when you turn a handle or key.

If something happens **as regular as**

汉语用**连锁反应**比喻若干个相关的事物，只要一个发生变化，其他都跟着发生变化。

我们是在亲眼目睹一场无法阻止的失业的连锁反应。

行政管理系统

由于行政指挥失效，供给品已不再能到达目的地，于是那些共和国和地区都已开始将其自身利益放在了首位。

羁绊；束缚
参见 7.1

这向这个国家提供了打破从属于别国的枷锁、走上发展道路的机会。

它将把我从一项坐在办公室的工作中解放出来，给我以从事其他项目，甚至旅行的自由。

受到某事束缚；被困于……

为了赶上最后期限，汉娜整个周末都不得不伏案工作。

（玩具等上面的）发条装置

极有规律地

clockwork, it happens very regularly.

7.9 If something such as a plan or arrangement works **like clockwork**, it happens or works correctly, with no problems or delays.

He soon had the household running like clockwork.

准确地；顺利地

他很快将家料理得井井有条。

cog

7.10 A **cog** is a wheel in a machine that fits into the edge of another wheel or part and makes it turn.

Cog is used metaphorically to refer to someone who is considered as a minor part of a large organization.

a small cog in the corporate wheel

齿轮

比较汉语中的**螺丝钉**，如：愿做革命的螺丝钉。

小人物

大公司里的一个小人物

engine

7.11 An **engine** is a machine with moving parts that uses a fuel to produce movement, for example in a road vehicle or aircraft.

Engine is used metaphorically to refer to something that causes a process to happen.

Industrialization is the most important engine of economic growth.

发动机；引擎

汉语用**火车头**比喻起带头作用或领导作用的人或事物。

驱动力；推动力

工业化是经济发展最重要的推动力。

engineer

7.12 When a vehicle, bridge, or building **is engineered**, it is constructed or built using scientific methods.

The verb **engineer** is used metaphorically to say that something has been arranged to happen, especially in a useful and skillful way.

Government officials managed to engineer a meeting between the two

设计（公路、铁路、桥梁或机械）

（尤指很巧妙地）安排，策划

政府官员设法安排了两位大使之间的会面。

ambassadors.

As far as I can remember, most of our early arguments were engineered by her simply because she felt like a fight and enjoyed one.

根据我记忆所及，我们早期的多数争论都是她有意策划好的，她这样做仅仅是因为她喜欢争吵，而且把它当作一种享受。

link

7.13 A **link** is one of the connecting rings in a chain.

（链的）一环

Link is used to refer to a connection between two or more people, places, facts, or events, especially when one is affected or caused by the other.

（尤指彼此影响或互为因果的）关系

汉语中，**环节**指相互关联的许多事物中的一个，如：主要**环节**、薄弱**环节**。

Police arrested a man believed to be the main link between crime rings.

警察逮捕了一名男子，据信其为犯罪团伙中的重要人物。

The link between smoking and cancer was established decades ago.

吸烟和癌症之间的关联在数十年前就已确立。

7.14 You may refer to a relationship between two or more people, organizations, or countries as a **link**.

（个人、机构或国家之间的）关系

At that time there was a close link between Scotland and France.

在那个时候，苏格兰和法国两国之间关系很密切。

The institution's goal is to foster stronger links between the scientific community and the world of industry.

该机构的目标就是使科学团体和工业世界之间的关系更加紧密。

7.15 You may use **the missing link** to refer to something such as a piece of information that is needed to connect two things or to complete an explanation, solution etc.

缺失的一环（联系两事物或完成某种解释或解决方案等所缺的一条信息）

Mr. Savimbi said that this was the vital missing link in all previous peace negotiations.

塞文毕先生说，从前所有的和平谈判都缺少这个极其重要的环节。

He has such creative thought and marvelous touch that he could just be the missing link in the English football

他具有如此的创见和非凡的机敏，因此，在那个英国足球经理的宏伟计划中，他会是一个他们所需要的重要人

manager's grand plan.

7.16 The weak link (in the chain) is the weakest part of a group, plan, or team.

<u>The weakest link in the chain</u> of administration was the way in which ships were armed.

Prison visiting has long been regarded as one of <u>the weak links in the security chain</u>.

（团体、计划或队伍中）薄弱的一环

管理程序中最薄弱的环节是装备轮船的方式。

探监长期以来已被视为保安程序中的薄弱环节之一。

machinery

7.17 Machinery is machines.

Machinery is used to refer to an established system for doing something.

the corporate decision-making <u>machinery</u>
the <u>machinery</u> of government
the <u>machinery</u> for resolving disputes

机器；机械
系统；体系；机制

公司的决策机制
政府机制
争端解决机制

mechanical

7.18 A mechanical device is operated by a machine or system of moving parts.

Mechanical is used metaphorically to describe actions or responses that are done without thinking or without any attempt to be original.

I found her purely <u>mechanical</u> explanations inadequate.

机械操作的；机械的

不动脑筋的；呆板的
汉语用**机械**比喻方式拘泥死板，没有变化，如：工作方法太**机械**。

我发现她那些完全不动脑筋的解释很不充分。

mechanics

7.19 Mechanics is the area of physics that deals with the forces such as gravity that affect all objects.

Mechanics is used to refer to the way in which something works or is done.

the <u>mechanics</u> of investigative reporting

机械学；力学

工作方法；工作技巧

调查报告的写法

mechanism

7.20 A mechanism is a machine or part of a machine.

机器；机械装置；机件

You may use **mechanism** to refer to a method or process for getting something done within a system or organization. （在系统或内部做事的）方法；技巧；过程

a *mechanism* for settling disputes between trading partners　贸易伙伴之间的争端解决机制

pump

7.21 To **pump** means to make liquid or gas move into or out of something, especially by using a pump.　（尤指用泵）抽取；抽吸；注入

If a liquid **pumps** from somewhere, a lot of it comes out in quick regular movements.　汩汩流出；大量涌出；流淌

Blood *was pumping* from a wound in his arm.　血液从他手臂上的伤口汩汩流出。

7.22 If you **pump** money **into** something, you invest a lot of money into it.　大量投资

She wants to *pump* money *into* her local football team.　她打算把钱大量投入到当地的足球俱乐部。

7.23 To **pump out** something means to produce a lot of it.　大量生产；大量制造

They get paid too much for *pumping out* work like that.　他们大量生产那样的产品，获得了巨额利润。

7.24 If you **pump up** something, you make it increase by a large amount.　大量增加

They have cut prices in an attempt to *pump up* sales.　他们试图通过降价来大幅度促进销售。

7.25 If someone is or gets **pumped up**, he feels very excited and enthusiastic about something.　充满激情的；热情高涨的；兴奋的　汉语用**打气**比喻鼓动；用**加油**比喻进一步努力。

The coach's job is to get everyone *pumped up* for the game.　教练的职责就是要让大家都热情高涨地投入比赛。

Schumacher's really *pumped up* for the race this weekend.　舒马赫确实已热情高涨地准备好参加本周末的比赛。

tick over

7.26 If an engine **ticks over**, it works while the vehicle is not moving.
If a system, business etc. **ticks over**, it continues working but without producing very much or without much happening.
The president's decision will keep the government <u>ticking over</u> until next Thursday.

（汽车引擎）空转；慢转

进展缓慢；呆滞

总统的决定将使这届政府继续勉强运作直至下星期四。

wheel

7.27 A **wheel** is a round object that turns round and round to make a car, bicycle, or other vehicle move.
You may refer to processes or forces that cause things to happen or cause progress to be made as **wheels**.
The <u>wheels</u> of government grind very slowly.
The media are important to a healthy, well-functioning economy; they are a commercial activity that oils the <u>wheels</u> of the economy.

轮子；车轮
参见 7.11

推动力；机构

政府机构运转十分缓慢。

对健康、运转良好的经济来说，媒体是重要的；媒体是种商业活动，是经济发展的润滑剂。

7.28 To **keep the wheels turning** means to make something continue to happen or operate.
For decades it was these people who <u>kept the wheels</u> of the British economy <u>turning</u>.

使继续进行；使继续运转

几十年来是这些人保持了英国经济的发展。

7.29 To **set the wheels in motion** or **start the wheels turning** means to do the thing that is necessary to make a process start.
Mr. Major <u>has set the wheels in motion</u>. Now let's get on with it.

使继续进行；使继续运转

梅杰先生已经开始了这项工作。现在让我们继续做下去吧。

Tools & working with tools

deadlock

7.30 A **deadlock** is a lock that closes with a small metal bar when you turn a key or handle.

单闩锁

Deadlock is used to refer to a situation in which neither person or group involved in a disagreement is willing to change their opinions or position.

僵局；僵持

Negotiations are finally due to begin after months of political deadlock.

几个月的政治僵局之后谈判终于在预定时间开始。

There are really fears that the meeting will end in deadlock.

确实担心会议将以僵局而告终。

forge

7.31 To **forge** means to heat metal until it is soft, then hit it with a hammer or pour it into a mould to form different shapes.

锻造
汉语用**千锤百炼**比喻多次的斗争和考验以及对诗文等做多次的精细修改。
参见 7.55

Forge is used metaphorically to talk about developing a successful relationship, especially in business or politics, with another country, organization, or person.

（与其他国家、组织或个人）缔结；发展（关系，尤指商业或政治关系）
汉语用**打造**比喻创造或造就，如：打造著名品牌。

The company wanted to forge alliances with other motor manufacturers.

公司希望和其他汽车制造商结成联盟。

During the 1970s, the US forged trade links with China.

美国于 20 世纪 70 年代与中国建立了贸易关系。

She forged a new career as a poet and songwriter.

诗人和歌词作者是她的新职业。

7.32 If you **forge ahead**, you make strong steady progress.

稳步发展；进展顺利

Export sales continue to forge ahead.

出口销售继续稳步发展。

grind

7.33 To **grind** a substance means to

磨碎；把……磨成粉状

break it into very small pieces or powder, by using a machine or by crushing it between two hard surfaces.

汉语用**榨取**比喻残酷剥削或搜刮，如：榨取民财。类似的表达方式还有**剥削**、**盘剥**、**压迫**等。

If you **grind** someone **down**, you treat him in a cruel way over a long period and gradually destroy his confidence or strength.

长期欺压；折磨；压迫

Don't let them grind you down.
Years of oppression had ground the people down.

别让他们欺压你。
人民年复一年地遭受着压迫。

7.34 If something boring or unpleasant **grinds on**, it continues happening for a long period of time.

令人厌烦地长期持续

The argument ground on for almost two years.

这场争论拖拖拉拉持续了近两年。

7.35 If you **grind** something **out**, you produce it in large quantities, especially when this is boring or difficult.

（尤指单调地或艰难地）大量生产

She grinds out romantic novels at the rate of five a year.

她以一年五部的速度苦心撰写爱情小说。

7.36 You may use **grind** to refer to something that is hard work, boring, and tiring because it takes a lot of your time and energy.

枯燥冗长的苦差事

the usual daily grind of household tasks
It's a long grind to the top of that particular profession.

令人厌倦的日常家务活
爬到那种行业的最高位置要经过漫长的艰苦奋斗。

grinding

7.37 You can describe a process which is extremely slow and boring or a situation which is tiring and unpleasant, and which continues for a long time, as **grinding**.

极端的（用于强调形势的恶劣）

Their grandfather had left his village a century ago in order to escape the

一百年以前，他们的祖父为了逃脱长时期的难以忍受的贫困而离开了他的

grinding poverty. 村子。

hammer

7.38 To **hammer** something means to hit it with a hammer.　　锤击；把……锤进

If you **hammer** someone or something, you criticize him/it severely.　　严厉批评；猛烈抨击

Her latest film *was hammered* by the critics.　　她最新拍摄的电影受到了影评家的猛烈抨击。

7.39 If you **hammer** your opponents, you defeat him easily.　　轻松击败

Our team *was hammered* 5-1.　　我队以 1：5 的悬殊比分败北。

7.40 If rain **hammers down**, a lot of it falls with great force.　　（大雨）倾盆

7.41 If your heart **hammers**, you feel it beating strongly and quickly.　　（心脏）剧烈跳动；怦怦跳

I was so scared my heart *was hammering* in my chest.　　我吓得心里怦怦直跳。

7.42 If you **hammer away at** something, you work hard in order to finish or achieve it.　　努力干；孜孜以求

She spent all weekend *hammering away at* her novel.　　她把整个周末的时间都用来写小说了。

7.43 When people **hammer out** an agreement, they finally decide on it after a lot of argument and discussion.　　（经讨论、争辩后）作出（决定），达成（协议）

A new deal *was hammered out* between the two banks.　　两家银行最终达成了新的协议。

7.44 If you **hammer home** a point, an idea etc., you repeat it many times in order to make people fully understand it.　　反复讲透；重点讲清（要点、想法等）

Today's march is meant to *hammer home* the fundamentalist's point of view.　　今天的游行是为了让人们了解原教旨主义者的观点。

instrument

7.45 An **instrument** is a tool or piece of　　仪器；器具

7 Machines and Tools

equipment used in science, medicine, or technology.
Instrument is used metaphorically to refer to someone or something that can be used in order to make something happen.
The government has a number of policy instruments it can use for this purpose.
an important instrument of quality control

手段；工具

政府有许多可用的政策手段来实现该目的。
质量监控的重要工具

key

7.46 A **key** is a small piece of metal used for opening or locking a door or container, or for starting the engine of a vehicle.
Key is used to refer to the thing that will do most to help you achieve something.
Proper planning is the key to success.
The key to our strength lies in our members.
7.47 **Key** is also used as an adjective to emphasize how important something is.
Foreign policy had been a key issue in the campaign.
This economic model has the following key features.

钥匙
汉语用**法宝**比喻用起来特别有效的工具、方法或经验，如：群众路线是我们工作的**法宝**。

关键；要诀

合适的计划是成功的关键。
我们实力的关键在于我们的成员。

关键性的；非常重要的

外交政策曾经是竞选活动中一个关键性的问题。

该经济模式有以下主要特点。

ladder

7.48 A **ladder** is a piece of equipment for reaching high places that consists of two long pieces of wood or metal joined by small pieces called rungs.
Ladder is used to refer to a system that has different levels through which you can process.
In that society, being a doctor was a

梯子
汉语用**垫脚石**比喻借以向上爬的人或物。

（发迹、晋升等的）阶梯，途径

在那个社会里，当一名医生就是在社

step up on the social <u>ladder</u>.
She was high enough on the corporate <u>ladder</u> to take time off whenever she wanted.

会阶梯上升了一级。
她在公司中的级别很高，只要她愿意随时可以休假。

lever

7.49 A **lever** is a long metal bar that you put under a heavy object to move it.

杠杆；撬棒

汉语用<u>杠杆</u>比喻起平衡或调控作用的事物或力量，如：发挥金融机构在经济发展中的<u>杠杆</u>作用。

Lever is used metaphorically to refer to something you use to influence a situation to get the result that you want.

手段；方法

Farmers may find a <u>lever</u> to persuade supermarkets to stock more local produce.

农民们或许能找到一个办法说服超市多进一些当地农产品。

The threat of sanctions is our most powerful <u>lever</u> for peace.

实施制裁的威胁是我们争取和平最有力的施压手段。

leverage

7.50 **Leverage** is the power that a lever gives you to move things.

杠杆作用；杠杆力量
参见 7.49

Leverage is used metaphorically to refer to the power to make someone do what you want.

力量；影响

diplomatic <u>leverage</u>
States may now have little <u>leverage</u> to force hospitals to hold down costs.

外交影响力
现在各州或许几乎没有什么权力能迫使医院降低费用。

lock

See **lock**: 6.28

nail

7.51 If you **nail** something somewhere, you fix it there securely with a nail or nails.

钉牢；钉住；把……钉上
汉语中，**钉子**可用来比喻难以处置或解决的事物，如：钉子户。还可用来比喻埋伏的人，如：安插钉子。

To **nail** someone means to catch him and prove that he has done something

抓获；戳穿；揭露

wrong or illegal.
The police haven't been able to nail the killer.
They finally nailed Capone for tax evasion.

7.52 If you **nail a rumor, lie etc.**, you show that it is not true.
I think we need to nail these lies about the deal.

7.53 If you **nail down** something, you reach a final and definite agreement or decision about it.
They're on the verge of getting the agreement nailed down.
All the parties seem anxious to nail down a ceasefire.

7.54 If you **nail** someone **down**, you force him to say clearly what he wants or what he intends to do.
She says she'll come, but I can't nail her down to a specific time.

polish

7.55 To **polish** something means to rub its surface in order to make it shine.

If you **polish** or **polish up** something such as a skill, you improve it by practicing.
He'd spent the summer polishing his flying skills.
I could do the job if I spent some time polishing up my Spanish.

sharpen

7.56 If you **sharpen** something such as a knife, tool etc., you make it have a

警方还没有抓到杀人凶手。

他们最终揭穿了卡彭逃税一事。

揭穿谣言、谎言等

我认为我们应该揭穿有关该交易的这些谎言。

确定；敲定；搞定
汉语用**板上钉钉**比喻事情已定，不能更改。
他们几乎就要敲定这个协议。

各方面似乎都渴望将停火之事敲定。

使……同意；让……表明意图

她说要来，但我无法让她确定具体什么时候来。

磨光；擦亮
汉语中，**琢磨**、**润色**有加工使精美之意。参见7.31
（通过练习）改进，提高（技巧）

他花了一个夏天的时间来提高飞行技巧。
如果我花点时间提高我的西班牙语水平，我就可以做这份工作。

使锋利；削尖
参见7.57

sharper edge or point.

If a sense or feeling **sharpens** or something **sharpens** it, it becomes stronger.

The sea air <u>sharpened</u> our appetites.

A series of attacks <u>have sharpened</u> fears of more violence.

（使感觉或感情）加强；加重；变得更明显

海上的空气增进了我们的食欲。

一系列的袭击事件加剧了人们对暴力行为升级的恐惧。

7.57 To **sharpen** something or **sharpen** something **up** means to improve it so that it is up to the necessary standard, quality etc.

The program will give young athletes the chance to <u>sharpen</u> their skills.

He needs to <u>sharpen up</u> before the Olympic trials.

（使）提高；（使）改善

汉语中，**磨砺**的本义为摩擦使尖锐，比喻磨练，如：他知道只有时时刻刻<u>磨砺</u>自己，才能战胜更大的困难。

该项目将为年轻运动员提供一次提高技能的机会。

在奥运会选拔赛之前，他需要进一步磨砺自己。

7.58 If disagreements **sharpen**, or if they **are sharpened**, they become stronger or more noticeable.

His speech served only to <u>sharpen</u> the differences between the two men.

（使）加剧；（使）尖锐

他讲话的结果只是加剧了两人之间的分歧。

7.59 If your voice **sharpens** or something **sharpens** it, it becomes high and loud in an unpleasant way.

"How is she?" Amy asked, anxiety <u>sharpening</u> her voice.

（使声音）变得尖锐，变得刺耳

"她好吗？"艾米问道，担心使她的声音变尖了。

springboard

7.60 A **springboard** is a strong board used for helping you to jump high in sports such as diving.

Springboard is used to refer to something that helps you to become successful.

The awards have been a <u>springboard</u> for many young photographers.

跳板；踏板

汉语用跳板比喻作为过渡的途径或工具，如：以展销为<u>跳板</u>向海外市场拓展。

（有助于成功的）跳板

这些奖项是很多年轻摄影家走向成功的跳板。

tool

7.61 A **tool** is something that you hold

工具；用具

7 Machines and Tools

in your hand and use to do a particular job.

Tool is used metaphorically to refer to someone who is used by another person or group, especially to do a difficult or dishonest job.

被人利用的人；（尤指）傀儡，爪牙

The prime minister was an unwitting tool of the president.

总理不知不觉被总统利用了。

weld

7.62 To **weld** two pieces of metal means to join them together by heating them and pressing them together.

锻接，焊接（金属）
参见 7.31

To **weld** people or things means to unite them into a strong and effective group.

使联合；使结合；使成整体

They had welded a bunch of untrained recruits into an efficient fighting force.

他们把一群未经训练的新兵组织成了一支有战斗力的部队。

The crisis helped to weld the party together.

这场危机促使整个党紧密地团结在一起。

Column 7

This column is adopted to help understand some metaphorical expressions of **machines & tools** that are unique to Chinese.

板上钉钉	that clinches it; that's final; no two ways about it
闭门造车	act blindly
锤炼；磨砺；磨练	① temper oneself; steel oneself ② (of an artist, writer, etc.) try to perfect one's skill or technique by strenuous effort; hammer out; polish
产业链	industrial chain—used metaphorically to refer to a set of enterprises that form a chain of production network
大刀阔斧	bold and resolute; drastic
刀子嘴	a sharp tongue; a sharp-tongued person
（钉）丁是丁，（铆）卯是卯	be strict/precise

钉子户	person or household who refuses to move and bargains for unreasonably high compensation when the land is requisitioned for a construction project
掉链子	off the chain — used metaphorically to talk about a situation when someone makes serious mistakes at critical moment, thus fails to meet the expectation of the audience, employers etc.
锻炼	① take exercise; have physical training ② temper; steel; toughen
孵化器	incubator; hatchery—used metaphorically to refer to something that functions as a incubator in any form of industrial production
幌子	① shop sign; signboard ② pretence; cover; front
火车头	① (railway) engine; locomotive ② person or thing which plays a leading role
拉锯战	seesaw battle
螺丝钉	a screw—used metaphorically to refer to someone who functions a tiny but indispensable (elementary) role in a system or organization
碰钉子	meet with a rebuff
切磋	learn from each other by exchanging views
琢磨	improve (literary works); polish; refine

8 Journeys, Traffic & Vehicles

Journeys

course

8.1 **Course** is a direction or route followed by a ship or an aircraft.

方向
汉语中，**转向**可用来比喻改变政治立场。

Course can be used metaphorically to talk about the way something develops or should develop.
Politicians are often obliged to steer a course between incompatible interests.
a speech that changed the course of history

发展；进程

政治人物常常被迫在互不相容的利益集团之间开辟航道。

一场改变了历史进程的演讲

8.2 If some liquid **courses**, it flows somewhere in large amounts.

流动；奔流；流淌
汉语中，**流**有向坏的方向转变之意，如：放任自**流**。

When an emotion or physical feeling **courses** through you, you suddenly feel it strongly.
Anger courses through him.
His smile sent waves of excitement coursing through her.

（情感、感情）涌动

怒火涌上他的心头。
他的微笑让她的心中涌起阵阵激动。

journey

8.3 **Journey** is an act of travelling from one place to another, especially when they are far apart.

Journey is used metaphorically to talk about a process of changing and developing

（尤指长途）旅行；行程
比较汉语中的**迷途知返**、**误入歧途**、**迷津**等。

历程；过程；进程

over a period of time.
our great <u>journey</u> through life 我们一生的漫长道路
a spiritual <u>journey</u> 精神之旅

halfway

8.4 A **halfway** place is at an equal distance between two points. 中间的；中途的

Halfway is used metaphorically to talk about middle time of a period. 中期的

At the <u>halfway</u> stage of the campaign, Bush had the lead. 在总统竞选的中期，布什领先。

8.5 If you say that something is **halfway decent**, you mean it is fairly, but not very, good. 还不错的；过得去的

It's the only <u>halfway decent</u> novel she's written in years. 这是她这么多年来所写的唯一一部还算过得去的小说。

8.6 If you say someone is **halfway there**, you are saying that he has an advantage that will help him to be successful. 具有优势；占得先机

If the interviewer likes you, you're <u>halfway there</u>. 如果面试的人喜欢你，那你就具备了优势。

8.7 If you **meet someone halfway**, you reach an agreement with him by giving him part of what he wants. 迁就某人；对某人让步

If he was prepared to apologize, the least she could do was <u>meet him halfway</u> and accept some of the blame. 如果他愿意道歉，她至少也会迁就他一点，承担一些责任。

travel

8.8 To **travel** is to go on a journey. （长途）旅行

If rumors **travel**, they spread from one place to another in a way that affects or influences a lot of people. 传播；流传

比较汉语中的**流言飞(蜚)语、飞(蜚)短流长、谣言四起**。

The news <u>traveled</u> quickly. 消息传得很快。
Rumors <u>travel</u> fast. 谣言传起来很快。

Words for roads

avenue

8.9 An **avenue** is a wide, straight road, often with trees on either side.　　大道；（尤指）林阴大道

Avenue is used metaphorically to refer to one of the methods you can use to achieve something.　　途径；渠道

Believe me; we have explored every possible avenue to find funds.　　相信我，每一个可能的集资渠道我们都找过。

byway

8.10 A **byway** is a quiet minor road that is not used by many cars or people.　　旁道；偏僻小路

Byways are used metaphorically to refer to the less important aspects of a subject.　　次要方面　比较汉语中的枝节。参见 4.19

a personal exploration of the byways of Indian history　　对印度历史次要方面的个人探究

See also **branch** 4.19, **highway** 8.11

highway

8.11 A **highway** is a road built for fast travel between towns and cities.　　公路

You can refer to all the different aspects of something as **the highways and byways**.　　各方面

the highways and byways of folk music　　民间音乐的大小流派

lane

8.12 A **lane** is a section of a wide road, which is marked by painted white lines to keep lines of traffic separate.　　车道

The fast lane is the exciting busy way of life that a successful person has. You can refer to this kind of life as **life in the fast lane**.　　忙碌刺激的生活方式

He told of <u>life in the fast lane</u>, when he made and lost millions.　　他讲起自己那段忙碌刺激的生活，那阵子的生意盈亏数额都以百万计。

8.13 You can say that someone is in **the slow lane** if he does not do many exciting or stressful things. You can refer to this kind of life as **life in the slow lane**.　　慢节奏的生活方式

Rather than moving over into <u>the slow lane</u> he has been having fun proving his critics wrong.　　他没有去过平静的、慢节奏的生活，而是一直在证明对他进行过批评的人们是错误的，并乐此不疲。

seven days of good food, fine wine, and <u>living in the slow lane</u>　　过了七天好吃好喝、平静放松的日子

line

8.14 A **line** is the direction or path along which someone or something moves or looks.　　（移动或注视的）方向，路线

汉语中，**路线**指思想上、政治上或工作上所遵循的根本途径或基本准则。

Line is used metaphorically to talk about an attitude or a belief, especially one that is stated publicly.　　（尤指公开表明的）态度；看法

The government is <u>taking a firm line</u> on terrorism.　　政府现在对恐怖主义采取强硬的态度。

The MP supported <u>the official line</u> on education.　　这位议员支持官方有关教育的表态。

8.15 You can refer to a method or way of doing or thinking about something as a **line**.　　方式；方法

I don't follow your <u>line of thinking</u>.　　我不理解你的思维方法。

The police are pursuing a new <u>line of enquiry</u>.　　警方正在实施一种新的调查方法。

8.16 If you want to stress that something is in every part and/or from the beginning, you can say that it is **all along the line**.　　全部地；处处；时时

He's been opposing me <u>all along the line</u>.　　他一直处处和我作对。

Our supporters have been magnificent all along the line.
我们的支持者们一直都非常棒。

8.17 If you say someone is **on the right lines**, you mean that he is generally correct.
基本正确的；对头的

You haven't got the right answer, but you're on the right lines.
虽然你没有得出正确的结论，但是你的方法是对头的。

8.18 If someone is said to be **out of line**, he behaves in a way that other people do not approve of.
出格；越轨
汉语用<u>出圈儿</u>、<u>出格</u>来比喻越出常规或一定范围，如：话说得<u>出圈儿</u>了。

That comment was way out of line.
那句评论非常不当。

path

8.19 A **path** is a track or way made by or for people walking over the ground.
（人走出来的）小径；（人走的）小道
参见 8.25

You can refer to the way that someone's life develops as his **path** in life.
（生活）道路；方式；发展路线

His father offered to give Alex 200 pounds a month so that he could follow his chosen path of becoming an artist.
亚历克斯的父亲提出每月给他 200 英镑，这样他就能按自己的选择朝着成为一名艺术家的目标努力。

Until their paths diverged Lennon and McCartney wrote many hits together.
伦农和麦卡特尼在分道扬镳之前一同写过许多成功之作。

8.20 You can refer to the choices that people or groups of people make or to the things that they choose to do in order to reach a particular situation, state, or condition, as a particular **path**.
（人们为实现某种特别的形势、状况或条件）所做的选择或所选择的道路

the right of every nation to choose its own path of social development
每个国家选择自己的社会发展道路的权利

The President said his country would continue on its path to full democracy.
总统说，他的国家将继续走上完全民主政治的道路。

8.21 If two people's **paths cross**, they meet each other by chance.
偶遇

Our paths first crossed when we were students at Yale.
我们的第一次偶遇是在耶鲁大学念书的时候。

rail

8.22 A **rail** is one of the pair of metal bars that a train travels on.
Rail is used metaphorically to talk about a normal situation or way of life.
The peace process seems to be finally back on the <u>rails</u>.

铁轨

正常的状态；规范的生活；正轨

和平进程好像最终又回到了正轨。

8.23 A person who **goes** or **runs off the rails** starts behaving in a way that is not socially acceptable.
A lot of kids from strict backgrounds <u>go off the rails</u> when they leave home.

（行为）越轨；不规矩
参见 8.18

许多家教严格的孩子离开家后，就不再规矩了。

8.24 If a campaign **goes off the rails**, it no longer works as planned or intended.
The campaign for independence seems to have <u>gone off the rails</u>.

偏离初衷

独立运动好像改变了初衷。

road

8.25 A **road** is a way that leads from one place to another, especially one with a hard surface that cars and other vehicles can use.
Road is used metaphorically to talk about a particular process or course of action.
I've tried being reasonable with him and I don't want to <u>go down that road</u> again.
<u>The road to</u> success is not always an easy one.
After weeks of illness he is finally <u>on the road to</u> recovery.
A hundred years ago feminists like Elizabeth Cady Stanton were advocating exercise as the best form of make-up and <u>the right road to</u> beauty.

路；道路；（尤指）公路
汉语用捷径来比喻能较快地达到目的的巧妙手段或办法，如：另寻捷径。类似的表达方式还有另辟蹊径等。

路子；方法；通往……的道路

我已经试图和他讲道理了，现在我不想再那样做了。

通往成功的道路并非总是一帆风顺。

他病了几个星期后，终于开始康复了。

一百年以前，像伊丽莎白·凯蒂·斯坦顿这样的女权主义者就主张锻炼，说锻炼是化妆的最好形式和美容的正确途径。

8.26 If you say that someone is **on the road to ruin**, you mean that you think that the thing he is doing or the way he is behaving will have very bad results for them.
Fans thought this vicious attack would put her <u>on the road to ruin</u>.
Staff became discontented, the boss was over-worked, team spirit sank to the lowest possible levels and the firm was <u>on the road to ruin</u>.

走上毁灭之路；大祸临头

影迷们认为，这个恶毒的攻击会逼她走上毁灭之路。
员工变得不满，老板过度劳累，协作精神降到了最低的限度，这家公司走上了灾难之路。

8.27 If you say that someone is **on the road to nowhere**, you think that he is going to fail in what he is doing. If you say that the way someone is behaving is **on the road to nowhere**, you think that his behavior will not achieve anything positive for him.
Any rational person must know that violence is <u>a road to nowhere</u>.
Half a century ago, you knew you were on <u>the road to nowhere</u> if you were made minister of education.

注定要失败的；无结果的；徒劳无功的

任何有理性的人都一定知道，暴力不能解决问题。
半个世纪以前你就知道，如果让你当教育部长，你将会一事无成。

8.28 **Down the road** is used metaphorically to talk about the future and what may happen.
Two years <u>down the road</u>, you might feel very differently.
It's a decision that may well have an impact further <u>down the road</u>.

将来；今后

再过两年，你可能会有完全不同的感受。
这是个很可能会对未来产生深远影响的决定。

8.29 **The end of the road** is used metaphorically to talk about the moment when someone or something has to stop, for example because he/it can not succeed or improve.

（由于失败或无进展等）停止；结束
汉语用**日暮途穷**来比喻到了末日，用**穷途末路**来形容无路可走，用**死胡同**来比喻绝路。

There is a growing feeling that the NLD may have reached <u>the end of</u> its current political <u>road</u>.

人们越来越感觉到，（缅甸）国家民主同盟也许在政治上已走上了穷途末路。

road hog
See **hog**: 3.86

route
8.30 A **route** is a way that buses, trains, or planes travel regularly.

路线；航线
参见 8.25

Route is used metaphorically to talk about a way of doing something that produces a particular result.

办法；途径，渠道

By the time she was sixteen she had decided that education would be the best <u>route</u> to a good job.

16 岁时她已确认，教育将是获得好工作的最佳途径。

I'll need to think carefully before deciding what <u>route</u> to take next.

在决定下一步怎么做之前，我需要仔细想一想。

track
8.31 A **track** is a path or road with a rough surface or railway line.

粗糙不平的小路；铁轨
参见 8.25

Track can be used metaphorically to talk about a way of achieving something.

途径

the fast <u>track</u> to wealth and prosperity
She is on the fast <u>track</u> to promotion.

通往财富和繁荣的捷径
她现在升迁在望。

8.32 If you **cover your tracks**, you hide any evidence that you were somewhere or did something.

隐匿行踪；掩盖活动

8.33 If you **keep track** of something, you have all the information you need about it.

掌握全部所需信息

We need a system to <u>keep track</u> of all our expenses.

我们需要一套记录所有支出的系统。

8.34 When you **lose track**, you forget something or do not have all the information you need.

忘记；未掌握所需信息

I've <u>lost track</u> of how many times he

我忘了他上周打过多少次电话。

called last week.

8.35 You can say someone **makes tracks** if he leaves a place.
It's getting late—I think we'd better make tracks.
离开
天色不早了，我想我们该走了。

8.36 Someone who is **on the right** or **on the wrong track** is one who is doing or thinking the right/wrong things.
The figures show we are on the right track.
正确的
错误的
这些数据表明我们是对的。

8.37 If someone is **back on track**, he goes in the right direction again after a mistake, failure, etc.
I tried to get my life back on track after my divorce.
重新步入正轨；恢复正常
离婚之后我力图使生活恢复正常。

8.38 If someone is **on track**, he is likely to be successful.
We are right on track to create two million new jobs.
有可能成功
我们有望创造出 200 万个新的就业岗位。

8.39 If you **stop something in its tracks**, you suddenly make it stop.
The opposition plans to stop the reform process in its tracks.
突然中止某事
反对党计划中止改革进程。

tunnel

8.40 A **tunnel** is an underground passage through which vehicles travel. You can use **light at the end of the tunnel** to talk about a sign that a difficult period will soon end.
隧道；地道
苦尽甘来；历尽艰辛之后的成功、愉快、幸福等

Traffic

bend

8.41 A **bend** is a curve or turn, especially in a road or river.
（尤指道路或河流的）拐弯，弯道
汉语用**转弯抹角**来比喻说话、做事不

直截了当，如：有什么话就直接说，别转弯抹角的。

If you say that someone **is** or **goes round the bend**, you are saying that he becomes crazy.

发疯

She's gone completely round the bend.
她完全疯了。

The children have been driving me round the bend.
孩子们快把我气疯了。

circle

8.42 A **circle** is a completely round flat shape.
圆；圆形

Circle can be used metaphorically to talk about a group of people who are connected because they have the same interests, jobs, etc.
圈子；阶层；界

She is well known in theatrical circles.
她在戏剧界赫赫有名。

8.43 An **inner circle** is the small group of people who have a lot of power in an organization.
核心集团

8.44 A **vicious circle** is a situation in which one problem causes another problem which then makes the first problem worse.
恶性循环

8.45 If a situation **comes**, **goes**, or **turns full circle**, it becomes the same again as it was at the beginning.
循环；又回到原处

He's back managing the club he first started out in, so his career has come full circle.
他又经营起当初起家的那家俱乐部，因此他的事业兜了个圈子又回到了原处。

8.46 If you **go around/round in circles**, you make no progress in spite of working for a long time.
在原地兜圈子；瞎忙；毫无进展
比较汉语中的原地踏步、裹足不前。

corner

8.47 A **corner** is a place where two roads or paths meet.
（道路的）拐角；街角

Corner can be used metaphorically to talk about a difficult situation that you can not easily escape from.

The government is in a <u>corner</u> on the subject of taxes.

They had forced me into a <u>corner</u>, and I had to admit the truth.

困境；绝路

政府在税收问题上陷入了困境。

他们把我逼上了绝路，我只好承认了这个事实。

8.48 If someone **turns the/a corner**, he begins to be healthy, happy, or successful again after a difficult period.

Has the economy finally <u>turned the corner</u>?

With this new job I feel I'm <u>turning a corner</u>.

好转；有起色

经济终于好转了吗？

有了这份新工作，我觉得自己的处境正在好转。

crossroads

8.49 A **crossroads** is a place where one road crosses another.

Crossroads is used metaphorically to talk about a point during the development of something when you have to make an important decision about what to do next.

He was at a <u>crossroads</u> in his career.

交叉路口；十字路口

转折点；重大的抉择时刻

他正处在事业的十字路口。

dead end

8.50 A **dead end** is a road or passage that has no way out at one end.

You can use **dead road** to talk about a situation in which no further progress is possible.

This line of investigation could prove to be a complete <u>dead end</u>.

死路；死胡同
参见 8.29
绝境；僵局

这种调查方法到头来可能是完全没有结果的。

8.51 A **dead-end job** is one with low wages and no hope of promotion.

没有前途的工作

green light

8.52 A **green light** is a signal that gives

（交通）绿灯

traffic permission.
You can refer to the official approval for a project to start as a **green light**. 准许；许可

The project has finally been given <u>the green light</u>. 该工程最终获得了批准。

U-turn

8.53 A **U-turn** is an act of turning a vehicle in order to travel in the opposite direction. （车辆的）掉头 参见 8.41

U-turn is used metaphorically to talk about a sudden and complete change of policy by a government or by someone in authority. 大转变；大转弯

The government was today accused of doing a <u>U-turn</u> after its decision not to raise petrol prices after all. 政府在决定不提高汽油价格后又作出了 180 度的大转变，因此今天受到指责。

Column 8.1

This column is added to help understand some metaphorical expressions of **traffic** that are unique to Chinese.

被引入歧途	be led astray
重蹈覆辙	turn from the right road and take the wrong one—give up an honest life for a dishonest one
独辟蹊径	off the beaten track—develop a new method or style of one's own
分道扬镳	part company
留后路	keep a way open for retreat; leave a way out
迷津	miss the ferry—stray from the right path
迷途知返	realize one's errors and mend one's ways
轻车熟路	drive in a light carriage on a familiar road—do something one knows well and can manage with ease
穷途末路	be in an impasse; have come to a dead end
上坡路	upward trend; steady progress
死路	the road to ruin (or destruction)

坦途	level road; highway
退路	room for maneuver; leeway
歪路	dishonest practices
弯路	roundabout way; detour
狭路相逢	(of adversaries) meet face to face on a narrow path—come into unavoidable confrontation
正路不走走斜路	turn from the right road and take the wrong one—give up an honest life for a dishonest one
直道而行	follow the straight path—act with rectitude
转弯抹角	beat about the bush; speak in a roundabout way
走上绝路	come to a dead end
走下坡路	be on the decline
走邪道	lead a depraved life; abandon oneself to evil ways

Vehicles

back seat

8.54 A **back seat** is a seat behind the driver of a car. If you say someone or something **takes a back seat**, you mean that he/it becomes less active or less important.

I'll happy to take a back seat when Robin takes over.

Other issues must take a back seat to this crisis.

8.55 A **back seat driver** is someone who keeps giving advice about things that he is not responsible for.

brake

8.56 A **brake** is the equipment in a car, bicycle, or other vehicle that you use for slowing down or stopping.

Brake is used metaphorically to talk about an action or situation that

（汽车的）后座

退居二线；退居次要位置

罗宾接管时，我将很高兴退居二线。

在这一危机面前，必须把其他问题放到次要位置上。

干涉与自己职责无关的事情的人；不负责任乱提建议的人

制动器；刹车；车闸

阻碍；抑制

prevents something from developing or making progress.

The high level of debt continued to put a *brake* on economic recovery. 巨额债务仍抑制着经济复苏。

Inevitably, insufficient funding acts as a *brake* on medical research. 资金不足不可避免地阻碍了医学研究。

coast

8.57 If a vehicle **coasts** somewhere, it continues to move there with the engine switched off or without anyone pushing or pedaling it. （汽车或自行车）靠惯性滑行

Coast is used metaphorically to talk about doing something without any real effort. 轻易得到；毫不费力地实现

Scotland *coasted* to a 31-12 win over Argentina. 苏格兰队31比12轻松战胜阿根廷队。

There was a time when Charles was *coasting* at school, and I should have told him to work harder. 曾有一段时间，查尔斯在学校学习不努力，只是打发日子，我当时本该叫他要更加努力学习。

drive

8.58 To **drive** is to control a vehicle so that it moves somewhere. 驾驶；驾车

If you **drive** someone, you force him into a bad situation or state. 迫使；逼迫

Desperation finally *drove* her to ask for help. 她走投无路，最后只得请求援助。

People are being *driven* to violence by police action. 人们被警方的行动逼得采用暴力。

8.59 If you **drive someone from/out of/off/away**, you force him to leave a place, usually the place where he lives. 迫使（某人离开）

This malicious gossip has *driven* her *out of* the village. 这些恶意中伤的谣言迫使她离开了村子。

8.60 **What someone is driving at** is what he is really trying to say. 某人说话的真正意图

8 Journeys, Traffic & Vehicles

I can see <u>what you're driving at</u>.
我能理解你说的意思。

8.61 If you **drive up** a price or amount, you make it rise to a higher level.
提高（价格）；增加（数量）

The government's policies are <u>driving up</u> interest rates.
政府的政策促使利率不断提高。

driving seat

8.62 A **driving seat** is a seat where the driver sits. If you say that someone is **in the driving seat**, you mean that he is controlling a situation.
驾驶座
掌控局面；处于主管地位

gear

8.63 The **gears** in a vehicle such as a car are the different speeds the engine can operate at.
（排）挡

If you **get** or **click into gear**, you start working effectively or making progress.
进入工作状态；开始进步；有进展

Suddenly my brain <u>clicked into gear</u> and I realized what was happening.
突然我的脑子开了窍，意识到正在发生什么事。

Her electoral campaign is finally <u>getting into gear</u>.
她的竞选活动终于有了进展。

8.64 To be **in** or **into top gear** means working very fast or effectively.
工作速度非常快；工作非常有效

The publicity machine was <u>in top gear</u> again yesterday as Madonna spent a day in Britain giving interviews to drum up interest in her new book.
昨天，当麦当娜花一天时间在英国接受访问以唤起人们对她的新书的兴趣时，大众宣传工具又以最快的速度运转起来。

From that moment on his career went <u>into top gear</u>.
从那一刻起，他的事业进入了发展最快的阶段。

8.65 If you **move up** or **shift up a gear**, you start working much more effectively or quickly, or with more energy.
开始更有效率地工作；开始更快地工作

It was a classic tennis match. Edberg won the first two sets, Becker <u>stepped up a gear</u> and won the next two, then lead 3-1 in the final set.
这是一场最精彩的网球比赛。埃德伯格先胜了两盘，贝克尔突然振奋精神赢了后两盘，然后在最后一盘中以 3 比 1 领先。

Pressure from the media was clearly going to <u>step up a gear</u> now.　　来自媒体的压力明显正在突然增大。

As she approaches her fortieth birthday, the Princess has <u>moved up a gear</u> in the pace of her life.　　公主在第 40 个生日快来到时突然加快了生活的节奏。

neutral

8.66 If a vehicle is in **neutral**, the engine is not in any gear and so it is not possible to drive or control it.　　（汽车的）空挡位置

If you say that you are **in neutral**, you mean that you are not making very much effort to do something, or are not really aware of what you are doing, because you are tired, or because you are thinking about other things.　　没有用心做的；不够努力的

I'm tired, my brain's <u>in neutral</u>.　　我感到疲劳，我的头脑一片空白。

This allows the practitioner to concentrate and work on areas that need particular attention, while holding stronger areas <u>in neutral</u>.　　这使那位开业律师得以集中精力在需要特别注意的领域进行工作，而对较强的领域暂且不管。

steer

8.67 To **steer** a vehicle is to control the direction it moves in.　　掌舵；驾驶
汉语用**掌舵**来比喻掌握方向。

Steer is used metaphorically to talk about influencing the way something happens or the way people behave.　　引导；影响

I try to <u>steer</u> my children <u>towards</u> healthier foods.　　我试图引导我的孩子吃比较健康的食物。

He <u>steered</u> the country <u>through</u> a transitional period to elections.　　他领导国家走过选举前的过渡阶段。

Ruth attempted to <u>steer</u> the conversation well <u>away from</u> work.　　鲁思试图使谈话的内容远离工作。

The single goal was enough to <u>steer</u> the club <u>to victory</u>.　　仅此一球足以帮助该俱乐部赢得胜利。

8.68 If you **steer clear of** someone or　　绕开；避开

something, you try to avoid him/it.
Tourists are advised to steer clear of the area until further notice.
旅游者得到建议，在未有进一步的通知前要避免进入该地区。
The singer has steered clear of drugs and alcohol for the past eighteen months.
这名歌手在过去的十八个月中已经戒除了毒品和烈酒。

8.69 If you **steer a course**, you behave in a particular way, especially when this involves making choice.
遵循
They tried to steer a middle course between overconfidence and undue pessimism.
他们试图在自负与过分悲观之间选择一条中间路线。

transport
8.70 If you **transport** people or things, you move them from one place to another, usually in a vehicle.
（通常指用车辆）运输，运送，搬运

If an event or scene **transports** you, it makes you imagine or feel as if you are in a different place or time.
使……觉得处于；使……仿佛置身于

The show transported Alvin back to nightclubs of the 1920s.
那场演出使阿尔文仿佛置身于20世纪20年代的夜总会。

veer
8.71 If a vehicle **veers**, it changes direction suddenly.
（尤指车辆等）突然转向

Veer is used metaphorically to talk about changing in a sudden or noticeable way, for example in a person's opinion or mood.
（突然或明显地）改变观点，改变情绪

After this defeat, the party veered sharply to right.
这次失败后，该党突然转向右翼。
The debate veered away from the main topic of discussion.
争论脱离了讨论的主题。
His emotions veered between fear and anger.
他的情绪变化不定，一会儿恐惧一会儿生气。

vehicle

8.72 A **vehicle** is a machine that is used for transporting people or goods from one place to another, such as a car or lorry.　　机动车辆

Vehicle is used metaphorically to talk about a way of expressing ideas or making something happen.　　（表达思想或使某事发生的）媒介；工具；手段

Art can be used as a <u>vehicle</u> for propaganda.　　艺术可以用作宣传的工具。

The play is an ideal <u>vehicle</u> for her talents.　　这部戏是她施展才华的理想机会。

Column 8.2

This column is adopted to help understand some metaphorical expressions of **vehicles** that are unique to Chinese.

翻车	run into difficulties
急刹车	bring to a halt
开倒车	back the car—turn back the clock
开快车	speed up the work
顺风转舵	take one's cue from changing conditions
顺水推舟	push the boat along with the current—make use of an opportunity to gain one's end

9 Market

advertise

9.1 To **advertise** means to try to persuade people to buy a product or service by announcing it on television, on the Internet, or in newspaper etc.

If you let people know something about yourself, you **advertise** it.
It's best not to <u>advertise</u> your own shortcomings.
If I were you, I wouldn't <u>advertise the fact that</u> you don't have a work permit.

（为……）做广告；登广告宣传
汉语用**兜售**比喻极力怂恿人接受某种观点、主张等，如：<u>兜售</u>地方保护主义错误言论。比较汉语中的**鼓吹、摇旗呐喊**等。

展现，宣传（自己的事）

最好不要宣扬你自己的缺点。

我要是你，决不会张扬自己没有工作许可证这件事。

afford

9.2 If you can **afford** something, you have enough money to be able to pay for it.

If you **can't afford** or **can ill afford** (to do) something, you should not do it because it will cause problems for you if you do.

Scientists are going abroad, taking with them skills that our country <u>can ill afford</u> to lose.
We <u>cannot afford</u> any more delays.

9.3 If you **afford** somebody something, you provide him with it.

The programme <u>affords</u> young people the chance to gain work experience.
The vaccination also <u>affords</u> protection

买得起

没有能力；承担不起（后果）

科学家们要出国，并随身带走了技能，这些是我们国家难以承受的损失。

我们不能再有任何耽误了。

提供；给予

这项计划给年轻人提供了获得工作经验的机会。

接种疫苗还能预防小儿麻痹。

against polio.

artificial

9.4 **Artificial** things are made by people and used instead of natural ones.

人造的；人工的

An **artificial** situation or quality exists because someone has made it exist, and not because it is really necessary.

人为的

Our new policies are designed to break down <u>artificial</u> barriers to women's advancement.

我们的新政策是要打破对女性晋升人为设置的障碍。

An interview is a very <u>artificial</u> situation.

面试是极不自然的场合。

9.5 Something that looks or sounds **artificial** does not seem real.

（看起来或听起来）假的；矫揉造作的

<u>artificial</u> manners

不自然的举止

To some people, the clarity of CD sound seems <u>artificial</u>.

对一些人来说，激光唱片听起来似乎有些假。

asset

9.6 **Assets** are the things that a company owns, which can be sold to pay debts.

资产；财产

汉语中，**财富**可用来泛指有价值的东西，如：自然<u>财富</u>、精神<u>财富</u>。

Asset is used metaphorically to refer to something or someone that is useful because it/he helps you succeed or deals with problems.

有价值的人或事物

Youth is a tremendous <u>asset</u> in this job.

在这种工作中，年轻是一个巨大的优势。

He is a definite <u>asset</u> to the team.

他无疑是该队的骨干。

bankrupt

9.7 A person or business that is **bankrupt** has officially admitted that he/it has no money and cannot pay what he/it owes.

（人或企业）破产的；倒闭的

汉语用<u>破产</u>比喻事情失败（多含贬义），如：阴谋<u>破产</u>。

Something that is **bankrupt** has no good qualities at all.

毫无优良品质的；沦丧到极点的

This is a <u>bankrupt</u> ideology.

这是个已毫无优点可言的思想体系。

a society that is morally <u>bankrupt</u>

bankruptcy

9.8 **Bankruptcy** is a situation in which a person or business becomes bankrupt. You can refer to a total lack of good qualities as **bankruptcy**.

moral <u>bankruptcy</u>

bargain

9.9 To **bargain** means to try to persuade someone to give you a better price or make an agreement that suits you better.
If you **bargain for** or **bargain on** something, you expect that it will happen and make it part of your plans.
We <u>hadn't bargained for</u> this sudden change in the weather.
When he agreed to answer a few questions, he got more than he <u>bargained for</u>.
I didn't <u>bargain on</u> finding them here as well.

buy

9.10 If you **buy** something, you get it by paying money.
Buy is used metaphorically to talk about getting something, usually by losing something else that is important.
attempts to <u>buy</u> peace with land
Increased profits <u>would be bought</u> at the expense of paying less attention to quality.

9.11 To **buy time** means to do something in order to get more time to do or finish something else.
Many feel that these latest negotiations are all part of a rebel plot to <u>buy time</u> or

道德沦丧的社会

破产；倒闭
参见9.7
（优良品质的）缺乏；沦丧

道德沦丧

讨价还价；洽谈；谈判
汉语用**讲价钱**比喻在接受任务或举行谈判时提出要求和条件。
预期；指望

我们没有预料到这样的天气突变。

他同意回答几个问题，不料却招来了一堆难以回答的问题。

我也没想到还会在这里遇到他们。

买；购买

获得；换取
比较汉语中的**收买人心**、**买好**、**买账**等。
以土地换和平的尝试
增加利润是以不注重质量为代价的。

赢得；争取（时间）

许多人觉得最近的这些谈判是争取时间或赢得更多支持的反叛阴谋的一部

try to win more support.

cheap

9.12 Something that is **cheap** is not expensive and not of good quality.

A **cheap** action or remark is unfair or unkind and does not deserve respect.

I'm not interested in scoring <u>cheap points</u> in this debate.

He said he realized it had been <u>a cheap trick</u> and he was sorry.

consume

9.13 If you **consume** something, you eat, drink or use it.

If a feeling or idea **consumes** you, it affects you very strongly, so that you can not think about anything else.

I <u>was consumed</u> with curiosity about my new neighbour.

9.14 If fire **consumes** something, it destroys it completely.

In 1541 a fire <u>consumed</u> most of the town and much of the castle.

consuming

9.15 A **consuming** feeling is so strong that you think of little else.

Football is a <u>consuming</u> passion for lots of kids.

consumption

9.16 **Consumption** is the process of buying or using goods.

If something is **for general, public, private etc. consumption**, it is intended to be heard or read by a particular group of people.

This report was never intended <u>for</u>

分。

便宜的；廉价的；劣质的
汉语中，贱有卑鄙、下贱之意。
卑劣的；卑鄙的；可耻的

我对这次辩论赛中靠不光彩手段得分的事不感兴趣。

他说他意识到这是个无聊的把戏，还说他很抱歉。

吃；喝；消费

使着迷；使全神贯注

我对新邻居充满了好奇。

毁灭；烧毁

1541年的一场火把镇子的大部分和城堡的相当一部分都烧毁了。

使人全神贯注的；强烈的

足球让许多孩子都非常着迷。

消费

供某人了解的

这份报告从来就未打算向公众公开。

public consumption.

cost

9.17 A **cost** is the amount of money that is needed in order to buy, pay for, or do something.

Cost is used metaphorically to talk about effort, loss or damage that is involved in order to do or achieve something.

He worked non-stop for three months, at considerable cost to his health.
The plant closed down at a cost of over 1,000 jobs.
She was determined to win at any cost.

价钱；价格；成本
汉语中，**价钱**可用以比喻条件、报酬等，如：他在工作中从来不讲价钱。

代价；牺牲；损失

他连续不断地工作了三个月，极大地损害了自己的身体健康。
工厂倒闭了，失去了一千多个岗位。
她决心不惜一切代价要获胜。

debt

9.18 A **debt** is an amount of money that you owe.

Debt is used metaphorically to refer to an obligation to be grateful to someone because he has done something for you.

I owe a debt of gratitude to my father, who has always supported me.
I would like to acknowledge my debt to my teachers.

债务；欠款

（欠下的）人情；恩义

我对父亲感恩不已，他总是支持我。

我想向老师表达我的感激之情。

discount

9.19 To **discount** means to reduce the price of something.

If you **discount** something, you consider that it is not important, possible, or likely.

Police have discounted the possibility that this was a terrorist attack.

打折扣；打折出售
汉语用**打折扣**来比喻不完全按规定的、已承认的或已答应的来做，如：要保质保量地按时交活儿，不能打折扣。用**掉价**比喻身份、排场降低。

认为……不重要；不重视；对……不全信

警方排除了这是一次恐怖袭击的可能性。

export

9.20 If you **export** goods, you sell and send them to another country.

If you **export** an activity, idea etc., you introduce it to another place or country.

American pop music <u>has been exported</u> around the world.

nations that <u>export</u> terrorism

出口；输出

传播；输出（思想或活动）

美国流行音乐已传播到世界各地。

恐怖主义输出国

fund

9.21 A **fund** is an amount of money that you collect, save, or invest.

A **fund of** something is a large supply of it.

She had <u>a huge fund of</u> knowledge, skill, and experience.

资金；基金；专款

储存；储备

她有极其丰富的知识、技能和经验。

legacy

9.22 A **legacy** is money or property that is given to you by someone when he dies.

Legacy is used metaphorically to refer to a situation that exists now because of events, actions, etc. that took place in the past.

The problems were made worse by the <u>legacy</u> of centuries of neglect.

Future generations will be left with a <u>legacy</u> of pollution and destruction.

遗产；遗赠财物

遗留问题；后遗症

汉语中，**遗产**可用来指某个国家或民族历史上遗留下来的物质财富或精神财富，如：文化<u>遗产</u>、文学<u>遗产</u>。

这些问题由于长期无人过问，情况变得更加严重。

留给子孙后代的将是环境的污染与破坏。

manufacture

9.23 To **manufacture** means to make goods in large quantities in a factory.

If you make up a story that is not true, you **manufacture** it.

He <u>manufactured</u> an alibi about his car breaking down.

（大量）生产；制造

捏造；杜撰；虚构

他编了一个汽车抛锚的借口。

package

9.24 If you **package** something, you put it into boxes or wrap it so that it can be sold.

包装；把……打包；把……装箱
汉语用**包装**比喻对人或事物从形象上装饰、美化，使更具吸引力或商业价值。

If you **package** someone or something such as a product or idea, you try to make him/it seem interesting and exciting to the public.

包装（产品或想法等）

Politicians these days are packaged to appeal to a mass market.

如今的政客们都进行了包装以吸引大众。

9.25 A **package deal** is a set of different things that are offered together and must be accepted together.

一揽子交易

The province wanted independence as part of the package deal.

该省想把独立当作一揽子交易的内容之一。

product

9.26 A **product** is something that is made, grown, or obtained in large quantities so that it can be sold.

制品；产品
汉语用**结晶**比喻珍贵的成果，如：劳动的结晶。

If something is the **product** of a particular situation, process etc, it is the result of that situation or process.

结果；产物；结局

The place is, of course, only the product of the poet's imagination.

这个地方当然只是诗人想象的产物。

The eastern frontier of France was the product of centuries of historical accidents.

法国东部边界是几百年历史变故的结果。

9.27 If someone is the **product** of a particular background or experience, his character is typical of that background or the result of that experience.

产物

These teenagers are typical products of the private education system.

这些少年是私立教育制度的典型产物。

property

9.28 Property is things that are owned by someone. 　所有物；财产

Property is used metaphorically to refer to a quality or power that a substance, plant etc. has. 　特性；特质

The water is said to have healing <u>properties</u>. 　那水据说具有治疗功能。

sell

9.29 If you **sell** something, you exchange it for money. 　卖；出售 参见 9.1

If you **sell** a new idea, plan etc., you try to make it become accepted. 　说服；使接受

I don't think we could <u>sell</u> the idea to our partners. 　我想我们无法让合作方接受这个想法。

Column 9

This column is adopted to help understand some metaphorical expressions of **market** that are unique to Chinese.

本小利微	small capital and little gain
变本加厉	be further intensified
不买账	not go for it
不名一文	penniless
不怕不识货，就怕货比货	just compare them and you will see which is better
不折不扣	hundred-percent; to the letter
吃老本	rest on one's laurels
重操旧业	take up one's old trade again
重打锣鼓另开张	start all over again
翻老账	rake up old scores
空头支票	empty promise
卖关子	keep people guessing
卖国求荣	turn traitor for personal gain
漫天要价	ask an exorbitant price
敲竹杠	overcharge

如意算盘	wishful thinking
一笔勾销	cancel
蝇头小利	a fly's head of profit; a pittance of profit; a petty profit

10 Theatres and Stage

curtain

10.1 A **curtain** is a piece of thick, heavy fabric that hangs in front of the stage in the theatre. The scene that a **curtain** rises or falls is often used metaphorically to talk about beginnings and endings.

幕,幕布
汉语中，**序幕**常被用来比喻重大事件的开端。如：卢沟桥事变拉开了全面抗战的**序幕**。**序曲**也可用来比喻事情、行动的开端。如：预赛获胜只是夺取冠军的序曲。

10.2 If **a curtain rises** or **is raised**, it means something begins to happen.
border incidents that were curtain-raisers to a full-scale war

开幕
引发一场全面战争的边境事件

10.3 If a **curtain falls**, it marks the end of something.
The curtain has fallen on her long and distinguished career.

闭幕；落幕
她那漫长而成绩斐然的职业生涯已告结束。

10.4 Similar meanings to 10.3 can be expressed with phrases like **bring down the curtain on** something and **bring the curtain down on** something.
His sudden decision to retire brought down the curtain on a distinguished career.

终止某事；结束某事；某事落下帷幕
他突然决定退休，结束了他成就斐然的职业生涯。

drama

10.5 A **drama** is a play for the theatre, television, or radio.

戏剧；电视剧
汉语用**好戏**指即将发生的热闹场景，如：您就等着看**好戏**吧。

In metaphorical meaning, **drama** means something unusual or exciting that happens.

激情；刺激

You couldn't help being thrilled by the drama of the situation.
你不禁会为这充满激情的场面激动不已。

10.6 When **a drama unfolds**, an exciting event is expected to happen.
发生戏剧性的事

A crowd had gathered to watch the drama unfold.
一群人聚拢过来观看那个戏剧性事件的发生。

10.7 If you **make a drama out of** something, you treat a particular situation as if it is more serious or exciting than it really is.
小题大做，夸大其词

play

10.8 If you **play** someone in a play, movie etc, you are asked to act the role of him or her.
扮演，饰演（角色）

The verb **play** is used metaphorically to talk about fulfilling or performing a function.
汉语中的**扮演**有充当、担任之意，如：在经济建设中扮演重要角色。
充当、担任

10.9 If you **play second fiddle to someone** or **something**, you are treated as less important than someone or something.
扮演次要角色，作某人的副手

10.10 If you **play a role in** something, you are involved in it, especially in a way that is important.
扮演重要角色，发挥重要作用；举足轻重

She played a key role in campaigning for equal opportunities in the workplace.
她在争取工作场所机会均等的运动中起到了关键作用。

prelude

10.11 A **prelude** is a short piece of music that introduces a longer piece of music.
（乐曲的）前奏，过门

Prelude is used to refer to an event that happens before and introduces a more important event.
（更重要事件的）序曲

The deal is a prelude to a merger of the two companies.
这笔生意是两家公司合并的序曲。

puppet

10.12 A **puppet** is a small model of a person or animal that you can move by pulling wires or strings or by putting your hands inside it. In metaphorical meaning, **puppet** means a person or group whose actions are controlled by another.

The occupying forces set up a <u>puppet</u> government.

木偶

汉语中的**傀儡**是指木偶戏里的木头人，可用来比喻受人操纵的人或组织。

傀儡

占领军建立了一个傀儡政府。

scene

10.13 A **scene** is a part of a play, book, and film etc. in which events happen in the same place or period of time.

Scene is used to refer to a place where something happens or a situation.

the <u>scene</u> of the crime

10.14 If someone or something **comes on the scene**, he/it starts to exist or to get involved in a situation or activity.

a band that first <u>came on the scene</u> in the 1980s

10.15 If an activity is **behind the scenes**, it is carried out secretly rather than publicly. If a person works **behind the scenes**, he is in a position to see the hidden workings.

These agreements have been drafted by officials <u>behind the scenes</u>.

<u>behind-the-scenes</u> negotiations

He prefers to work <u>behind the scenes</u> as a director.

10.16 To **set the scene** is used metaphorically to talk about creating the conditions that make it possible for an

（戏剧、书、电影等的）片断，场面，情节，镜头

某事发生的地点；局面

犯罪现场

走上（历史）舞台

于 20 世纪 80 年代首次登场的乐队

在幕后

汉语中，**幕后**用以比喻躲在后面指挥、策划、活动的地方，多含贬义，如：<u>幕后</u>交易、<u>幕后</u>操纵。

这些协议是官员们秘密草拟的。

秘密谈判

他宁愿作为导演在幕后工作。

（为……）提供条件

参见 6.29

event to happen.
The unjust peace agreement <u>set the scene</u> for another war.
这项不公正的和平协议导致了另一场战争。
Let me just <u>set the scene</u> by telling you a little about the school.
让我告诉你有关这所学校的一些情况，给你提供背景知识。

10.17 If someone **makes** or **causes a scene,** there is a noisy argument or a strong show of feelings in a public place.
（在公众场合的）吵闹，发脾气
比较汉语中的**搅局**。

Shh, will you stop <u>causing a scene</u>?
嘘，别当众大吵大闹啦！

10.18 **steal the scene**
抢镜头
See also 10.28
参见 10.28

show

10.19 If you **put on a show** or **make a show**, you pretend to have particular feelings.
假装；演戏

They <u>made a show</u> of affection for the sake of the children.
他们为了孩子，假装还恋着对方。

10.20 A person who **steals the show** is one who is in a subordinate role or position but becomes the main focus of attention or plaudits.
大出风头，意外地博得赞赏（或受人注目）

He did all the work, but his wife <u>stole the show</u>.
所有的工作都是他做的，但出尽风头的却是他妻子。

10.21 If you say someone **put up a good** or **put up a poor show**, you mean the person did something well or badly.
表现得很好
表现得很差

They <u>put up a poor show</u> against the stronger team.
他们在与强队的比赛中表现很差。

string

10.22 A **string** is a thin rope on puppet or instrument.
细绳
汉语用**束手束脚**比喻做事顾虑多，不敢放手去干。

Strings are used metaphorically to refer to limiting conditions.
限制条件
比较**束缚**，如：思想**束缚**。

If there are any strings involved, I'm really not interested.
如果有任何限制条件，那我就真的没兴趣了。
offer official aid without strings attached
无条件提供官方援助

10.23 If you **have** someone **on a string**, you are able to control him or her.
能操纵（或支配）某人
She has really got him on a string.
她真是牵着他的鼻子走。

10.24 If you **pull strings**, you use your influence in order to get something you want or to help someone, especially when this is unfair.
运用影响获得好处；（尤指）走后门
汉语用**走后门**比喻用托人情、行贿等不正当的手段，通过内部关系达到某种目的。
Jack pulled strings and got us a room at the crowded hotel.
杰克走了后门，在客满的旅馆里为我们开到了一个房间。

10.25 The person who **pulls the strings** is the real actuator of what another does.
在幕后牵线，幕后操纵
参见 10.15
Some appeared on the stage, while others pulled the the strings behind the scenes.
有人在前台表演，有人在后台指挥。

10.26 If you **have more than one string to your bow**, you have more than one plan, idea, or skill if the first one is not successful.
有多手准备；有后备方案（或想法、技巧）
比较汉语中的**留一手**。
To survive as an actor you need more than one string to your bow.
作为一名演员，如果要生存就必须要多才多艺。

stage

10.27 A **stage** is the part of a theatre where the actors or musicians perform. In metaphorical meaning, **stage** refers to the place or situation in which something happens, especially in politics.
舞台
汉语中，**舞台**用来比喻供人开展活动、发挥才能或施展抱负的场所（多指抽象的），如：政治舞台；在军事舞台上导演出威武雄壮的话剧来。
参见 10.28

the European political stage
欧洲政治舞台
the stages of a famous battle
一次著名战役的战场
Those diseases now occupy the centre of the medical stage.
那几种疾病成了医学界注意的中心。

10.28 To **set the stage for** something means to prepare for it or make it possible.
set the stage for a protracted struggle

创造条件；作好准备
汉语用**出台**比喻某些政策法规予以公布或解决问题的措施予以实施。
准备作长期斗争

rehearsal
10.29 A **rehearsal** is an occasion when you practise for the performance of a play, concert, opera etc.
Rehearsal is used metaphorically to talk about a practice session preparatory to many activities.
The earlier revolts had just been dress rehearsals for full-scale revolution.

排演；排练

演练；演习

那些初期的反抗活动只不过是大规模革命行动的演习。

tone
10.30 Your **tone** is the quality of your voice that shows what you are feeling.

声调；腔音；语气
汉语中，**高调**可比喻脱离实际的议论或说了而不去实践的漂亮话，如：唱高调。**低调**比喻缓和的或比较消沉的论调；也有和缓而不张扬的意思，如：低调处理。

Tone can be used to refer to the general character of a place or event.
The positive tone of the evening had changed completely.
Trust you to lower the tone of the whole conversation.

气氛；氛围

晚上的良好气氛已彻底改变了。

你肯定会让整个谈话煞风景的。

10.31 **Tone** is also used to refer to a general attitude shown by a piece of writing.
Much of his writing has a rather strident tone to it.
Their next letter was more optimistic in tone.

（作品的）风格，笔调

他的很多作品笔调都相当尖刻。

他们的下封信笔调乐观了一些。

well-rehearsed
10.32 If you say something is **well-**

计划周密的

rehearsed, you mean it is carefully planned.
I figured I'd better be prepared with a well-rehearsed explanation.

汉语用**滴水不漏**形容说话、做事十分周密,没有漏洞。
我想我最好准备好圆满的解释。

Column 10

This column is adopted to help understand some metaphorical expressions of **theaters & stage** that are unique to Chinese.

唱独角戏	go it alone
唱对台戏	enter into rivalry with someone
唱反调	speak or act contrary to
唱高调	say fine-sounding things; affect a high moral tone
唱双簧	collaborate with each other
丑角	(in real life) clown; comedian; buffoon
重演	recur; react; repeat
粉墨登场	make oneself up and go on stage—embark upon a political venture
各吹各的号,各唱各的调	each blows his own bugle and sings his own song—each does things in his own way
好戏	great fun (used sarcastically)
开场白	opening (or introductory) remarks
拿手好戏	one's specialty; one's forte
潜台词	what is actually meant (in one's speech); implication
上台	assume power; come (or rise) to power
台柱子	soul member (of an organization); mainstay; pillar
下台	fall out of power; leave office
序幕	prologue (to a major event, etc.); prelude
一唱百和	when one starts singing, the others join in—meet with general approval
一唱一和	sing the same tune; echo each other

11 Clothes

belt

11.1 A **belt** is a narrow piece of leather, cloth etc. that you wear around your waist, for example to keep your clothes in place or for decoration.
You can refer to an area of land where there is a particular industry, activity etc. as a **belt**.
the corn belt
the city's commuter belt
a belt of trees
11.2 A comment that is **below the belt** is cruel and unfair.
That was distinctly below the belt.

cap

11.3 A **cap** is a type of soft hat with a peak.

You can refer to a limit on the amount of money that you can spend or charge as a **cap**.
Airlines began to impose a $50 cap on commissions for domestic flights.
The government introduced new spending caps for local authorities.
11.4 If the government **caps** a local authority or council, it limits the amount of money that the authority is allowed to

腰带；皮带
汉语中，带有地带、区域之意，如：温带、黄河地带等。
参见 6.4
（某种工业、活动等的）地带，地区

玉米产区
城市通勤者聚居区
一片林带
（评论）不公正的，卑劣的

那显然是不公正的。

（有帽舌的）帽子
汉语用帽子比喻罪名或坏名义，如：批评应该切合实际，有内容，不要光扣大帽子。
（支出或收费的）限额，上限
参见 6.11

航空公司开始把国内航班手续费的上限规定为 50 美元。
政府为地方当局规定了新的支出限额。
规定（收费或支出）的上限；规定……的限额
参见 6.11

spend.

The Department of the Environment is capping local authorities' spending.
环境部正在限定地方当局的支出限额。

The interest rate has been capped at 11.5 percent.
利率上限规定为 11.5%。

使圆满完成；使结束
参见 10.1

11.5 If someone says that a good or bad event **caps** a series of events, he means that it is the final event in the series.

His victory in the world championship capped a brilliant week's skiing.
他在世界锦标赛上的胜利给一周精彩的滑雪比赛画上了圆满的句号。

The festivities were capped by a presentation to all the committee members.
庆典活动以对全体委员的致词作为圆满结束。

被……所覆盖

11.6 If something **is capped** with another, it has the other on its top.

The mountains were capped with snow.
山顶覆盖着积雪。

coat

外套

11.7 A **coat** is a piece of clothing with long sleeves that you wear over your other clothes when you go outside.

汉语中，衣可以指包在物体外面的一层东西，如：笋衣、糖衣等。

覆盖层；涂层

You can refer to a layer of something such as paint that you put onto a surface as a **coat**.

All the door needs is a new coat of paint.
这扇门只需涂上一层新漆。

在……上涂（或盖）

11.8 If you **coat** something **with** a substance or **in** a substance, you cover it with a thin layer of the substance.

The wind had coated everything with a layer of sand.
这阵风使所有的东西上都落了一层沙。

hat

帽子
参见 11.3

11.9 A **hat** is a piece of clothing that you wear on your head.

角色；职位

If you say someone is wearing a particular **hat**, you mean that he is performing a particular role.

She has to <u>wear several different hats</u> in her position.

她在这个岗位上要身兼数职。

Of course, when I say this, <u>I'm wearing my teaching hat</u>.

当然，我是作为教师来说这些话的。

11.10 If you say that you are ready to do something **at the drop of a hat**, you mean that you are willing to do it immediately, without hesitating.

立即；毫不迟疑地；乐意地

He is willing to cancel the order <u>at the drop of any hats</u>.

他愿意随时取消订货。

She loves playing the piano and will give you a tune <u>at the drop of a hat</u>.

她爱弹琴，并乐意随时为您奏一曲。

11.11 If you tell someone to **keep** a piece of information **under** his **hat**, you are asking him not to tell anyone else about it.

对某事保密

<u>Keep it under your hat</u> for the moment.

请暂时保密。

mend

11.12 If you **mend** a piece of clothing, you repair a tear or hole in it.

缝补；修补

If you try to **mend** divisions between people, you try to end the disagreements or quarrels between them.

结束（争论）；弥合（分歧）

The Secretary of State and Chinese Foreign Minister met in an attempt to <u>mend</u> strained relations.

国务卿和中国外交部长会晤，试图消除两国之间的紧张关系。

11.13 If one country tries to **mend fences** with another, it tries to end a disagreement or quarrel with the other country. You can also say that two countries **mend fences**.

言归于好；重修旧好

比较汉语中的**亡羊补牢**。

The object of the meeting was primarily to <u>mend fences</u>.

这次会议的目的主要是为了言归于好。

11.14 If a relationship or situation is **on the mend** after a difficult or unsuccessful

正在好转

period, it is improving.
Do you think the economy really is <u>on the mend</u>? — 你认为经济真的在好转吗？

11.15 If you are **on the mend** after an illness or injury, you are recovering from it. — 正在康复

She's been very ill, but luckily she's <u>on the mend</u> now. — 她病得很重，但幸运的是她现在正在康复。

needle

11.16 A **needle** is a small, very thin piece of polished metal that is used for sewing. — 针；缝衣针

汉语用**针锋相对**比喻双方策略、论点等尖锐地对立，用**一针见血**比喻话说得简短而能切中要害。

If someone **needles** you, he annoys you continually, especially by criticizing you. — （用言语）刺激，激怒

He takes delight in <u>needling</u> his nearest rival. — 他喜欢用言语来刺激与他实力最接近的对手。

shoe

11.17 **Shoes** are objects that you wear on feet, usually over socks. — 鞋；鞋子

汉语用**穿小鞋**比喻受人（多为有职权者）暗中刁难、约束或限制。

If you **fill someone's shoes**, you take his place by doing the job he was doing. — 接替某人的工作

比较汉语中的**衣钵**。

Not many people could <u>fill the old man's shoes</u>. — 没有人能够接替那位老人的工作。

11.18 If you talk about being **in someone's shoes**, you talk about what you would do or how you would feel if you were in the situation. — 处于某人的处境

What would you do if you were <u>in my shoes</u>? — 如果你处于我的处境，你会怎么办？

sock

11.19 **Socks** are pieces of clothing which cover your feet and ankles and — 袜子

are worn inside shoes.
If you tell someone to **pull his socks up**, you mean that he should start working or studying harder, because he has been lazy or careless recently.

We should pull our socks up and see whether by more efficient approaches we can improve our work.

多加努力；多多用功

我们要加紧努力，看是否能用更为有效的方法改进工作。

suit

11.20 A **suit** is a set of clothes made from the same cloth, usually a jacket with trousers or a skirt.

一套衣服；服装

You can refer to something that someone does well as his or her **strong suit**.

某人的特长

Tact has never been his strong suit.

他向来处事不够老练。

11.21 To **follow suit** means to do what someone else has done.

跟着做；跟风

They began to offer takeout food, and other restaurants followed suit.

他们开始提供外卖，其他饭店纷纷效仿。

thread

11.22 A **thread** is a long thin fibre used for sewing pieces of cloth together or for weaving.

线

Thread is used to refer to an idea or condition that exists in all the different parts of something and connects them.

（贯穿始终的）主线，思路

There is a common thread running through all the problems.

所有这些问题都有一个共同的特点。

11.23 If something **is hanging by a thread**, it is in a very dangerous situation and may not continue.

千钧一发；岌岌可危；命悬一线

His son's life was hanging by a thread.

他的儿子生命垂危。

11.24 If you **lose the thread**, you stop concentrating so that you do not

走神

understand what someone is saying.
More than once she <u>lost the thread</u> and had to ask them to speak more slowly.   她多次走神，只好求他们说慢一点。

11.25 If you **pick up the threads**, you start doing something again that you had stopped doing.   继续从事；重新开始

I <u>picked up the threads</u> of ordinary life again.   我重新开始过普通生活。

tie

11.26 A **tie** is a narrow piece of cloth that a man wears around his neck under the collar of a shirt. It is tied with a knot.   领带
参见 6.4

You can use **tie** to refer to a relationship or connection between people or things.   关系；纽带；联系

The treaty should strengthen <u>ties</u> between the two countries.   该条约应该会加强两国之间的联系。

Family <u>ties</u> have become weakened.   家族关系弱化了。

the <u>ties</u> of marriage that united the kings   使诸王联系在一起的姻亲关系

11.27 **Tie** is used metaphorically to talk about a result of a game or competition in which each person or team has the same number of points, votes etc.   平局；平分；相同的票数
比较汉语的扯平、拉平。

The game finished in a <u>tie</u>.   比赛以平局结束。

There was a <u>tie</u> for fourth place.   有并列第 4 名的。

11.28 If something **ties** you to a particular place or situation, you cannot leave it.   束缚；约束；使……无法离开
参见 7.1

Many young mothers feel <u>tied</u> to the home and children.   许多年轻母亲觉得受到家庭和孩子的束缚。

An open ticket means you <u>are not tied</u> to returning on a particular day.   未注明往返日期的机票意味着你不一定非得某一天回来。

11.29 If two players or teams in a game **tie**, they both have the same number of points.   （比赛）打成平局，得分相同
参见 11.27

The game <u>was tied</u> 1-1 after extra time. 加时赛后，比赛打成 1 比 1 平。
They <u>tied</u> for first place, with a time of 25.64 seconds. 他们并列第 1，成绩为 25′64″。

wear

11.30 To **wear** means to have something on your body as clothing, decoration, or protection. 穿戴；佩带

If something **wears**, or **wears thin**, it gets thinner or weaker because it has been used a lot. 磨损；变旧

His shoes <u>were wearing</u> at the heel. 他的鞋后跟磨薄了。
The carpet <u>has worn very thin</u> in places. 地毯有几处被磨得很薄。

11.31 If something such as a feeling or explanation **wears thin**, it becomes gradually weaker or harder to accept. （感情）逐渐变弱；（解释）难以接受

After 50 pages, the reader's patience starts to <u>wear thin</u>. 读了 50 页后，读者开始有些不耐烦了。

11.32 If something **wears well**, it stays in good condition even after a lot of use. 经久耐用

The carpet <u>is wearing well</u>, isn't it? 这地毯很耐用，是不是？

11.33 If a person **wears well**, he looks attractive and healthy even though he is not young. 不显老

He was at least 50, but <u>he'd worn well</u>. 他至少有 50 岁了，但不显老。

11.34 To **wear** someone **down** means to make him gradually lose his energy or confidence. 使精疲力竭；使失去信心

They <u>were worn down</u> by the stress of feeding five children. 养活 5 个孩子的压力使他们精疲力竭。

11.35 To **wear** something **down** means to make it gradually disappear or become thinner by using or rubbing it. （使）磨损；（使）磨薄

The old stone steps <u>had been worn down</u> by years of use. 古老的石阶由于多年的使用已经磨损了。

11.36 If a sensation or feeling **wears** （情感或感觉）逐渐消失

off, it disappears slowly until it no longer exists or has any effects.

The numbness in his shoulder was starting to <u>wear off</u>. 他肩膀上麻木的感觉开始慢慢消失。

I got bored with the job once the novelty <u>wore off</u>. 新鲜感一消失，我就对工作感到厌烦了。

11.37 If something **wears on** you, it is annoying, and makes you tired. 烦扰（某人）；使疲倦

Your constant complaining <u>is really wearing on</u> me. 你没完没了的抱怨真让我心烦。

Column 11

This column is adopted to help understand some metaphorical expressions of **clothes** that are unique to Chinese.

给（某人）穿小鞋	to give someone tight shoes to wear—make things hard for someone by abusing one's power; make it hot for someone
穿新鞋，走老路	tread the old path in new shoes—make no real change
穿一条裤子	share the same pair of trousers—band together; collude; gang up
穿针引线	act as a go-between
戴高帽子	flatter; lay it on thick
戴帽子	be branded as; be labeled

12 Games and Sports

also-ran

12.1 In a horse race, an **also-ran** is a horse that took part but that did not do very well.
Also-ran is used metaphorically to refer to people who are not successful, especially those who lose an election or competition.
It is the second largest party but it is likely to remain the also-ran forever if it goes on like this.

（赛跑中）未获名次的马
汉语用驽马比喻没有才能的人。

失败者；（尤指竞选或比赛的）落选者

它是第二大党，但这样下去它就可能永远做陪衬。

angling

12.2 **Angling** is the sport of catching fish.

垂钓
汉语中，钓可用来比喻用手段猎取（名利），如：沽名钓誉。

If someone **is angling for** something, he is trying to get it, and he is using indirect methods rather than asking for it directly.
Are you angling for promotion? Finding out which type of worker you are, and how your colleagues see you, are the first steps to getting ahead at work.
It sounds as if he's just angling for sympathy.

（尤指采用间接方法）试图得到

你的意思是想要升职？要使自己工作表现突出，第一步就是要明确你自己属于工人中的哪一类，你在同事们心目中的形象如何。
听起来他好像只是在博取同情。

bait

12.3 **Bait** is food used for attracting and catching fish, birds, or animals.
Bait is used metaphorically to refer to

（钓鱼、捕鸟或猎兽用的）饵
汉语用钓饵来比喻引诱人的事物。
诱饵；诱惑（物）

something that is offered in order to persuade someone to do something or buy something.

Interest-free credit is on offer and customers are taking the <u>bait</u>.
顾客们都受诱惑接受了提供的无息贷款。

12.4 If one person **baits** another, the first person deliberately tries to make the second angry by saying or doing unpleasant, cruel, or annoying things. You can refer to this action as **baiting**.

故意激怒

挑衅行为

All through the interval, Ray <u>was baiting</u> poor Jack, questioning him time and again about whether he wanted to change his mind.
整个间歇期间,雷都在逗弄可怜的杰克,不断地问他是否要改变主意,企图引他发火。

Black sportsmen are the latest victims of racist <u>baiting</u>.
黑人运动员是最近种族主义挑衅行为的受害者。

card

12.5 **Card** game is the activity of playing games with a set of 52 **cards**.

扑克牌

If you say that someone will achieve success if he **plays** his **cards right**, you mean that he will achieve success if he acts skilfully and uses the advantages that he has.

办事高明;应对得当;做事有心计

If she <u>played</u> her <u>cards</u> sensibly there was a new and decent life ahead of her.
如果她明智地行事处世,她将来能过上体面的新生活。

12.6 If you say that someone **has played all** his **cards**, you mean that he has tried all the possibilities open to him, without success.

竭尽所能
汉语用**黔驴技穷**比喻仅有的一点伎俩也用完了,用**山穷水尽**比喻陷入绝境。

I <u>haven't played all my cards</u> yet. We can still make a deal.
我并没有到穷途末路的地步。我们仍然能做一笔交易。

12.7 If you say that someone **holds** or **has all the cards**, you mean that he is able to control a particular situation

能控制局面;应付自如;占上风
比较汉语中的**占先手**。

because he has an advantage over other people.

The 150,000-strong army <u>held all the cards</u> over the presidential election last week.

上个星期，拥有15万人的军队控制着总统选举的整个局面。

12.8 If you say that someone **keeps** or **plays** his **cards close to** his **chest**, you mean that he does not tell other people about his ideas or plans for the future.

（对自己的想法、计划等）守口如瓶，秘而不宣

The big companies <u>were playing</u> their <u>cards close to</u> their <u>chests</u> last night about where the money goes.

昨夜那些大公司始终回避资金流向的问题。

12.9 **Put** or **lay** your **cards on the table** is used as a metaphor to talk about a situation in which someone decides whether or not to reveal ideas, plans, or intentions which he had previously kept secret.

摊牌

I'm going to <u>put</u> my <u>cards on the table</u> and make you an offer.

我打算将我的想法全部说出来，向你提出一个建议。

He says he needs a little more information; he wants to see a few more <u>cards on the table</u>.

他说他需要更多一点信息；他要了解更多的情况。

12.10 To **play the ... card** means to use a particular quality, argument etc. in order to gain an advantage.

使出……的一招；打出……的招牌

politicians who <u>play the</u> nationalist <u>card</u> in order to get votes

为赢得选票而打出民族主义者幌子的政客

See also **trump 12.58**

checkmate

12.11 A **checkmate** in chess is an attack that your opponent's king cannot escape from, so that you win the game.

（国际象棋中的）将死，将军
汉语用**将军**比喻给人出难题，使人为难，如：他**将**了我一军。

Checkmate is used metaphorically as a verb to talk about a situation in which

打败；战胜

one person defeats another, often in a clever or cunning way.
He had to find out what this girl was up to so he could <u>checkmate</u> her.
他必须弄明白这个女孩想干什么，这样他就有可能打败她。
He would have to <u>checkmate</u> the dirty tricksters at their own game.
他将不得不在这些肮脏的骗子自己玩的把戏中击败他们。

chess
12.12 **Chess** is a game for two people played on a chess board.

国际象棋
汉语中，一些围棋术语也常被用作隐喻，如：**布局**、**收官**等。
博弈（斗争）

You can refer to a situation in which people are trying to gain advantages over each other in a cunning way as a **chess game** or a **game of chess**.
The application is very much part of the long <u>chess game</u> which has been going on between the two communities since 1974.
应用在很大程度上是那盘下了很长时间的棋的一部分，这盘棋从1974年以来就一直在两个社区之间进行着。
A deadly <u>game of chess</u> is being fought on London's streets between the terrorists and the police, with the public as pawns.
恐怖主义分子和警方之间的一场殊死的斗争正在伦敦的街道上进行，而公众则成了小卒。

favourite
12.13 When people gamble on a horse, the **favourite** is the horse that is considered to be the most likely to win.

最有可能赢得比赛的马

Favourite is used as a metaphor to talk about the person or organization that is believed to be most likely to be successful in a particular situation, especially in a very competitive situation.
The Mayor of Ankara is the current <u>favourite</u> for the succession.
The Americans are hot <u>favourite</u> to win the title.

（比赛中）最有希望获胜者，夺冠热门

安卡拉的市长是目前最有可能继任的人选。
美国队是有望赢得这一桂冠的热门队。

fish

12.14 To **fish** means to try to catch fish, for example using a net or a fishing rod. If you **fish** for something, you try to find it by feeling inside a bag, a box etc.
She stopped and fished for her door key.
Matthew started fishing around in a file of papers.
When I said I was overweight, I wasn't fishing for compliments.

捕鱼；钓鱼
参见 12.2
搜索；寻找

她停下来找门钥匙。
马修开始在一堆文件中到处搜寻。
当我说我超重时，我不是在拐弯抹角地寻求赞扬。

gamble

12.15 To **gamble** means to risk money or something valuable in the hope of winning more if you are lucky or if you guess something correctly.
Gamble is used metaphorically to talk about doing something that involves risks but may result in benefits if things happen as you hope they will.
The improved atmosphere persuaded some foreign investors to gamble on a recovery.
Mr. Bush is gambling that his idea will attract support from the public.

12.16 **Gamble**, as a noun, is used to refer to an action or plan that involves risks but will bring important benefits if it is successful.
His bankers opposed the move, but the gamble paid off.

打赌；赌博

投机；冒险；碰运气

氛围的改善促使一些国外投资者想碰运气挽回损失。
布什先生把赌注压在他的想法会吸引公众的支持上。

赌博；投机；冒险

他的银行经营者反对那一举措，但是这一冒险成功了。

game

12.17 A **game** is an activity that you do for fun that has rules, and that you can win or lose.
Game is used to refer to an activity or

游戏

儿戏；玩笑

situation that someone seems to be treated less seriously than it should be treated.

Marriage is just a *game* to them.

They are playing political *games* with people's safety.

12.18 **The game is up** is used for saying that the truth has been discovered, especially when someone has been doing wrong and will have to stop.

He narrowed his eyes as the blue lights of the police car filled the cab. Sensing *the game was up*, he pulled over.

12.19 In sport, a team's **game plan** is the strategy they intend to use during a match or competition in order to win it. **Game plan** is used metaphorically to talk about the actions someone intends to take and the policies he intends to adopt in order to achieve a particular thing.

Yesterday's attack on the city shows that the militants have their own *game plan*.

  See also **play** 12.32

goal

12.20 **Goal** is the net or structure that you try to get the ball into in games such as football and basketball.

Goal is used metaphorically to refer to something that you hope to achieve.

Our *goal* is to provide a good standard of medical care.

You should set *goals* for yourself at the beginning of each school year.

I haven't yet reached my *goal* of losing 2

婚姻对他们来讲不过是儿戏。

他们简直就是拿人们的安全玩政治游戏。

（尤指某人做了错事并不得不收场时）完蛋了，事已败露

警车那蓝色的灯光射进出租汽车，刺得他眯起了眼睛。他感到戏该收场了，于是把车停了下来。

行动策略

昨天对这个城市的攻击表明，激进分子有他们自己的行动策略。

球门；球篮
汉语中，箭靶的中心称为*的*，如：目的、众矢之*的*。
目标；目的

我们的目标是提供高水准的医疗保健服务。
你应该在每学年开始时为自己确立目标。
我还没有实现减掉2英石的目标。

stone.

12.21 An **own goal** is one that you accidentally score against your own team.

Own goal is used metaphorically to refer to something you do that accidentally harms you, often when you intend to harm someone else.

Because of the legislation I could not employ a woman. Women have made themselves unemployable. They have scored an <u>own goal</u>.

乌龙球
参见 5.54

蠢事，错事，自打嘴巴

按照法规我不能雇用妇女。妇女已经使她们自己无法受雇。她们这是自作自受。

goalpost

12.22 A **goalpost** is one of the two posts that the ball must go between to score a goal in games such as football.

Goalposts is used metaphorically in the expression **move the goalposts** to talk about a situation in which one person or group of people behaves unfairly in order to gain an advantage over another person or group of people.

They seem <u>to move the goalposts</u> every time I meet the conditions that are required.

球门柱

移动球门柱，改变规则（增加某人做某事的难度）

每当我满足了他们提出的要求时，他们都似乎有意改变条件，使我永远无法达到目的。

hunt

12.23 When people or animal **hunt**, they chase and kill wild animals for food or as a sport.

If you **hunt** for someone or something, you try to find or catch him/it by searching carefully or thoroughly.

Detectives <u>have been hunting</u> for clues to the murder's identity.

He began by <u>hunting</u> around for

打猎；射杀（猎物）
汉语中，猎有搜寻、物色之意，如：猎奇、猎取。

搜寻；追捕

侦探一直在搜寻有关谋杀犯身份的线索。

他从四处搜索信息着手。

information.

hunted

12.24 If someone has a **hunted** look, he looks worried, as if he is expecting something unpleasant to happen soon.

（表情）焦虑的，十分惊恐的

He had a <u>hunted</u> look about him, as if he expected someone to kick open the door at any minute.

他看起来忧心忡忡，好像在期待什么人随时把门踢开。

lottery

12.25 A **lottery** is a game designed to raise money by selling lottery tickets that people buy hoping that their numbers are chosen by chance in the draw so that they win a money prize.

抽彩给奖（筹款法）；彩票游戏

Lottery is used to refer to a situation where everything depends on luck or chance. This word shows that you do not think a situation like this is fair.

赶巧的事，碰运气的事（该词表示认为类似的情形不公平）

The standard of care you get in hospital is a bit of a <u>lottery</u>.

你在医院得到什么水准的护理全靠碰运气。

Some people think that marriage is a <u>lottery</u>.

有些人认为婚姻靠的是运气。

marathon

12.26 A **marathon** is a race that is run over a distance of 42 kilometres or about 26 miles.

马拉松（长跑）

If you use **marathon** to describe an event or task, you are emphasizing that it takes a long time to complete and is very tiring.

耗费精力和毅力的持久活动；马拉松式的活动

The meeting turned out to be a bit of a <u>marathon</u>.

这场会议有点像马拉松。

marathon negotiations

马拉松式的谈判

neck and neck

12.27 If two horses are **neck and neck**

（赛马比赛中）并驾齐驱

as they approach the end of a race, they are both ahead all the other horses, but they are so close together that it is difficult to tell which one is going to win.
If two political parties or two candidates for a position are **neck and neck**, they are involved in a close race, competition, etc.
The candidates are running <u>neck and neck</u> in their election.

比较汉语中的**不相上下、不分伯仲、平分秋色、棋逢对手**。

难分高低；不相上下

这场选举中候选人难分高下。

odds

12.28 **Odds** are the chances used for calculating how much money you will get if the person or thing you bet on wins a race or competition.
Odds is used to talk about the chances of something happening.
The <u>odds</u> of getting hit by a falling satellite are very small.
The <u>odds</u> are they won't succeed.
The <u>odds</u> were always in favour of a South Africa victory.
The <u>odds</u> were stacked against him, but he never gave up.
12.29 You may refer to difficulties or conditions that make success unlikely as **odds**.
Against all the <u>odds</u>, we won our case on appeal.
Left alone, they were fighting against overwhelming <u>odds</u>.
Nobody realized he was facing impossible <u>odds</u>.

投注赔率

（某事发生的）机会，可能性

被坠落的卫星砸中的可能性是极小的。
他们可能不会成功。
南非队一直有获胜的可能。

他难以成功，但他从不放弃。

困难；不利条件

尽管困难重重，我们还是上诉打赢了官司。
他们孤身作战，正与莫大的困难作斗争。
没有人意识到，他正面临着不可逾越的障碍。

outsider

12.30 In a horse race, an **outsider** is a horse that is thought unlikely to win or even to come in second or third place.

不大可能获胜的赛马

Outsider is used to metaphorically to refer to someone who seems very unlikely to be successful in a particular situation, especially a competitive situation.

没有可能获得成功的人

Until the election campaign started, he was an unknown rank <u>outsider</u>, having left the country twenty-one years ago.

他在 21 年前离开了这个国家。在竞选运动开始之前，他完全是个不为人知的小人物。

pawn

12.31 In chess, a **pawn** is one of the smallest and least valuable pieces.

（国际象棋中的）卒

You may refer to a person who is being used by someone who is more powerful to help him achieve an aim as a **pawn**.

爪牙；小卒

We are just <u>pawns</u> in her ambitious plans.

我们只不过是她野心勃勃的计划中的棋子罢了。

play

12.32 If you **play** a game, you take part in it. The noun **play** is used to talk about how someone plays a game.

参加（体育运动或比赛）
游戏，玩耍

If you believe in **fair play**, you think that everyone should be treated fairly, and that rules should be followed carefully.

公平竞赛

He described the circumstances of the ban as a departure from the basic principles of <u>fair play</u>.

他将禁令的情况描述为对公平竞赛的基本原则的背离。

12.33 If you say that someone does not **play fair**, you mean that he behaves dishonestly or deceitfully, even though he may not actually have broken any rules or laws.

公平地比赛

He had a reputation as a quiet and amiable man who <u>played fair</u>.

他享有办事公平、沉默寡言、对人和蔼的盛誉。

12.34 If you say that a person or organization **plays by the rules**, you mean that he/it follows the correct procedures for doing something, rather than doing things in a way that may be easier and more successful, but which is not acceptable to other people.

按规则办事

The town's road safety officer spends his days ensuring that motorists <u>play by the rules</u>.

这个镇的道路安全官员花了数天时间确保司机们按交通规则驾驶汽车。

France is not complaining; it just wants everyone else to <u>play by EC rules</u>.

法国不是在抱怨；它只是要所有别的人也都按欧洲共同体的规则办事。

12.35 If you can **play** a particular kind of **game**, you understand the way to do something in order to be successful or to gain an advantage in a particular situation.

遵守规则；办事公道；做事讲道德
汉语把在规定的界限边缘而不违反规定做事比喻为**打擦边球**，如：按规矩办事，不打政策擦边球。

Her willingness to <u>play the game</u> by the usual rules of the establishment had hardly been rewarded.

她愿意按这个现存社会体制的常规行事，可是，她的这一表示几乎没有得到什么回报。

Bankers don't generally expect that a customer knows how to <u>play the game</u>, which makes it easier for us to fight back.

银行家们一般不指望客户懂得金融业的基本知识，这一点使我们能比较方便地进行反击。

12.36 If you **play** a particular person's **game**, you behave in a way that he will approve of, in order to gain advantage for yourself, even though you may not agree that it is the right way to behave.

按某人的意图办事

If he is to win their financial support he must <u>play</u> their <u>game</u>.

如果要赢得他们的资助，他必须按他们赞同的方式办事。

12.37 If one person **plays games** with another, the first person is not honest

玩弄；糊弄；耍诡计

with the second one and this may cause problems for the second person if he does not understand the situation.

They were just using her, *playing games* with her as if what she felt and what she had actually done didn't matter a bit.　他们只是在利用她、玩弄她，似乎她的感受如何、她实际上做了什么都根本无关紧要。

掩饰（真实感情）

12.38 If people **play games** or **play a game** involving their relationships with other people or their feelings, they express their feelings dishonestly, in order to make other people feel a particular emotion or behave in a particular way. For example, someone might pretend to be very unhappy in order to make other people feel sorry for them.

Stop *playing games* and tell him what you really feel.　别再闹着玩了，把你真实的感受告诉他。

Two people *playing* this *game* will obviously have an unhealthy relationship.　要是两个人都耍手腕，他们之间显然会有一种不健康的关系。

player

12.39 A **player** is someone who takes part in a game or sport.　选手

Player is used metaphorically to talk about a person, organization, or country that influences a situation, especially in business or politics.　（尤指商场或政坛中的）竞争者，重要力量

Scottish companies could become major *players* in the world market for green technologies.　苏格兰的公司可能会成为全球绿色技术市场的主角。

Germany is seen as a key *player* within the European Union.　德国被视为欧盟中的一股关键力量。

playing field

12.40 A **playing field** is a grassy area where sports such as football, hockey,　球场

or cricket are played.

A **level playing field** is a situation that is fair because no one involved in it has an advantage over anyone else.

American businessmen ask for a <u>level playing field</u> when they compete with foreign companies.

平等的竞争环境

美国商人在与外国公司竞争时要求竞争环境公平。

running

12.41 If a horse **makes the running** in a particular race, it runs very fast so that it seems likely to win and all the other horses have to try hard to keep up with it.

一马当先

If someone **makes the running** in a situation, especially a competitive one such as an election, he does things better or faster than the other people involved, so that the other people have to work harder to try to compete with him.

先声夺人
比较汉语中的**领跑**、**领先**。

From now on it's space-based astronomy that's going to <u>make the running</u>.
The other two actors <u>have been making the running</u>.

今后具有竞争力的将是以太空为基础的天文学。
另外两位演员的发展势头一直很好，比别人更有竞争力。

sail

12.42 If a boat **sails**, it moves across the surface of a sea, lake, river etc.

（船只）航行
汉语用**顺风转舵**比喻顺着情势改变态度（多含贬义），用**顺水推舟**比喻顺应趋势办事。

If you **sail through** a situation, you are able to cope with it very well without appearing to make very much effort.

顺利通过

She <u>sailed through</u> the first interview.

她顺利通过了第一次面试。

12.43 If you say that a task was not all **plain sailing**, you mean that it was not easy or straightforward.

一帆风顺
参见12.42

We know it won't be <u>plain sailing</u> in the final because there are no easy games at this level.

我们知道决赛不会是一帆风顺的，因为在这一水平上的比赛都很艰难。

show your hand

12.44 In some card games, you **show your hand** at the end of the game to see who has cards of the highest value and has therefore won.

亮出底牌；摊牌

If someone **shows his hand**, he lets other people know what he plans to do, what he is thinking, or what he has, especially when he might prefer to keep this secret.

摊牌

On domestic politics he seemed unwilling to <u>show his hand</u> too clearly.

Events in Russia are now forcing the US President to <u>show his hand</u>.

他似乎不愿意将其在国内政治方面的情况对外说得太清楚。

俄罗斯所发生的事件现在正迫使美国总统摊牌。

skate

12.45 If you **skate**, you move over a surface using skates.

滑冰

If you **skate over** or **skate around** a difficult subject or situation, you do not talk about it or think about it in detail.

一笔带过；回避

Many important issues <u>have been skated over</u> in this report.

When pressed, he <u>skates around</u> the subject.

在这份报告里很多重要问题都被一笔带过。

迫于压力，他对这个题目避而不谈。

12.46 If you say that someone is **skating on thin ice**, you mean that he is doing something risky that may have unpleasant or serious consequences for him.

履薄冰；冒风险
比较汉语中的**玩火**。

I <u>had skated on thin ice</u> on many assignments and somehow had, so far, got away with it.

我曾在许多任务上冒过风险，不过后来我还是以某种方式侥幸渡过了难关。

sport

12.47 **Sport** is used to refer to games such as football, tennis, and athletics in which individuals or teams compete against each other in physical activities.　　运动；体育比赛

If you say that someone is a **good sport**, you mean that even when he has bad luck he is cheerful and friendly.　　体育道德好的人

They thought you were being such a good sport about it.　　他们认为你在这件事上展现出如此良好的风度。

He is really not in the mood to be a jolly good sport.　　他实在是没有情绪表现得快乐而有风度。

12.48 If you say that someone is a **bad sport**, you mean that when he has bad luck or does not succeed in something that he is doing, he is bad-tempered about it and does not cope with it well.　　体育道德差的人

To be a bad sport means to risk almost certain humiliation by the lads at the pub.　　发脾气意味着冒这样的风险：几乎肯定会遭到酒馆里那些小伙子的羞辱。

sporting

12.49 If you have a **sporting chance** of succeeding in doing something, it is not likely you will succeed, but it is possible, so you think it will be worth trying.　　可能成功的机会

There's no reason why you can't make it. You've got a sporting chance. I've got none.　　你没有理由说明你为什么不能成功。你有一个成败各半的机会。而我没有。

stake

12.50 A **stake** is an amount of money that you risk losing when you try to guess the result of a race or competition.　　赌注；赌金

Stake is used metaphorically to refer to the degree to which you are involved in　　利害关系

something and want it to succeed.
He has a huge stake in making the peace process work.

他与和平进程的推进有很大的关系。

12.51 If you say that something is **at stake**, you mean that it is being risked in a particular situation and may be lost or damaged if the people involved are not successful.

在危急关头；濒于险境

At stake is the loss or failure of the world trade talks.

无法预料的是世界贸易谈判的损失或失败。

12.52 If you say that the **stakes** are **high**, you mean that the people involved are likely to lose or gain a great deal, depending on whether or not they are successful.

（高）风险

By arresting the organisation's two top leaders the government and the army have now raised the stakes.

逮捕了该组织的两名最高领导人后，政府和军队的风险现在更大了。

Magazine publishing is a high-stakes game.

发行杂志是一种高风险的赌博。

12.53 **Stake** is also used as a verb to talk about risking losing or damaging something valuable in order to obtain or achieve something.

拿……当赌注；冒险
汉语用**孤注一掷**比喻在危急时刻把全部力量拿出来冒一次险。

The government has staked its reputation on eliminating the deficit.

政府拿自己的声望作赌注来消除赤字。

I'd stake my life on his loyalty.

我拿命担保他的忠诚。

12.54 **Stakes** is used for talking about a competition or comparison that seems like a race.

争夺（赛）

Who are the main contenders in the party leadership stakes?

在该党领导人的争夺战中谁是主要的竞争者？

stalemate

12.55 In chess, **stalemate** is a situation when the game ends because neither

（棋局的）僵棋，和棋

player can make a legal move or win the game.

Stalemate is used to refer to a situation in which progress is impossible because the people or groups involved cannot agree.

Management and the unions have reached a <u>stalemate</u> in their negotiations.

僵局；僵持

资方和工会在谈判中陷入了僵局。

toy

12.56 A **toy** is an object that a child can play with, especially a model of a real thing such as a car or animal.

玩具

You may refer to a piece of equipment that you enjoy using as a **toy**.

喜欢使用的东西；爱物

He parked the car right next to the windows of the conference room. Perhaps he didn't want to take his eyes off his new <u>toy</u>.

他将汽车就停放在会议室的窗户底下。也许他不想让自己的眼光离开他的这个新宝贝。

12.57 If you say that you **are toying with** the idea of doing something or the notion of doing something, you are considering it in a way that is not serious or definite.

不大认真地考虑；不大有把握地考虑

I've been <u>toying with</u> the idea of setting up in business.

我一直在琢磨经商这个想法。

She <u>had toyed with</u> the notion of going abroad that spring.

那年春天她曾有过出国的念头。

trump

12.58 In some card games, **trumps** is the suit which is chosen to have the highest value during a particular game. If someone **comes up trumps** or **turns up trumps**, he does what is necessary to succeed, especially when success does not seem likely.

（牌戏中的）一套王牌

汉语用**撒手锏**比喻在最关键时刻使出的最拿手的本领，也说**杀手锏**。

使出绝招；亮出王牌

Time was short but he <u>came up trumps</u> under pressure.
时间很紧，但他在压力之下仍获得出乎意料的成功。

At least you will discover where your true affections lie when certain people <u>turn up trumps</u>.
当某些人获得成功时，至少你会发现你真正钟爱的是什么人。

12.59 In cards, if you **trump** someone, you beat him by playing a trump card.
出王牌赢（牌）

If you **trump** someone, or **trump** something he has done, you beat him by doing something similar but better than the thing that he has done.
（由于拥有别人没有的优势而）打败，赢

The research team did not want <u>to be trumped</u> so they had to publish their findings quickly.
研究组不想被人超越，所以他们必须赶快发表他们的发现。

trump card

12.60 A **trump card** is one of the cards of the suit that has been chosen to be trumps, and which will beat any card of another suit.
王牌
参见 12.58, 7.46

Trump card is used as a metaphor to talk about an advantage that someone has that will help him to be more successful than anyone else.
独有的优势；独门法宝；王牌

Low wages are the country's <u>trump card</u> at this stage of its economic development.
低工资是这个国家在其经济发展现阶段的一张王牌。

unsporting

12.61 If you describe someone's behaviour as **unsporting**, you think that he behaves unfairly or selfishly, especially in a competitive situation.
无体育道德的；自私的；不公平的

They fined me 2,700 francs which I thought was rather <u>unsporting</u> of them.
他们罚了我 2 700 法郎，我认为他们这种做法相当不公平。

Column 12

This column is adopted to help understand some metaphorical expressions of **games & sports** that are unique to Chinese.

活棋	agreeable and invigorating atmosphere; move that creates such an atmosphere
僵局	deadlock; impasse; stalemate
开局	① (of a chess or ball game) start; begin; ② beginning
妙招	clever trick; ingenious device
棋逢对手	be well-matched in a contest
棋高一着	be superior to one's opponent (in chess or otherwise); outmatch one's opponent
全国一盘棋	take the whole country into account
舍车保帅	give up a chariot to save the marshal (in Chinese chess)—make minor sacrifices to safeguard major interests
死棋	a hopeless case; a stupid move
摊牌	force one's opponent to show his hand; force a showdown
戏法人人会变，各有巧妙不同	magicians are many, but each has his tricks
一招不慎，满盘皆输	one careless move and the whole game is lost; one wrong move spoils the entire game
有板有眼	rhythmical; measured; orderly; systematic

13 War

attack

13.1 When you **attack**, you use violence to harm a person, animal or place.
攻击，进攻，袭击
汉语也用**针砭**比喻发现或指出错误，以求改正，如：针砭时弊。

You can say a person **attacks** if he or she severely criticizes someone or something for his/its ideas or actions.
猛烈抨击；用语言攻击；非难

Opponents <u>attacked</u> the government's plan to increase road tax.
反对者强烈批评政府增加道路税的计划。

The deputy Prime Minister last night <u>attacked</u> the decision as foolish.
副总理昨晚批评这项决定是愚蠢的。

13.2 If you **attack** something like a problem or a meal, you begin working on it or doing it in a determined way.
干劲十足地开始（做）；奋力做
汉语中，攻有致力研究、学习之意，如：专攻、攻读、攻外语等。

We need to <u>attack</u> the problem now before it gets worse.
我们必须现在就花大力气解决问题，以免事态恶化。

She was just about to <u>attack</u> a plate of spaghetti when the phone rang.
她正要狼吞虎咽地吃一盘意大利面条时，电话突然响了。

13.3 **Attack** is also used as a noun to metaphorically refer to strong criticism.
强烈的批评；猛烈的抨击

This book is widely seen as an <u>attack</u> on the education system.
这本书被普遍视为对教育体制的强烈抨击。

He was outraged by the personal <u>attacks</u> launched against him.
他为针对自己而发动的人身攻击感到愤怒。

The school has come under <u>attack</u> for failing to encourage bright students.
这所学校因未能鼓励聪明学生而受到非难。

battle

13.4 A **battle** is a fight between two armies in a war.
战役；战斗

Battle is used metaphorically to talk about a competition, an argument or a struggle between people or groups of people trying to win power or control.

竞争；较量
比较汉语中的<u>斗法</u>、<u>斗智</u>、<u>斗嘴</u>。

The couple are locked in a bitter legal <u>battle</u> over custody of their children.

这对夫妇在争夺孩子监护权的法律较量中打得难解难分。

Supermarkets are cutting prices in a desperate <u>battle</u> to win customers.

超市竞相降低价格，不顾一切地争夺顾客。

13.5 If you say that someone **fights a losing battle**, you mean that he is trying to do something that will probably fail.

打一场不会赢的战斗；做可能徒劳的事

She tries to get him to go, but she knew she was <u>fighting a losing battle</u>.

她试图让他走，但她知道这可能是徒劳的。

13.6 You can use **battle** as a verb to talk about the action of trying very hard to achieve something difficult or to deal with a difficult situation.

奋斗；（与……）争斗

Many species of birds are <u>battling</u> extinction.

许多种类的鸟都在为摆脱灭绝的命运而苦苦挣扎。

She described how they had <u>battled</u> against huge waves to save their friends.

她描述了他们如何为了营救朋友而与巨浪搏斗。

Surgeons <u>battled</u> to save the man's life.

外科医生奋力抢救那个人的生命。

The two leaders are <u>battling</u> for control of the government.

两位领导人在为控制政府而争斗。

13.7 If two people or groups **battle it out**, they compete with each other until there is a definite winner.

决出胜负
比较汉语中的**一决雌雄**。

Twelve teams will <u>battle it out</u> latter in the year to see who will become the champion of Europe.

12 支队伍将在今年晚些时候进行比赛，以决定谁将成为欧洲冠军。

battlefield

13.8 A **battlefield** is a place where a battle takes place or where one took place in the past.

战场
汉语中，**战场**指两军交战的地方，也用于比喻，如：抗洪<u>战场</u>。

Battlefield is used metaphorically to talk about a situation in which people disagree and cause problems for each other.
Life at home was something of a battlefield.

争执；斗争

家庭生活在某种意义上是一种斗争。

besiege

13.9 If a city or castle is **besieged**, it is surrounded with military force and people there are prevented from getting food and supplies, as a way of getting control of it.

包围；围困

If you **are besieged with** letters, demands or requests, they are in a larger amount than you can deal with.

使应接不暇；使手忙脚乱

The department has been besieged with enquiries from students from all over the country.

全国各地学生的咨询使系里应接不暇。

blitz

13.10 A **blitz** is a sudden military attack. **Blitz** is used metaphorically to refer to a special effort to finish a job or to deal with a problem quickly and thoroughly.

闪电战；闪击战；突然袭击 突击；闪电式行动

汉语中，**突击**用来比喻集中力量、加快速度，在短时期内完成某项工作，如：连续突击了两个晚上才把稿子写完。

It's time we had a blitz on the paperwork.
We had a leafleting blitz the day before the election.

该是我们突击文书工作的时候了。
我们在选举的前一天进行了一场闪电式的散发传单宣传。

bombard

13.11 To **bombard** is to attack a place for a long time by using large weapons, bombs etc.

轰炸；炮击（某地）
汉语用**放炮**比喻发表激烈抨击的言论，如：发言要慎重，不能乱放炮。

If someone **bombards** another one, the former one attacks the latter one with a lot of questions, criticisms, etc. or by

连珠炮似地提问；大肆抨击；提供过多信息

giving him too much information.
She <u>bombarded</u> him faxes and called his office repeatedly.
她连续不停地给他发传真并且反复打他办公室的电话。
We have been <u>bombarded</u> with letters of complaint.
我们接二连三收到了大批的投诉信。

conquer

13.12 To **conquer** is to take control of land or people using soldiers.

征服；占领；攻克

If you **conquer** a situation or emotion, you gain control of it by making a great physical or mental effort.

克服；控制

The only way to <u>conquer</u> fear is to face it.
克服恐惧的唯一方法就是正视恐惧。

13.13 You can use **conquer** to metaphorically talk about the action of earning the love, admiration, or respect of someone.

赢得；征服
汉语中，征服也有使人信服或折服的意思，如：艺术家的精彩表演征服了观众。

His gentle nature had <u>conquered</u> their hearts.
他的温文尔雅征服了他们的心。

He set out to <u>conquer</u> the literary world of London.
他决心赢得伦敦文学界的赞誉。

crossfire

13.14 **Crossfire** is bullets coming from two directions, fired by two people or armies who are shooting at each other.

交叉火力
比较汉语中的**腹背受敌**。

Crossfire is used metaphorically to talk about a situation in which people are arguing, and the results of this affect other people who are not directly involved.

（可能偶然影响未直接参与者的）激烈影响

When two industrial giants clash, small companies can get caught in the <u>crossfire</u>.
两大企业争斗之下，小公司遭受池鱼之殃。

defuse

13.15 If you **defuse** a bomb, you stop it

拆除（炸弹的）引信

from exploding by removing its fuse.

If you say someone **defuses** tension, anger or a crisis, he makes the situation more relaxed by making people feel less angry or less worried.

The government is trying to defuse tensions over cuts in public spending.

缓和

政府正尽力缓和公共开支削减问题上的紧张气氛。

dynamite

13.16 **Dynamite** is a substance used for causing explosions.

You can refer to someone or something that is very impressive or exciting as **dynamite**.

The abortion issue is political dynamite.

炸药

引起轰动的人；引起轰动的事物

堕胎问题在政治上是个爆炸性的问题。

fire

13.17 If a weapon **fires** or someone **fires** it, someone uses it to shoot.

If you **fire questions at someone**, you ask him questions, especially those that are difficult for him to answer.

Reporters fired questions at her as she left the court house.

开火；发射

汉语用**开火（炮）**比喻进行抨击或开展斗争，如：向腐败现象开火。

提问（尤指难以解答的问题）

她离开法院的时候，记者们向她连珠炮似地提出了很多问题。

firestorm

13.18 A **firestorm** is a very large fire that is caused by bombs.

You can refer to a sudden expression of strong protests or criticism as a **firestorm**.

A continuing economic slide could well touch off a firestorm of protest from the left.

（炸弹爆炸引起的）风暴性大火

（突然爆发的）强烈抗议，猛烈抨击

经济持续恶化很可能会激发左派的强烈抗议。

front line

13.19 The **front line** is the area where two armies face each other and fight

（战争的）前线

during a war.
People **in, at** or **on the front line** are 在第一线的
those who are doing the hardest or most
important work.
These dedicated people are <u>on the front</u> 这些富有献身精神的人工作在医疗服
<u>line</u> of health care. 务的第一线。
front-line
13.20 Something that is **front-line** is 前线的
directly involved in fighting during a
war.
A **front-line** person is with a leading or 主要的；重要的
important position in an activity.
a <u>front-line</u> campaigner in the 1987 1987年大选中一位重要的活动家
election
invade
13.21 If you say one country **invades** 武力入侵；侵占；侵略
another country, you are saying that the
former one sends an army into the latter
in order to get control of it.
Invade is used metaphorically to talk 进入；（尤指）涌入，大批进入
about the action of entering a place,
especially in large numbers or in a way
that causes problem.
Demonstrators <u>invaded</u> the government 大批示威者闯进了政府办公楼。
buildings.
As the final whistle blew, fans began 比赛结束的哨声一响，球迷便开始冲
<u>invading</u> the field. 入球场。
13.22 To **invade** someone's life, privacy 干扰，侵犯（某人的生活）
etc. is to get involved in his life without
his permission or in an unpleasant way.
Closed-circuit TV cameras seem to be 闭路电视摄像机似乎正在侵入我们生
<u>invading</u> every aspect of our lives. 活的各个方面。
Investigators were spying on people's 调查者正在秘密监视人们的家庭并侵
homes and <u>invading</u> their privacy. 犯他们的隐私。
The memory of their last meeting kept 他们最后一次见面的记忆在他的思绪

invading his thoughts.
中一直挥之不去。

invasion

13.23 **Invasion** is an occasion when one country's army goes into another country to take control of it by force.

入侵；侵略

Invasion is used metaphorically to refer to a situation in which a large number of people or things come to a place at the same time, especially in an annoying way.

（尤指令人厌烦的）涌入，大批进入

The shops prepared for an *invasion* of last-minute Christmas shoppers.
各商店做好了准备迎接圣诞节前最后一批蜂拥而入的购物者。

13.24 You can refer to the occasion when someone finds out or uses information about your private life, especially illegally as **invasion of privacy**.

（尤指非法的）干涉隐私，侵犯隐私

The actress described the photographs of her as an *invasion of privacy*.
那位女演员认为她的这些照片是对隐私权的侵犯。

kill

13.25 To kill a person or living thing means to make him/it die.

杀死；弄死

If you **kill time**, an hour etc., you spend time doing a particular activity while you are waiting for something.

消磨（时光）；打发（时间）

We *killed a few hours* watching videos.
我们看录像打发了几个小时。

Shopping can be a good way to *kill time* at the airport.
在机场，购物可能是消磨时间的一个好方法。

13.26 If you **kill** something, you stop it from continuing.

制止；扼杀；消灭

The group effectively *killed* speculation that a merger was about to take place.
该集团有效地消除了人们关于要合并的疑虑。

The nurse will give you something to *kill* pain.
护士会给你一些止痛药。

Jack can really *kill* a conversation with his ideas on politics.
杰克的政治观点真的会使谈话无法继续下去。

launch

13.27 If you **launch** something such as a missile, space vehicle, satellite etc., you send it into the air or into space.

发射（导弹、太空飞行器、人造卫星等）

Launch is used metaphorically to talk about the action of starting an activity, especially an organized one.

发动，发起（尤指有组织的活动）

The police confirmed that an enquiry has been <u>launched</u> into the incident.

警方证实对该事件的调查已着手展开。

13.28 If you **launch** a new product or service, you start selling it to the public.

发行；将（新产品或新服务）投放市场

The company announced it will <u>launch</u> a new version of its software in January.

该公司宣布它将在1月份将其新版软件投放市场。

13.29 If you **launch into** something, you start something such as an explanation, project, or attack with a lot of enthusiasm.

（积极地）开始（解说、工程或袭击等）

He immediately <u>launched into</u> a detailed account of his trip.

他立即开始详尽地描述他的旅行见闻。

powder keg

13.30 **Powder keg** is used metaphorically to refer to a dangerous situation that may suddenly become very violent.

火药桶；危险的局面；一触即发的情势

salvo

13.31 A **salvo** is an act of firing a number of guns or other weapons at the same time.

（火炮或其他武器的）齐射，齐发，齐鸣

An **opening salvo** is the first in a series of questions, statements etc. that you use to try to win an argument.

开篇第一炮

The newspaper article was the <u>opening salvo</u> in what proved to be a long battle.

报上那篇文章是一场长期论战的开篇第一炮。

This statement provoked a <u>salvo</u> of accusations.

这项声明激起一片谴责声。

shot

13.32 A **shot** is the act of firing a gun.

射击；开枪

Shot is used metaphorically to refer to something you say or do as an attack.　（话语或行动上的）一击

At the door she could not resist a parting shot.　到门口时她忍不住说了句狠话。

The supermarket fired the first shot in a price war today.　今天，这家超市打响了价格战的头一炮。

sword

13.33 A **sword** is a weapon with a short handle and a long sharp blade.　剑；刀

A **double-edged sword** or **two-edged sword** is used to refer to a situation with as many bad qualities or effects as good ones.　双刃剑

The increase in tourism has been a double-edged sword for island residents.　旅游业的发展对海岛的居民而言是一把双刃剑。

time bomb

13.34 A **time bomb** is a bomb that can be set to explode at a particular time.　定时炸弹

Time bomb is used metaphorically to talk about a situation that is likely to cause serious problems in the future.　潜在危险；隐患

Rising unemployment is a political time bomb for the government.　日益严重的失业问题对政府来说是一枚政治上的定时炸弹。

troop

13.35 A **troop** is a group of soldiers.　部队

Troop is used metaphorically to refer to a large group of people going somewhere.　（前往某地的）一大群人

A troop of guests was moving towards the house.　一群客人朝那房子走去。

troops of school children　大群大群的学生

war

13.36 There is a **war** when two or more countries fight.　战争

War is used metaphorically to refer to a determined and organized effort to　（为控制或消灭疾病、犯罪等而进行的）斗争

control or stop something, for example a disease or crime.
This is a major victory in the <u>war</u> against drugs.
We will continue to wage <u>war</u> on organized crime.

这是反毒品斗争的一次重大胜利。
我们将继续同有组织的犯罪活动作斗争。

13.37 **War** is used metaphorically to talk about a situation in which countries, organizations, or businesses compete with each other to gain economic power or control.

竞争；争夺

This could easily start a trade <u>war</u>.
the <u>war</u> for supremacy in the fast-food industry

这很容易引发一场贸易战。
快餐业的霸权之争

13.38 You can refer to a situation in which two people or groups continuously criticize each other in public because they disagree seriously about something as **a war of words**.

舌战；论战
比较汉语中的**唇枪舌剑**、**口水战**、**斗口**等。

Column 13

This column is adopted to help understand some metaphorical expressions of **war** that are unique to Chinese.

鞍马劳顿	travel-worn
按兵不动	take no action
安营扎寨	camp
暗箭伤人	injure someone by underhand means
败笔	a faulty stroke in calligraphy or painting; a faulty expression or flaw in writing
搬救兵	call in reinforcements; ask for help
背水一战	fight to win or die
毕其功于一役	accomplish the whole task at one stroke
兵不血刃	win victory without firing a shot
不攻自破	collapse of itself
不堪一击	collapse at the first blow

步步为营	consolidate at every step
草木皆兵	a state of extreme nervousness
城下之盟	a treaty signed under coercion
重整旗鼓	rally one's forces
出奇制胜	defeat one's opponent by a surprise
大刀阔斧	drastic
大动干戈	go to war
大张旗鼓	in a big way
单刀直入	speak out without beating about the bush
单枪匹马	all by oneself
反败为胜	turn the tide
反戈一击	turn against one's own side
放空炮	talk big; spout hot air; indulge in idle boasting
决战	decisive engagement
决一死战	fight to a finish
厉兵秣马	get ready for battle
火药味	aggressive
临阵磨枪	start to prepare at the last moment
临阵脱逃	sneak away at a critical juncture
明枪暗箭	both open and covert attacks
拿着鸡毛当令箭	treat one's superior's casual remark as an order and make a big fuss about it
强弩之末	a spent force
杀手锏	sudden thrust of the mace — one's trump or master card
虾兵蟹将	ineffective troops
偃旗息鼓	cease all activities
以卵投石	court defeat by fighting against overwhelming odds
真刀真枪	the real thing
左右开弓	be ambidextrous
化干戈为玉帛	bury the hatchet
将计就计	beat someone at his own game
精兵简政	better staff and simpler administration

14 Weather

avalanche

14.1 An **avalanche** is a mass of snow, ice and rock that falls down the side of a mountain.
雪崩

You can refer to a large amount of something which appears at once as **an avalanche of** that thing, especially when you are not expecting it, and it is difficult to deal with.
大量的；如雪片般涌来的

We received an avalanche of letters in reply to our advertisement.
我们登出广告后收到了雪片般飞来的大批答复信件。

breeze

14.2 A **breeze** is a pleasant, refreshing wind.
微风；和风
汉语用**和风细雨**比喻方式和缓、不粗暴。

If something is said to be a **breeze**, it is extremely easy.
轻而易举；非常容易

Everyone thought the test was a breeze.
每个人都认为测试非常容易。
It was a breeze.
这事不费吹灰之力。

14.3 **Breeze,** as a verb, can be used metaphorically to talk about moving in a cheerful and confident way.
轻盈而自信地走

She just breezed in and asked me to help.
她一阵风似地飘然而至，要求我帮她。
He breezed into the meeting and took charge.
他自信地走进会场主持会议。

14.4 If someone **breezes through** a difficult situation, he copes with it very easily or confidently.
轻松通过；轻松完成

The first time I appeared on television I was so terrified I didn't say a word. Now I just <u>breeze</u> through talk shows.

第一次上电视时，我怕得一句话也说不出来。现在我可以轻轻松松地做完电视访谈节目。

breezy

14.5 When the weather is **breezy**, there is a fairly strong but pleasant wind blowing.

通风良好的；有微风的

Breezy is used as a metaphor to describe people or their behaviour when they seem lively and confident.

轻松自信的；愉快的

She gave a bright <u>breezy</u> smile as she came in.

她走进来时露出轻松自信的微笑。

14.6 **Breezy** can be used in a negative way for saying that someone is too informal and not careful enough.

漫不经心的；过于散漫的

a <u>breezy</u> attitude towards work

对待工作漫不经心的态度

chilly

14.7 A **chilly** day is cold enough to be unpleasant.

寒冷的

汉语用凉比喻灰心或失望，如：听到这消息，他心里就凉了。参见 17.15

Chilly can be used metaphorically to talk about being unfriendly.

冷淡的；不友好的

<u>chilly</u> politeness

冷淡的客套

The visitors got a very <u>chilly</u> reception.

客人们受到了非常冷淡的接待。

cloud

14.8 A **cloud** is a white or grey mass of very small drops of water in the sky.

云；云雾
参见 14.18

Cloud is used metaphorically to refer to something unpleasant that spoils an activity.

（引起不愉快的）阴云，阴影

a <u>cloud</u> of uncertainty

疑虑的阴影

A <u>cloud</u> of suspicion is hanging over him.

有一团疑云笼罩着他。

14.9 If something **casts a cloud over** your situation, it makes you less hopeful

使……蒙上阴影；给……带来不愉快

14 Weather

and optimistic.
Violent protests <u>cast a cloud over</u> the president's visit. 暴力抗议给总统的访问蒙上了一层阴影。

Her arrival <u>cast a cloud (of gloom) over</u> the party. 她的到来给聚会蒙上了一层阴影。

14.10 You can refer to something that is likely to spoil a situation as **a cloud on the horizon**. 可能的麻烦；威胁

The only <u>cloud on the horizon</u> is the possibility of a hostile takeover. 唯一令人担忧的就是可能出现恶意接管。

14.11 If someone or something is **under a cloud**, people are suspicious of him/it because he/it seems to have done something wrong. 名誉受损

I'll probably live the rest of my life <u>under</u> this <u>cloud</u>. 也许我将要在人们怀疑的阴云下度过我的余生。

His economic reform program has come <u>under a cloud</u> because of a stock market scandal. 由于股票市场的一个丑闻，他的经济改革计划罩上了怀疑的阴云。

14.12 If something **clouds the issue**, it makes it more complicated or confusing. 使变复杂；使变混乱

Unanswered questions have further <u>clouded the issue</u>. 未予解答的问题使事情更为复杂。

14.13 If something **clouds** a situation which would normally be good, it spoils it. 破坏（活动、事件或局面）

Her political future was <u>clouded</u> by allegations of misconduct. 对她滥用职权的指控给她的政治前途蒙上了一层阴影。

14.14 If you say that something **clouds** your judgment or thoughts, you mean that it stops your judgment from being as good as usual. 干扰（思考）；把（某人）搞糊涂

Make sure that personal motivation is not <u>clouding</u> your judgment. 一定不要让个人因素干扰你的判断。

14.15 If your face or eyes **cloud** or （脸色）阴沉下来；（眼神）变得忧伤

cloud over, they show a negative emotion.

Her face <u>clouded over</u> in confusion at his curt tone.

The tramp's eyes <u>clouded over</u> and he seemed to lose interest.

他唐突的口气使她不知所措，脸色也沉了下来。

流浪汉的眼睛黯然失色，他似乎已失去了兴趣。

deluge

14.16 A **deluge** is a very heavy fall of rain.

暴雨；大雨

You can refer to a lot of things all happening or arriving at the same time as **a deluge of** them.

同时涌来的大量事物

The company received <u>a deluge of</u> complaints about the defective product.

公司收到许许多多对这种有缺陷产品的投诉。

14.17 If you **are deluged with** things, you have a lot of them to deal with.

应接不暇

The commission <u>has been deluged with</u> complaints.

委员会对潮水般涌来的投诉应接不暇。

fog

14.18 When there is **fog**, there are tiny drops of water in the air which form a thick cloud and make it difficult to see through.

雾

汉语用云消雾散、烟消云散比喻事物消失干净，用云烟过眼比喻事物很快就消失了。

Fog is used metaphorically to refer to a state of confusion, in which things are not clear.

迷惘；困惑

汉语用一头雾水形容摸不着头脑、糊里糊涂。

He went through the day with his mind in a <u>fog</u>.

整整一天，他的头脑都是昏昏沉沉的。

She shook of the <u>fog</u> of sleep.

她甩头克制自己的睡意。

14.19 If you **fog** someone, you make him confused.

使困惑；使迷惑

If you **fog** the issue, you make it confusing.

使人困惑；使费解

My brain was <u>fogged</u> by sleep.

我睡得昏头昏脑。

Your questions are only <u>fogging the</u>

你的提问只能使这个问题变得费解。

issue.

foggy

14.20 When it is **foggy**, there is fog, so it is difficult to see.
多雾的；有雾的
参见 14.18

Foggy is used metaphorically to refer to a state of being confused or not clearly remembered.
模糊的；糊涂的

Still foggy with sleep, she groped her way down the hallway.
她仍旧睡意朦胧，摸索着走过过道。

a foggy memory
模糊的记忆

14.21 If you say you do **not have the foggiest idea** or **notion** about something, you mean you do not know anything at all about it.
一无所知；根本不明白
汉语用**云山雾罩**形容说话漫无边际，使人困惑不解。

I don't have the foggiest idea why he called me.
我压根儿不知道他为何打电话给我。

freeze

14.22 If water **freezes**, it gets very cold and changes into ice.
结冰
参见 14.23

If you say a person **freezes**, you mean he stops moving and keeps completely still.
呆住；发愣；一动不动

Kate froze in horror when she saw all the blood.
凯特看到那滩血时吓呆了。

I stood frozen to the spot, unable to believe my eyes.
我站在那里一动不动，无法相信自己的眼睛。

14.23 **Freeze**, as a noun, can be used metaphorically to refer to an official decision to prevent any increase in the number, level, or rate of something.
冻结
汉语用**冻结**比喻阻止（人员、资金等）流动或变动，也比喻暂不执行或发展，如：冻结双方关系。

a pay freeze
薪金冻结

There has been a freeze on the number of police officers.
警官人数有定额。

frosty

14.24 When the weather is **frosty**, it is
霜冻的；严寒的

extremely cold.

If you behave in a **frosty** way, you look unfriendly and show your disapproval of someone or something.
冷淡的；冷若冰霜的

a *frosty* look
冷冰冰的样子

The latest proposals were given a *frosty* reception.
对最新的建议反应冷淡。

gale

14.25 A **gale** is a very strong wind.
大风；强风

Gale is used metaphorically to refer to a sudden loud noise of people laughing.
一阵笑声

His speech was greeted with *gales* of laughter.
人们对他的演讲报以阵阵笑声。

gust

14.26 A **gust** is a sudden strong wind.
一阵强风；一阵狂风

Gust is used metaphorically to refer to a sudden strong expression of emotion.
（感情的）迸发；爆发

a *gust* of anger
大发脾气

hail

14.27 **Hail** consists of small balls of ice that fall like rain from the sky.
冰雹

A **hail of** something is a large number of things such as bullets or questions that come at you quickly or with force.
（冰雹似的）一阵；一连串

The riot police were met with a *hail of* stones and petrol bombs.
防暴警察遭到了密集的石块和汽油弹的攻击。

Officials sneaked out through a side door to avoid a *hail of* protest.
官员们通过一扇侧门偷偷地溜出去，以避免抗议浪潮。

haze

14.28 **Haze** is small drops of water in the air that make it difficult to see clearly.
薄雾；霾
参见 14.18

Haze is used metaphorically to refer to a situation or condition which makes it
迷惑；糊涂

汉语用**雪上加霜**比喻一再遭受灾难，损害愈加严重。

difficult for you to think clearly.
She sat by herself in a <u>haze</u> of nostalgic bliss.

hazy
14.29 A **hazy** day is not clear because there is smoke, dust or water in the air.
Hazy is used metaphorically to talk about things that are difficult to understand or remember.
<u>hazy</u> memories
They did not know what they were fighting for, apart from a <u>hazy</u> notion of freedom.

她独自坐在那儿，沉浸在一种怀旧的幸福之中。

雾蒙蒙的；烟雾弥漫的
参见 14.20
（记忆）模糊的；朦胧的

模糊的记忆
除了一个模糊的关于自由的信念外，他们不知道究竟是在为什么战斗。

hurricane
14.30 A **hurricane** is a violent storm with extremely strong winds and heavy rain.
A **hurricane** of an emotion such as grief or anger is a very strong sense of this emotion that seems likely to affect a lot of people in a negative way.
the <u>hurricane</u> of grief and anger that swept the nation
14.31 A **hurricane** of something such as insults or criticism is a large number of serious insults or a lot of criticism that seems likely to seriously hurt and upset someone.
a <u>hurricane</u> of abuse
Many small businesses will not survive the economic <u>hurricane</u>.

飓风

强烈的，极度的（悲痛、愤怒等）

举国上下的极度悲伤和愤怒

铺天盖地而来的（诋毁、批评等）

铺天盖地而来的诋毁谩骂
许多小企业难以渡过这次严重的经济风暴。

icily
14.32 If people speak or behave **icily**, they obviously dislike each other and are very unfriendly but not actually rude

冷冷地；冷漠地

to each other.
"I don't see that it's any of your business," Sandra said *icily*.

“我看不出这关你什么事，”桑德拉冷冷地说道。

icy

14.33 **Icy** weather is very cold. An **icy** road is covered with ice.

寒冷的，冰封的

Icy is used metaphorically in showing that you do not like someone and do not want to be friendly with him.

冷漠的；冷冰冰的

Baker's voice was cold, his dark eyes icy.

贝克的声音冷冰冰的，黑黑的眼睛流露出冷漠。

lightning

14.34 **Lightning** is the bright flashes of light that you see in the sky during a storm.

闪电

If **lightning** is used as an adjective, it means very quickly.

极快的

Police made a lightning raid on the house.

警方突然查抄了那座房子。

14.35 If you do something **at** or **with lightning speed**, you do it extremely quickly.

很快地；飞快地

These guys move around at lightning speed.

这些人快速地移动着。

mist

14.36 **Mist** consists of a large number of tiny droplets of water in the air that make it difficult to see.

薄雾；雾气
参见 14.18

Mist is used metaphorically to talk about something difficult to understand.

难以透彻理解的事物；迷雾

A mist of prejudice spoiled his judgment.

偏见的迷雾损害了他的判断能力。

14.37 You can use **the mists of time** or **history** to refer to a period of time so long ago that people cannot remember it.

时间/历史的迷雾

The program looks through the mists of time to examine the lives of our earliest ancestors.
这个节目透过时间的迷雾审视我们最早的祖先的生活。

The origins of the organization are lost in the mists of time.
这个组织的起源已经湮没在时间的迷雾中。

rain

14.38 **Rain** is water that falls in small drops from clouds in the sky.
雨，雨水

A rain of something is a large number of something falling or moving through the air together.
（降雨般的）一阵，倾泻物

a rain of bullets
一阵弹雨

shower

14.39 A **shower** is a short period of rain.
阵雨；阵雪

A shower of something is a large number or amount of it moving through the air or falling together.
大量洒落的东西

A log in the fire broke, sending out a shower of sparks.
火里边有根木头迸裂了，火星四溅。

14.40 If you **shower** someone with something, you give him a large number of it.
大量给予

He showered her with flowers and jewellery.
他送给她许多鲜花和珠宝首饰。

Susan showered kisses on the baby.
苏珊狂吻婴儿。

14.41 If something **showers**, it falls in large quantities.
大量散落；像雨点般落在（某物上）

Bullets showered the building.
子弹像雨点般打在大楼上。

snow

14.42 If it **snows**, snow falls from the sky.
下雪；降雪

汉语用雪藏比喻有意掩藏或保留，如：把主力雪藏起来；也可用以比喻搁置不用，如：这几篇批评文章遭到雪藏。
参见 14.23

If someone **is snowed under** with work,
被工作压得喘不过气；忙得不可开交

he has more work than he can deal with.
Arnold <u>was</u> really <u>snowed under</u> with work.
He <u>was snowed under</u> with thousands of letters when he was doing his television show.

比较汉语中的**疲于奔命**。
阿诺德的工作实在多得使他难以应付。
在他进行电视表演时,收到成千上万封信,使他无法应付。

storm

14.43 A **storm** is very bad weather in which it rains and the wind blows strongly.

暴风雨
汉语用**风暴**比喻规模大而气势猛烈的事件或现象,如:革命的风暴。

You can refer to a sudden violent outburst or display of strong feeling as a **storm**.

感情的猛然爆发或激烈表现

His proposal was met by a <u>storm</u> of protest.

他的建议遭到激烈的反对。

14.44 **Storm** is used metaphorically to talk about a situation in which many people are upset or excited.

激动;骚动;风潮;风暴
汉语用**风潮**比喻很多人为达到某种目的而采取的各种集体行动,如:闹风潮。

The photos caused a <u>storm</u> when they were first published in Italy.
The ministers hadn't realized the extent of the <u>storm</u> that was gathering when they planned this special meeting.
They put on a show of unity for their first public appearance together since the <u>storm</u> broke.

这些照片在意大利首次出版时引起了剧烈的争议。
部长们没有意识到,在他们计划召开这个特别会议时,人们正在集聚的愤懑已到了何种程度。
在那个丑闻发生后第一次公开共同亮相时,他们表现出团结一致的样子。

14.45 If a person or an organization **weathers** or **rides the storm**, he/it experiences a difficult period and reaches the end of it without being harmed or damaged too much.

渡过难关

The government appears to have <u>weathered the storm</u>.

看起来政府已渡过难关。

14.46 If something new **takes** a country

在某地大获成功;完全征服(某群人)

or group of people **by storm**, it becomes very popular very quickly.
Jazz took London and Paris by storm in the 1920s.
爵士乐在 20 世纪 20 年代风靡伦敦和巴黎。

14.47 If you say that something **goes down a storm**, you mean that it is very popular.
I know there are some absolutely beautiful things to photograph which would go down a storm.
深受欢迎；深受喜爱

我知道，那里有一些绝对美丽的东西值得拍摄，它们将会让摄影爱好者们为之着迷。

14.48 If someone **storms**, he says something in a very angry way.
"What are you saying?" she stormed at me.
非常生气地说；怒骂

"你在说什么？"她对我大发脾气。

14.49 If someone **storms** somewhere, he goes there in a way that shows he is very angry.
Rob stormed out of the house and slammed the door.
气冲冲地去（某处）

罗布气冲冲地走出屋子，砰的一声关上了门。

stormy

14.50 A **stormy** weather is one with a lot of rain and strong winds.
有暴风雨的；风暴的

A **stormy** relationship, meeting etc is full of strong and often angry feelings.
激烈的；愤怒的；多风波的

a stormy relationship
The couple had had a series of stormy arguments and the police had been called in recently.
一波三折的关系
这对夫妻间已发生了一连串激烈争吵，最近还把警察都叫来了。

The meeting could be a stormy affair, with the debate centering on the country's financial scandals.
由于那场以国家的财政丑闻为中心的辩论，这次会议可能会充满火药味。

sunny

14.51 When it is **sunny**, the sun is shinning.
阳光充足的；阳光明媚的

Someone who has a **sunny** personality
开心的；快活的；快乐的

is cheerful and friendly, and makes the people around him feel happy.
It was always good to see her <u>sunny</u> smile.
Disappointing employment figures, showing a 9.5% rise, spoiled the market's <u>sunny</u> mood.

看到她快乐的笑容总是会令人开心。

令人失望的就业数字显示出9.5%的增长，它破坏了市场的乐观气氛。

tempest

14.52 A **tempest** is a severe storm with strong winds and heavy rain.

Tempest is used metaphorically to talk about a situation in which people are very upset or excited.

I hadn't foreseen the <u>tempest</u> my request would cause.

暴风雨
参见 14.43, 14.44
骚动；风波
汉语用风波、风浪比喻纠纷或乱子，如：政治风波。
我没有预见到我的要求会引起的巨大麻烦。

tempestuous

14.53 Someone or something that is **tempestuous** is full of strong emotion.

a <u>tempestuous</u> relationship

（情绪）强烈的，骚动的，狂暴的

动荡不定的关系

thunder

14.54 **Thunder** is the loud noise that you sometimes hear in the sky during a storm.

You can refer to a loud noise as **thunder**.

the <u>thunder</u> of the sea on the rocks

14.55 If something **thunders**, it makes a very loud noise.

An express train <u>thundered</u> through the station.

14.56 You can say that someone **thunders** when he says something in a very loud, angry voice.

To his friends he was gentle: he

雷；雷声
汉语中，雷声大，雨点小比喻话说得很有气势或计划定得很大而实际行动却很少。

雷鸣般的巨响

海水撞击礁石的响声
发出轰响声，发出雷鸣般的响声

快速列车呼啸着穿过车站。

怒喝；大声斥责；怒吼

对朋友他是温和的：他为反对不公正

thundered against injustice but he wept with those who wept.

thunderous

14.57 Something that is **thunderous** is very loud.

His speech was greeted by *thunderous* applause.

whirlwind

14.58 A **whirlwind** is a very powerful dangerous wind that spins extremely fast, carrying away anything in its path.

Whirlwind is used metaphorically to talk about something that happens very quickly and unexpectedly, so the people involved have little control of what happens and how they feel.

The next day they flew to Washington DC where they began a *whirlwind* of public appearances.

After a *whirlwind* of romance the couple announced their engagement in July and were married last month.

wind

14.59 A **wind** is a natural current of air that moves fast enough for you to feel it. You can use **winds of change** to refer to actions or influences that will lead to important political or social changes.

The *winds of change* are sweeping away corruption and cynicism.

的行为大声疾呼，但他也与流泪的人们一起流泪。

雷鸣般的

他的演说受到了雷鸣般掌声的欢迎。

旋风

旋风般的突发事件；匆忙的事情

次日他们乘飞机到了华盛顿市，在那里他们开始连续不断地在公共场合露面。

经过一段旋风式的浪漫爱情之后，这两个人在七月份宣布订婚，并于上个月结婚了。

风

参见 14.43, 14.44

改革之风；变革的行动；变革的影响

改革之风正在扫除贪污腐败和愤世嫉俗。

Column 14

This column is adopted to help understand some metaphorical expressions of **weather** that are unique to Chinese.

放冷风	spread slanderous rumors
无风不起浪	There are no waves without wind; there's no smoke without fire.
饱经风霜	weather-beaten; having had one's fill of hardships
干打雷，不下雨	all thunder but no rain—much noise but no action
和风细雨	like a gentle breeze and light rain—in a gentle and mild way
呼风唤雨	summon wind and rain—exercise magic powers; stir up trouble
及时雨	timely rain—help rendered in the nick of time; timely help
见（听）风是雨	take wind as the forerunner of rain—jump to hasty conclusions
久旱逢甘雨	have a welcome rain after a long drought—have a long-felt need satisfied
闷雷	unpleasant surprise; shock
平地一声雷	a sudden clap of thunder—a sudden rise in fame and position; an expected happy event
迅雷不及掩耳	A sudden peal of thunder leaves no time to cover the ears; as sudden as a flash of lightning
天有不测风云	A storm may arise from a clear sky—something unexpected may happen any time.
狂风恶浪	violent winds and fierce waves—grave perils; great hazards

15 Colour

black

15.1 Something that is **black** is of the darkest colour that there is, like the colour of the sky at night when there is no light at all.
If someone is in a **black** mood, he feels very miserable and depressed.
She alone could cheer him up when he was in the blackest depression.
15.2 If you describe a period of time as **black**, you mean that it is a very unhappy or unsuccessful period, possibly the worst you have ever experienced.
Last Wednesday was one of the blackest days of my political career.
the blackest month of the war
15.3 **Black humor** involves laughing at frightening or unpleasant things as death or war.
black humor that lightens the carnage
15.4 **Black** thoughts or acts are very cruel or wicked.
I think their crime is a blacker one than mere exploitation.

blacken

15.5 To **blacken** something means to make it black or very dark in colour.
If you **blacken** someone's **reputation**, **name**, **character**, you do or say unpleasant

黑色
汉语中，黑有秘密、非法和不公开的意思，如：黑市、黑话、黑社会等；也可形容坏、狠毒，如：心黑。
痛苦，压抑；情绪低沉

在他最为消沉的时候，只有她才能让他高兴起来。
不幸的，糟糕的，倒霉的（时期）

上星期三是我政治生涯中最倒霉的日子之一。
战争期间最黑暗的一个月
黑色幽默

使大屠杀显得轻松可笑的黑色幽默
残忍的，邪恶的
我认为他们的罪行是一种更残忍的行为，而不仅仅是剥削。

（使）变黑
汉语用抹黑比喻丑化，如：干吗要往自己脸上抹黑。
败坏某人的声誉、名声、品德

things in order to make other people have a bad opinion of him.

Why have they gone to such lengths to blacken her name?

他们为什么要花这么大的力气去毁坏她的名誉?

Column 15.1

This column is adopted to help understand some metaphorical expressions of **black** that are unique to Chinese.

背黑锅	be made a scapegoat; be unjustly blamed
黑交易	shady deal
黑心	wicked; sinister; evil mind
黑帮	reactionary gang; sinister gang; cabal
黑道	dark deeds (as of robbers)
黑店	an inn run by brigands
黑户	unregistered household; unregistered resident; a shop without a license; an illegal shop
黑话	(bandits') argot; (thieves') cant; double-talk; malicious words
黑会	a clandestine meeting
黑货	smuggled goods; contraband
黑幕	inside story of a plot, shady deal, etc.
黑钱	ill-gotten money
黑枪	illegally possessed firearms; a shot fired from a hiding-place
黑手	a vicious person manipulating someone or something from behind the scenes; evil backstage manipulator
青眼（有加）	favor; good graces

blue

15.6 **Blue** is the colour of the clear sky or the deep sea.

蓝色
汉语中用青来形容人恐惧、愤怒或患病时的脸色, 如: 脸色铁青。

Blue is used metaphorically to talk about feeling rather sad.

沮丧的；悲伤的；忧郁的

She usually calls her mother when she's feeling blue.

她情绪低落时通常会给母亲打电话。

His prospects of getting a job look

他得到工作的希望不大。

rather blue.

brown

15.7 **Brown** is the colour of chocolate or coffee.

If you are in **brown study**, you are in a condition of being deep in thought.

brown years in boarding houses

colour

15.8 The **colour** of something is the way it looks because of the way it reflects light.

Colour is used metaphorically to talk about qualities that make something more lively or interesting.

The old town is full of colour, character and attraction.

15.9 If you **add**, **give** or **bring colour to** something, you make it more interesting or exciting.

Her acting added warmth and colour to the production.

local colour

15.10 If you do something **with flying colours**, you do it extremely well.

15.11 If you **give a false colour to** a fact, you distort it.

colourful

15.12 An object that is **colourful** has bright colours or a lot of different colours.

A **colourful** character is someone who behaves in a lively and amusing way, but who may shock some people.

Joe, who worked for a number of years with us, was a colourful and unique

棕色

沉思，遐想；神不守舍

寄宿舍里沉闷的岁月

色；颜色

汉语中的**色彩**隐喻往往离不开光的使用，比如：增光添彩、蓬荜生辉等等。

特色

这座古老的城镇充满了情趣、特色和吸引力。

为……增色；使……生动

汉语用**渲染**比喻夸大地形容，如：一件小事，用不着这么渲染。参见7.55

她的表演给这出戏增添了生气和趣味。

（文学作品的）乡土色彩

成功地

歪曲

色彩丰富的，引人注目的

活泼有趣的，性格独特的

乔和我们在一起工作了好几年，他是一个活泼有趣、性格非常独特的人，

character not afraid to speak his mind. 他敢于坦率地说出自己的想法。

15.13 If someone has had a **colourful** past or a **colourful** career, he has been involved in exciting, but slightly shocking or illegal activities. 参加过许多不光彩活动的

have a <u>colourful</u> career 有过声名狼藉的经历

15.14 A **colourful** story is full of exciting details. 惊险的，富有传奇色彩的

The explorer described his <u>colourful</u> experiences with the natives. 探险家叙述了他在土人中间惊险的经历。

15.15 **Colourful** language is rude or uses offensive language. 粗鲁伤人、令人讨厌的话

There was much hostility and a great deal of <u>colourful</u> language was used. 人们相互之间怀有强烈的敌意，用了许多粗鲁肮脏的语言。

colourless

15.16 Something that is **colourless** has no colour at all. 无色的

Colourless is used metaphorically to say that someone or something that is not very interesting or exciting. 无趣的；不刺激的；呆板的
汉语用**无味**形容没有趣味，如：枯燥无味。参见5.26

Some people find him lacking in personality, <u>colourless</u> perhaps. 一些人觉得他缺乏个性，也许是没什么与众不同的鲜明特征。

green

15.17 **Green** is the colour of grass in spring and summer. 绿色
汉语中，**绿色食品**指无公害、无污染的安全营养型食品；**绿色通道**泛指简便、安全、快捷的途径或渠道。

If you say a method, scheme etc. is **green**, you mean that it is designed to protect the environment or limit damage to environment. 环保的

Thousands of people have turned to the bike as the most economic, <u>greenest</u> and quickest way to travel. 成千上万的人已经改骑自行车，将它作为最节约、最符合环境保护要求和最快捷的旅行方式。

15.18 A **green** person is one who lacks 无经验的

15 Colour

of training or experience, especially because of being young.
a <u>green</u> hand
She wasn't so <u>green</u> as to expect suspicious characters to look suspicious.

15.19 If you are **green with envy**, you feel very unhappy because you wish you had something that someone else has.
I'm <u>green with envy</u> when I go to Bristol and see their facilities.
In a <u>green</u> rage, Boris stamped out of the room.

grey

15.20 **Grey** is the colour of ashes or of clouds on a rainy day.

Many people consider grey to be a dull and uninteresting colour, and **grey** is used metaphorically to talk about people or things that are dull or uninteresting.
Life seemed <u>grey</u> and pointless after she'd gone.

15.21 **Grey** can also be used metaphorically to talk about being unclear and therefore not easy to deal with.
a <u>grey</u> area in environment law
a government department run by little <u>grey</u> men

pink

15.22 **Pink** is the colour between red and white.

If you are **in the pink**, you are healthy

汉语用**新**、**生**、**嫩**等来比喻缺乏经验，如：<u>新</u>手、<u>生</u>手、太<u>嫩</u>等等。
生手
她没有幼稚到以为可疑分子看上去就是一副可疑相。

嫉妒，妒忌
汉语中关于嫉妒的隐喻常与**红色**或**火**（**热**）相关，如：眼<u>红</u>、眼<u>热</u>、妒<u>火</u>等等。
我去布里斯托尔见到他们的设备，真是羡慕极了。
鲍里斯怒气冲天，跺着脚从房里走出去。

灰色
灰色在汉语中也可用来比喻中间的、中性的、不清楚的，如：<u>灰色</u>收入。

单调乏味的

她走后，生活显得既单调又无意义。

无明确含义的；难以处理的

环境保护法的灰色区域
由无名之辈掌管的政府部门

粉红色；淡红色
汉语用**红润**形容健康的面色。**粉色**，也称**桃色**，则用以形容跟不正当的男女关系有关的，如：<u>桃色</u>新闻。
健康快乐的；红光满面的

and happy.
purple
15.23 **Purple** is the colour between red and blue. Purple can be used as a symbol of royal.

紫色
汉语文化中，象征皇室的是黄色，而紫色可以用来形容炙手可热的人，如：红得发紫。

born to the *purple*
出身王室或显贵

15.24 **A purple passage** is a piece of writing that is written in a very emotional or complicated style.
辞藻华丽的段落

red
15.25 **Red** is the colour of blood.

红色
汉语中，红色多用来象征顺利、成功或受人重视、欢迎，如：红运、开门红。

If you are **in the red**, you have spent more money than there is available.
亏欠；赤字

Their bank account was *in the red* again.
他们的银行账户上又出现赤字了。

The company has gone thousands of dollars *into the red*.
公司已经出现了几千美元的亏损。

15.26 If you **go red**, you become red in the face because you are embarrassed.
（困窘得）脸红

He tries to deny it, but he *went* very *red*.
他竭力否认，但还是羞愧得满脸通红。

15.27 **A red rag to a bull** is something that will make someone very angry.
激怒人的东西

A mere mention of his shortcomings is *a red rag to him*.
稍一提及他的缺点，他就会大怒。

15.28 If you **roll out the red carpet for** someone, you take the person as an important visitor.
热烈欢迎某人

He was sort of expecting *the red carpet* and not the fisheye.
他多少以为自己会受到隆重欢迎，而不是挨白眼。

15.29 If you **see red**, you get very angry.
生气，发脾气

When he started criticizing my work, I really <u>saw red</u>. | 他竟批评起我的工作来了，我立即火冒三丈。

Column 15.2

This column is adopted to help understand some metaphorical expressions of **red** that are unique to Chinese.

红白喜事	weddings and funerals
红榜	honour roll (or board)
红得发紫	(of a person) extremely popular
红火	flourishing; prosperous
红极一时	be well-known for a time; enjoy popularity for a time
红心	a red heart—a heart loyal to the cause of proletarian revolution

white

15.30 **White** is the palest colour that is like the colour of snow or milk.

白色

汉语中的白色用来隐喻美德，如：清清白白。使用时常与"冰"或"玉"相联系，如：冰清玉洁（白）。但白色也会与消极的意义相联系，如丧事就被婉称为白事。此外，白也有徒然的意思，如：白费力气。

15.31 If you describe someone's character as **white than white**, you mean that you have not heard any bad reports about his behavior and he has a reputation for always behaving honestly and morally.

道德高尚；品行端正

There was no point in inventing a <u>white than white</u> character.

生造一个行为诚实、品行端正的人没有什么意义。

15.32 **A white lie** is one told to avoid making someone upset, not for your own advantage or in order to harm someone else.

善意的谎言

15.33 If you **go** or **turn white**, you look very pale because you are frightened,

（因害怕、生气或生病而）脸色发白的，苍白的

angry or ill.
You can also use **(as) white as a sheet** to describe a person who is extremely pale.

Luke's face was <u>white with anger</u>.

She suddenly turned deathly <u>white</u> and fainted.

yellow

15.34 **Yellow** is the colour of gold.

Yellow can be used metaphorically to talk about being cowardly.

I knew you were quiet, but I didn't know you were <u>yellow</u>.

面无血色的；脸色像白纸一样的

卢克气得脸色发白。

她脸色突然变得像死人一样苍白，接着就晕倒了。

黄色
胆小的
黄在汉语中作动词时指事情失败或计划不能实现，如：买卖黄了。
我知道你不大说话，但我不知道你胆小。

16 Light and Darkness

Light

bright

16.1 If the weather is **bright**, the sun is shining and there is a lot of light.

明亮的；光亮的
汉语中，明有清楚、明白之意，如：讲明；也有公开、显露之意，如：明说。

A **bright** person is intelligent and usually young and likely to do well at school or in their careers.

聪明的；伶俐的
汉语中，明也可用来表示眼光正确、对事物现象看得清，如：聪明、英明、明察秋毫等。

She was married to a bright young lawyer.
她嫁给了一位聪明的年轻律师。

one of the brightest students in the class
班上最聪明的学生之一

16.2 A **bright idea** is clever. This word is often used for showing that you think an idea is stupid.

好主意（该词常用于指愚蠢的主意）

Whose bright idea was that, then?
那么，那是谁的好主意？

This is pretty much a guaranteed waste of time. But it was the captain's bright idea.
这简直是浪费时间。不过，这是船长的一个"聪明"主意。

16.3 If you describe something as **bright**, it is happy and lively.

欢快的；有活力的

She gave him a bright smile.
她给了他一个灿烂的微笑。

His eyes were bright and hopeful.
他的眼里流露出快乐和希望。

16.4 If the future looks **bright**, you think that something will be successful.

有前途的；有希望的

I'm sure there is a very bright future for
我相信你在这家公司有光明的未来。

you in this company.
The team's prospects don't look very <u>bright</u>.

这支球队的前景看来不太乐观。

16.5 You can refer to something that is good as a **bright spot** when everything else seems bad.

亮点（指其他事都很糟时的一件好事）

The one <u>bright spot</u> is that they have promised to reexamine the case.

唯一值得高兴的是他们答应重新审查这个案子。

The win last week was the only <u>bright spot</u> in their last ten games.

上周的胜利是他们最近十场比赛中唯一振奋人心的一次。

16.6 If you **look on the bright side** of a situation, you concentrate on the positive aspects of it and try not to think about the negative ones.

看事物的光明面；看事物好的一面

I tried to <u>look on the bright side</u>, to be grateful that I was healthy.

我试图从好的方面看，为我健康的身体感到庆幸。

brighten

16.7 If something **brightens**, it starts to have more color or light.

发亮；发光

If something or someone **brightens** a situation, or **brightens up** a situation, it/he makes it more pleasant.

使……愉快；（使）增添乐趣
比较汉语中的**蓬荜生辉**。

A personal letter <u>will</u> usually <u>brighten up</u> a person's day.

一封私人来信往往就能使人一天心情愉快。

Fresh flowers <u>will brighten up</u> any room in the house.

鲜花会使屋里的任何房间都亮丽生色。

16.8 If your spirits **brighten**, or if something **brightens** them, you begin to feel more happy and optimistic.

开颜；高兴

Her eyes <u>brightened</u>.

她的眼睛亮了起来。

She frowned anxiously, then suddenly her face <u>brightened</u>.

她忧虑地皱着眉头，然后突然脸上露出喜色。

brilliant

16.9 **Brilliant** light or colour is very bright and strong.

明亮的；鲜亮的
参见 16.11

16 Light and Darkness

A **brilliant** idea, performance, career etc. is extremely skillful, impressive or successful.
技艺高超的；杰出的；非常成功的
What a brilliant idea!
真是个绝妙的主意！
It was a brilliant save by the goalie.
这是守门员一次非常精彩的扑救。
a brilliant legal career
极为成功的律师生涯

16.10 A **brilliant** person is very intelligent.
聪颖的；才华横溢的
a brilliant young scientist
一位才华横溢的青年科学家
She has one of the most brilliant minds in the country.
她是全国最有才气的人之一。

dazzle

16.11 If a very bright light **dazzles** you, it stops you from seeing properly for a short time.
（强光）使目眩，使眼花
比较汉语中的光耀、荣耀、耀武扬威等。

If someone or something **dazzles** you, he/it impresses you a lot, for example with his/its beauty, intelligence or skill.
（用美貌、智力或技能）使倾倒，使赞叹
He was dazzled by the warmth of her smile.
她那温柔的微笑使他神魂颠倒。

dazzling

16.12 A light that is **dazzling** is very bright and makes you unable to see properly for a short time.
耀眼的；眩目的
参见 16.11

If you describe something as **dazzling**, you mean that it is very impressive and attractive.
令人赞叹的；给人印象深刻的
a dazzling display of oriental dance and music
使人陶醉的东方音乐、舞蹈表演

light

16.13 **Light** is brightness from the sun or from a light, which allows you to see things.
光；光线；光亮
参见 16.1

If facts **are brought to light** or **come to light,** people discover them.
发现（某事物）；（某事物）被发现
汉语用曝光比喻隐秘的事（多指不光

New evidence in this case <u>has</u> recently <u>come to light</u>.
最近发现了这个案子的新证据。

These facts <u>have</u> only just <u>been brought to light</u>.
这些事实刚刚才被披露出来。

16.14 To **cast**, **shed** or **throw light on** something means to make a problem, etc. easier to understand.
使（问题等）较容易理解

Recent research <u>has thrown</u> new <u>light on</u> the causes of the diseases.
最近的研究可以使人进一步了解导致这种疾病的原因。

16.15 If something such as an idea, plan, or rule **sees the light of day**, it starts to exist.
（想法、计划、规定等）出台，颁布

He's written a lot of good material that <u>has</u> never <u>seen the light of day</u>.
他写了许多鲜为人知的好材料。

lighten

16.16 To **lighten** means to become brighter or less dark, or to make something brighter.
（使）变亮；（使）明亮；点亮
汉语中，点有启发之意，如：<u>点拨</u>、<u>点明</u>等。

If a situation or someone's mood **lightens**, or someone or something **lightens** it, it becomes more relaxed.
（使）放心；（使）减轻；（使）缓和

My mood gradually <u>lightened</u>.
我的心情渐渐好起来。

She told a joke to <u>lighten</u> the atmosphere.
她讲了个笑话以缓和气氛。

shine

16.17 If the sun **shines**, it produces a bright light and the weather is usually warm.
（太阳）发光；照耀
参见 16.11

If people's eyes or faces **shine**, they look extremely happy or excited.
（眼睛或脸）发亮；露出喜色（或兴奋之情）

The child's face <u>was shining</u> with excitement.
那个孩子的脸上洋溢着兴奋之情。

16.18 If someone **shines** at a skill or activity, he does it extremely well, so that other people notice him and are
显身手

impressed by him.
It's time we gave some of the younger players a chance to shine.
该是我们给一些年轻球员机会展示才能的时候了。

16.19 If a good feeling or quality **shines through**, it is very noticeable.
（好的感情或素质）显露无遗，表现明显

Perlman's musical talents shone through at an early age.
帕尔曼的音乐才华在他早年就已显露无遗。

Darkness

dark

16.20 If it is **dark**, there is little or no light.
黑暗的；无光的
汉语中，暗有隐秘不露、秘密之意，如：暗藏；也有糊涂、不明白的意思，如：偏信则暗。用黑暗比喻（社会状况）落后、（统治势力）腐败。

If you describe something as **dark**, you mean that it is morally bad, dangerous, or frightening.
凶恶的；危险的；可怕的

I always suspected there was a darker side to his character.
我总怀疑他的性格有阴暗的一面。

16.21 A **dark** time is one in which people feel frightened, unhappy, and without hope.
（时期）感到阴郁的，忧愁的，黑暗的

during the darkest days of war
在战争的那些最黑暗的日子里
This was the President's darkest hour.
这是总统感到最无望的时刻。

16.22 A **dark** look or remark is angry and threatening.
（神情或话语）凶恶的
汉语中，黯然用以形容心里不舒服，情绪低落的样子，如：神色黯然。

16.23 **Dark** thoughts are sad because you believe that something bad is going to happen.
（思想）悲观的

He had been reluctant to go home to the bungalow, with the dark thoughts still going round in his head concerning the
他曾不愿回到他家所住的平房，因为萨拉·埃利斯去世的阴影仍然笼罩在他的心头。

death of Sarah Ellis.

16.24 A **dark** secret or mystery is kept well hidden, especially because people would not approve if they knew about it.

隐秘的；深藏的
参见 16.20

There are no dark secrets in our family. 我们家没有隐秘。

16.25 A **dark** place is distant and mysterious because very little information is known about it.

（地方）偏远神秘的

in some dark corner of his mind 在他头脑中的某个神秘角落

16.26 If you have **dark** feelings or thoughts, you are very sad or worried.

沮丧的；痛苦的

He felt the same dark mood coming over him as had taken control last night. 他感到，昨天夜里控制了他的那种坏情绪又回来了。

dark despair 无奈的绝望

16.27 If you are **in the dark** about something, you know very little about it.

（对某事）一无所知的

We are still very much in the dark about how the money was lost. 对于钱是怎么丢掉的我们仍然一无所知。

You've kept us in the dark about what happened that night. 你一点儿都不让我们了解那天晚上发生的事。

darken

16.28 If something **darkens**, or if something **darkens** it, it becomes darker.

（使）变暗；（使）变黑

To **darken** a person or a situation means to make him/it become less hopeful or positive.

（使）变得阴郁；（使）变得阴沉

The mood was darkened further by a gloomy economic forecast. 心情被令人失望的经济预测搞得更加阴郁不欢。

It was a tragedy that darkened his later life. 这场悲剧给他后来的岁月蒙上了阴影。

Her mood darkened at the news. 听到这消息，她的心情暗淡起来。

Philip's face darkened. 菲利普的脸阴沉了下来。

darkly

16.29 If you do something **darkly**, you do it in a threatening or unpleasant way.
He hinted darkly that all was not well.

威胁地；险恶地；负面地

他悲观地暗示并非一切都顺利。

dim

16.30 Dim light is not bright.
A **dim** recollection, awareness etc. is a memory or understanding that is not clear in your mind.
I had a dim recollection of a visit to a big dark house.
He only had a dim awareness of the issue involved.

（光）暗淡的；昏暗的
模糊的；不大明白的
参见 16.20

我依稀记得去过一栋黑暗的大房子。

他只是模模糊糊地知道所涉及的问题。

16.31 If the chances of something good happening are **dim**, it is not likely to happen.
Their hopes of victory were starting to look dim.

（好事）不太可能发生的，渺茫的

他们对胜利抱有的希望开始变得渺茫。

16.32 If a light **dims**, or if you **dim** it, it becomes less bright.
If feelings or hopes **dim**, or **are dimmed**, they become weaker.
Her passion for dancing never dimmed over the year.

（使）暗下来；（使）变微弱

（使）（感情）减弱；（使）（希望）变渺茫

这些年来她对跳舞的热情一直不减。

gloom

16.33 Gloom is darkness in which it is difficult to see clearly.
Gloom is used metaphorically to refer to the feeling of having no hope.
a time of high unemployment and economic gloom
There is general gloom about the future of the farming industry.

昏暗；阴暗
参见 16.20

悲观；忧郁

高失业率和经济不景气的时期

对农业的未来普遍存在悲观的态度。

gloomy

16.34 If a place is **gloomy**, it is dark in a way that makes you feel sad.

阴暗的；幽暗的
参见 16.20

If you describe someone's mood as **gloomy**, you mean that he is unhappy and does not seem hopeful about the future.

沮丧的；悲观的

He became very gloomy and depressed.

他变得非常沮丧抑郁。

16.35 If a situation is **gloomy**, it makes you feel that things will not improve.

无望的；使人气馁的

gloomy prospects

黯淡的前景

The economic news is gloomy.

经济消息令人失望。

shadow

16.36 A **shadow** is an area of darkness that is created when something blocks light.

阴影；暗影

Shadow is used metaphorically to refer to the bad effect or influence that something has, which makes other things seem less enjoyable, attractive, or impressive.

阴影；（坏）影响

These countries will need assistance as they emerge from the shadows of war.

这些国家需要国际社会帮助他们摆脱战争阴影。

The new leader wants to escape from the shadow of his predecessor.

新任领导想要摆脱前任的影响。

He's always lived in the shadow of his brother.

他一直生活在哥哥的阴影中。

16.37 To **shadow** someone means to follow him closely in order to understand or know what he is doing.

尾随；（尤指）跟踪

Guards shadowed the escaped prisoners for several miles before capturing them.

警卫们跟踪了那些越狱者好几里才抓到他们。

Column 16

This column is adopted to help understand some metaphorical expressions of **light & darkness** that are unique to Chinese.

暗下决心	make up one's mind secretly
暗地里	secretly; inwardly; on the sly
暗处	a secret place; a covert place; cover
暗含	imply
暗号	a secret signal (or sign); countersign; watchword
暗疾	a disease one is ashamed of; unmentionable disease
暗器	hidden weapon
暗无天日	complete darkness—total absence of justice
暗喜	feel pleased but not show it
暗语	code word
明处	in the open; in public
明察暗访	observe publicly and investigate privately—conduct a thorough investigation
明来暗往	have overt and covert contacts with someone
明朗	clear; obvious
明镜高悬	a clear mirror hung on high—an impartial and perspicacious judge
明枪暗箭	spear thrusts in the open and arrows shoot from hiding—both open and covert attacks
明人不做暗事	an honest man does nothing underhand
明升暗降	a promotion in appearance but a demotion in fact
明修栈道，暗渡陈仓	pretend to advance along one path while secretly going along another; do one thing under cover of another
明一套，暗一套	act one way in the open and another way in secret
明争暗斗	both open strife and veiled struggle; overt contention and covert struggle
明珠暗投	a bright pearl cast into darkness—① a person of talent or a thing of value unrecognized ② a good person fallen among bad company
弃暗投明	forsake darkness for light—leave the reactionary side and cross over to the side of progress

17 Temperature

blaze

17.1 If a fire **blazes**, it burns strongly and brightly.
If someone's eyes **blaze**, they show a sudden strong emotion, especially anger.

熊熊燃烧
参见 5.13
（眼睛）流露出强烈的感情（尤指愤怒）

Her eyes <u>blazed</u> with fury.
她的眼里充满怒火。

17.2 If something **is blazed across** or **all over** a newspaper etc., it is written in a way that everyone will notice.

大肆宣扬；炒作
汉语用 煽风点火 比喻鼓动别人做某种事（多指坏的）。类似的表达方式还有 煽动、煽情 等。

The story <u>was blazed all over</u> the daily papers.
那个传闻被各家报纸炒得沸沸扬扬。

17.3 If someone or an organization **blazes a trail**, he/it is the first to do or to discover something that others follow.

作开路先锋；领先

The department <u>is blazing a trail</u> in the field of laser surgery.
这个部门正在为激光外科领域开辟一条新路。

17.4 If someone does something **in a blaze of** publicity or attention, he gets a lot of publicity or attention when he does it.

公众瞩目

The president launched his anti-drugs campaign <u>in a blaze of</u> publicity.
总统发动的反毒品战役引起轰动。

The career that began <u>in a blaze of</u> glory has ended in his forced retirement.
这项以辉煌开始的事业已经随着他的被迫退职而告结束。

blazing

17.5 If people have **a blazing row**, they argue in a very noisy and excited way.

激烈的争吵
比较汉语中的 热烈。

He walked out after *a blazing row* with his wife.

boiling point

See **boiling point**: 5.19

burn

17.6 If a fire **burns**, it produces heat and flames.

燃烧；烧
汉语用**发热**比喻不冷静，如：头脑<u>发热</u>。

If a part of your body **burns**, or if something **burns** it, it feels unpleasantly hot.

火辣辣地痛；发烫

Your forehead's <u>burning</u>. Have you got a fever?

你的前额很烫。你发烧了吗？

Her cheeks <u>burned</u> with embarrassment.

她的面颊羞得发烫。

17.7 If you **are burning with** rage, desire etc, you feel a particular emotion or a great need very strongly.

有强烈的感情；渴望
汉语用**欲火**比喻强烈的欲望（多指情欲），如：<u>欲火</u>中烧。

I <u>was burning with</u> curiosity, but didn't dare ask what happened.

我非常好奇，但不敢问发生了什么事。

17.8 If a fire **burns out**, or if it **burns itself out**, it stops burning.

（火）熄灭

If a strong feeling **burns out**, or if it **burns itself out**, you stop feeling it.

（使）（强烈感情）消失

His rage had been intense, but it had <u>burned itself out</u>.

他勃然大怒，但后来自己就消气了。

burning

17.9 A **burning** ambition, desire, need etc. is very strong.

强烈的
比较汉语中的**炽烈**、**强烈**等。

He's always had a <u>burning</u> ambition to start his own business.

他总是雄心勃勃地想自己开业。

17.10 A **burning issue** or **question** is very important and urgent.

很重要的迫切问题；当务之急
参见 5.19

The <u>burning question</u> is: can the Internet be regulated?

亟待解决的问题是：能对因特网进行管理吗？

burn-out

17.11 If someone becomes **burnt-out**, he has worked so hard for a long time or has been under such a lot of stress that he has become exhausted or ill and cannot carry on.
Some were simply burnt-out, exhausted.

筋疲力尽的；疲惫不堪的
汉语用**油尽灯枯**比喻生命的终止；用**风烛残年**比喻随时可能死亡的晚年；用**风中之烛**比喻随时可能死亡的人或随时可能消灭的事物。
一些人简直已经累垮了，筋疲力尽。

chill

17.12 If you **chill** something or if it **chills**, you lower its temperature so that it is quite cold but does not freeze.

（使）变冷；冰镇
参见 14.23

If you **are chilled** or if something **chills** you, you feel extremely frightened or worried.
They looked across at me, chilled by what Mark had said.
It was a thought that chilled me to the core.

（使）非常害怕；（使）非常担心
他们被马克所说的吓坏了，都朝我这边看。
这种想法使我不寒而栗。

17.13 If a situation or relationship **chills**, or if something **chills** it, it becomes less friendly.
The border dispute between the two countries chilled their relations for decades.

（使）沮丧；（使）扫兴；（使）消沉
两国之间的边界争端使它们几十年来的关系都很冷淡。

chilly

See **chilly**: 14.7

chilling

17.14 Something that is **chilling** makes you feel frightened, especially because it is cruel, violent, or dangerous.
The chilling truth is that the killers are still out there.
The proposed law would have a chilling effect on freedom of expression.

令人胆寒的；令人担心的；令人沮丧的
令人胆寒的事实是，那些杀手仍然逍遥法外。
提议的这项法律将对言论自由有消极的影响。

cold

17.15 Something that is **cold** has a lower temperature than usual.

冷的；寒冷的
汉语用**冷**比喻灰心或失望，如：心灰意**冷**；用**冷言冷语**比喻含有讥讽意味的话。参见 14.7

Someone who is **cold** or with a **cold** expression does not show emotion and seems unfriendly.

冷淡的；不友好的；无同情心的

He was <u>cold</u> and uncaring about it, as if it wasn't important.

他对它的态度非常冷漠，似乎它并不重要。

He used to say to me in a <u>cold</u>, calculating way, "I'm not going to leave any bruises."

他从前总是用一种冷漠、诡诈的口吻对我说："我不准备留下任何伤痕。"

17.16 If you **pour** or **throw cold water on** something, you give reasons for not being in favour of it.

泼冷水；批评；责备
汉语用**泼冷水**比喻打击人的热情或让人头脑清醒。

She immediately <u>poured cold water on</u> his plans to expand the business.

她马上给他扩展业务的计划泼了冷水。

coldly

17.17 If you do something **coldly**, you do it without any emotion or warm feelings.

冷淡地；冷漠地；不友好地

The speech was received <u>coldly</u>.

讲演受到了冷落。

coldness

17.18 **Coldness** is used to refer to lack of warm feelings or unfriendly behaviour.

冷淡；冷漠；不友好的举止

She was hurt by the <u>coldness</u> in his voice.

他说话的冷漠语气让她很伤心。

cool

17.19 If you say something, such as water or air, is **cool**, you mean it is cold but pleasant.

凉爽的；凉快的

If someone's behaviour to you is **cool**, it is not friendly or enthusiastic.

冷漠的；冷淡的

The presidential candidate got a <u>cool</u>

总统候选人受到了冷遇。

reception.

17.20 **Cool** people are calm and relaxed. 冷静的；沉着的；从容的
She tried to remain <u>cool</u>, calm, and 她试图保持冷静、沉着、镇定。
collected.
He has a <u>cool</u> head. 他头脑冷静。

17.21 **Cool** is sometimes used to express 时髦的；酷的
your approval towards someone or
something in fashion.
one of Britain's <u>coolest</u> young designers 英国最酷的年轻设计师之一

17.22 If a feeling such as love or anger （爱、怒等感情）冷下来，平息
cools, it becomes less strong.
Later, when tempers <u>had cooled</u>, they 后来，怒气平息以后，他们坐下来谈
sat down and talked. 了谈。
Her enthusiasm quickly <u>cooled</u>. 她的热情很快就冷了下来。

17.23 You can say someone **cools down** （使）冷静下来
if he becomes less angry or excited.
Just try to <u>cool down</u> and think 请你尽量冷静下来，理智地想一想。
rationally.

17.24 If the economy has **cooled**, （经济发展）降温；变缓
people are buying and selling less than
previously.
The hope must be that the economy has 这个希望一定是，经济发展的降温已
<u>cooled</u> sufficiently to relieve inflationary 足以减轻通货膨胀的压力。
pressures.

17.25 If something such as a tense （使）冷静下来
situation **cools off**, it becomes less tense
and the people involved become calmer.
Let him <u>cool off</u>, you can talk about it 先让他冷静下来，那件事你们可以稍
later. 后再谈。
I'm really busy, but when things <u>cool off</u> 我真的很忙，不过等忙完这阵儿以后，
I'll come to see you. 我会去看你的。

fiery

17.26 Something that is **fiery** looks like 如火的；似火的
fire. 参见 5.13
People who are **fiery** become angry 易怒的；急躁的；火爆的

very easily and quickly.
a fiery young man 动辄发怒的年轻人
He'll have to keep his fiery temper under control. 他将不得不控制自己火爆的脾气。

17.27 A **fiery** speech or piece of writing shows or encourages anger or excitement. 充满激情的
About twenty thousand people heard a fiery speech from the Secretary General. 约两万人听到了秘书长充满激情的演说。

Fire
17.28 **Fire** is the hot, bright flame produced by things that are burning. 火
汉语的火可比喻紧急，如：火速；也比喻发怒，如：冒火。另外，火也有兴旺、兴隆之意，如：买卖很火。
参见 5.13, 17.9

You can refer to strong feelings especially anger or enthusiasm as **fire**. 强烈的感情（尤指怒气或热情）
His words were full of fire and passion. 他的讲话中激情洋溢。

17.29 If you **come under fire**, you are criticized severely for something you have done. 受到严厉批评；遭到猛烈批判
The health minister has come under fire from all sides. 卫生部长受到来自各方的责难。
The government will come under fire again when the latest crime figures are released. 一公布最新的犯罪数字，政府就会再次受到批评。

flame
17.30 **Flame** is the burning gas that you see coming from a fire. 火焰；火舌
参见 5.13, 17.9, 17.28
Flame is used metaphorically to talk about a sudden strong feeling. 激情；突然的强烈感情
a flame of passion 突然的激情
He accused the president of fanning the flames of violence. 他指责总统煽动暴力行为。

17.31 If your face **flames**, it becomes red, especially because you are （脸尤因羞愧或愤怒而）变红

embarrassed or angry.
His cheeks flamed. 他的双颊变红了。

flare

17.32 If a fire **flares**, the flames suddenly become larger and brighter. 突然烧旺；闪耀
参见 5.13, 17.9, 17.28

If tempers **flare**, people suddenly become angry or violent. 突然发怒；突然爆发

Tempers flared during the debates. 在辩论中人们突然发起脾气。

17.33 If fighting or trouble **flares** or **flares up**, it begins or becomes worse. （战斗或困境）开始，恶化，加剧

Trouble flared in Greece, Cyprus, and the Czech Republic. 希腊、塞浦路斯及捷克共和国的问题加剧了。

It looked as if long-feared violence might flare up. 看来人们长期担心的暴力活动似乎会加剧。

17.34 If an illness or medical condition **flares up**, it becomes worse. （疾病或症状）恶化，加剧

In moments of stress, his asthma always flares up. 在有压力的时候，他的哮喘总会加剧。

17.35 You can use **flare-up** to refer to a situation in which someone suddenly becomes angry or violent. （怒气或暴力活动的）突然爆发

a flare-up of tension between the two sides 双方剑拔弩张

A flare-up along the border threatened the peace talks. 边境突发的暴力事件威胁着和谈。

17.36 You can refer to an occasion when a disease suddenly returns after you have not had it for some time as a **flare-up**. （疾病的）突然复发
汉语用死灰复燃比喻已经停息的事物又重新活动起来（多指坏事）。

a flare-up of malaria 疟疾的突发

flicker

17.37 If a flame or light **flickers**, it does not burn evenly, or it goes on and off. （火焰、灯光）摇曳，闪烁
汉语用闪烁比喻（说话）稍微露出一点想法，但不肯说明确，如：闪烁其词。

If an emotion, a thought etc. **flickers**, you feel it for a very short time.
Though we knew our army had been defeated, hopes still <u>flickered</u> in our hearts.
A little smile <u>flickered</u> around the corners of his mouth.

17.38 A **flicker of** an emotion is one that someone experiences only for a very short time.
They both saw the <u>flicker of</u> annoyance on the prince's face.

闪现；一闪而过
虽然我们知道我们的军队当时已经被打败，但我们的心里仍然闪烁一线希望。
他的嘴角掠过一丝微笑。

（情感的）闪现；掠过
他俩都看见王子脸上闪过厌烦的神色。

freeze
See **freeze:** 14.22

heat
17.39 **Heat** is the quality of being hot.

热；热度
汉语中，**热**有情意深厚之意，如：热爱；也可形容非常羡慕或急切想得到，如：热衷；还可指受人欢迎的，如：热门儿。
参见 17.6, 17.7

You can refer to strong and angry feelings as **heat**.
He felt the <u>heat</u> of my glare.
Professional counselling is one way of taking the <u>heat</u> out of getting a divorce.
The chairman tried to take the <u>heat</u> out of the situation.

愤怒，气愤
他感觉到了我目光中强烈的愤怒。
专业咨询是缓和离婚局面的一种办法。
主席尽力平息人们的激愤情绪。

17.40 You can use **the heat** to refer to pressure and criticism intended to force someone to do what you want.
Many producers are beginning to feel <u>the heat</u> from their larger customers.

压力；批评
许多生产商开始感觉到来自较大买主的压力。

17.41 You can say **"the heat is on"** when people are under a lot of pressure

有巨大的压力

to do something.
The heat was really <u>on</u> at work. 工作确实压力很大。
We kept going just that little bit better than our rivals when <u>the heat was on</u>. 在有巨大压力时，我们保持着比对手刚好多出一点儿的优势。

17.42 The heat of something is the busiest time or the most difficult part of it. 最忙的时刻；最艰难的阶段
汉语用白热化比喻事态、感情等发展到最紧张激烈的阶段。
In <u>the heat of</u> the debate, she forgot to be nervous. 在辩论的白热化阶段，她忘记了紧张。

17.43 If you are **in the heat of the moment**, you are too angry or excited to think carefully. 盛怒之下；一时情急
We both said things we didn't mean <u>in the heat of the moment</u>. 我俩一时情急，都说了些违背本意的话。

17.44 If something **heats up**, it becomes warm or hot. 加热；变热；（使）变暖
If a situation **heats up**, it becomes dangerous or full of problems. （形势）变得激烈；激化；加剧
The dispute was already <u>heating up</u>. 当时争论正在激化。

heated

17.45 A **heated** room, building etc. is made warm enough for people to use. 温的；暖的
参见 17.39
A **heated** discussion or argument is one in which people get angry and excited. （讨论或争论）热烈的，激烈的
They were engaged in a <u>heated</u> debate about the problem. 他们就这个问题进行了激烈的辩论。

17.46 Someone who gets **heated** becomes angry and excited as he speaks. 愤怒的；激动的
Robert grew <u>heated</u> as he spoke of the risks. 谈到这些风险时，罗伯特变得越来越激动。

heatedly

17.47 If people speak or argue **heatedly**, they feel very strongly about the discussion and become angry with each other. 愤怒地；激动地；情绪激烈地

His advisers have argued <u>heatedly</u> over whether to support them.

他的顾问们已经就是否支持他们激烈地争吵起来。

hot

17.48 Something that is **hot** has a high temperature.

热的；烫的；温度高的
参见 17.39

Someone or something that is **hot** is very popular or fashionable.

最新的；风行的；风靡一时的

the <u>hot</u> new look in women's fashion

女装的最新款式

one of Hollywood's <u>hottest</u> young directors

好莱坞最走红的年轻导演之一

17.49 In informal speech, people sometimes use **hot** to show that they think something is very good, strong or successful.

极好的

Now he runs the <u>hottest</u> nightclub in Hollywood.

他现在经营好莱坞最红火的夜总会。

17.50 In informal speech, people sometimes use **hot** to describe property which has been stolen and difficult to get rid of because they can easily be recognized.

偷来（因容易识别）而难以销赃的

I'd never have touched those CDs if I'd known they were <u>hot</u>.

早知道那些光盘是偷来的，我绝不会碰的。

17.51 Someone who has a **hot temper** becomes angry very easily.

脾气暴躁；火暴性子

Our coach has a really <u>hot temper</u>.

我们的教练脾气确实很暴躁。

17.52 A **hot** issue is important and causes arguments because people strongly disagree.

热门的

Tax cuts have become a <u>hot</u> topic in this election campaign.

减税成了这次总统竞选的热门话题。

17.53 If something **hots up**, it becomes more lively or exciting.

变得活跃起来；变得激动起来

The debate on electoral reform <u>hotted up</u> yesterday.

昨天关于选举改革的辩论变得很热烈。

hotly

17.54 If you do something **hotly**, you do it in an excited and angry way.

（情绪）强烈地；激动地

Rumours of a split have been hotly denied by the band's manager.

有关解散的谣言遭到乐队经纪人的强烈否认。

17.55 If something is **hotly** contested, there is a lot of competition for it or a lot of disagreement over it.

（竞争）激烈地

This year's final will be as hotly contested as ever.

今年决赛的竞争将会与往年一样激烈。

ignite

17.56 If you **ignite** something, you make it start to burn.

使……燃烧；点燃

If you **ignite** a fight or argument, you start it.

引发，激起（争斗或辩论）

At least this episode has ignited a lively debate on the issues.

至少这个插曲引发了一场对这些问题的热烈争论。

17.57 If you **ignite** a particular feeling in someone, you start it.

激发（某种情感）

His teaching ignited my interest in Russian literature.

他的教学激发了我对俄罗斯文学的兴趣。

Books can ignite the imagination in a way that films can't.

书籍能以电影无法做到的方式激发想象力。

lukewarm

17.58 Something that is **lukewarm** is not hot or cold enough to be enjoyable.

不冷不热的；微温的

Lukewarm is used metaphorically to talk about behaviour or attitude that is not very enthusiastic or interested.

不热情的；冷淡的

Involvement in the war has received only lukewarm support.

卷入这场战争并未得到多少支持。

She was lukewarm about the plan.

她对这个计划不大感兴趣。

melt

17.59 If something solid **melts** or if heat **melts** it, it becomes liquid.

（使）融化；（使）熔化

汉语中，**软化**可用来指态度、意志等

If a feeling, an emotion etc. **melts** or **melts away**, it becomes gentler and less strong.
The tension in the room began to <u>melt</u>.
My fear <u>melted</u> when I saw his kind expression.
I suddenly felt sorry for him and my anger <u>melted away</u>.
Her trusting smile <u>melted</u> his heart.

由坚定变成动摇，如：态度逐渐<u>软化</u>。
（使）软化，变得柔和

屋里的紧张气氛开始缓和。
看到他友善的表情，我的恐惧渐渐消失了。
我突然对他感到内疚，火气就渐渐消了。
她那信任的微笑使他的心变软了。

roasting
17.60 If you say it is **roasting**, you mean it is so hot that you feel uncomfortable.

燥热的；灼热的

17.61 If you give someone a **roasting**, you criticize him severely.

严厉批评

scalding
17.62 **Scalding** water, tea, coffee etc. is very hot.

灼热的；滚烫的

A **scalding** attack is very severe.
a scalding attack on the government's policies

严厉的；尖锐的
对政府政策尖锐的抨击

smoulder
17.63 If something **smoulders**, it burns slowly without a flame.

（无明火地）慢慢燃烧；闷燃

If someone **smoulders** or if his feelings **smoulder**, he has strong feelings that he does not fully express.
There is a <u>smouldering</u> anger in the black community throughout the country.
Baxter <u>smouldered</u> as he drove home for lunch.

（怒气）郁积；压在心头

在全国的黑人社区中都有愤怒的情绪在积聚。

巴克斯特开车回家吃午饭时内心生着闷气。

spark
17.64 A **spark** is a very small piece of burning material.

火花

You can refer to the quality of being lively and original as **spark**. 生气；活力

The performance was short on <u>spark</u> and creativity. 表演缺少活力和创造力。

17.65 A **spark of** something positive such as hope is a small amount of it which makes a situation seem more pleasant or more likely to improve. 一丝；略微

A tiny <u>spark of</u> anger flared with her. 她心里腾起一丝怒意。

For the first time she felt a tiny <u>spark of</u> hope. 她首次看到一线希望。

17.66 If one thing **sparks** or **sparks off** another, the first thing makes the second thing happen. 导致；引起；触发；激发

The protests were <u>sparked</u> by the firing of two restaurant employees. 抗议是由解雇两名饭店雇员引发的。

The trial <u>sparked off</u> widespread rioting in London. 这次审判引起了伦敦大范围的暴乱。

Your article <u>sparked off</u> happy memories for me. 你的文章勾起了我美好的回忆。

tepid

17.67 Water or liquid that is **tepid** is slightly warm. 温的；不够热的

A feeling, reaction etc. that is **tepid** shows a lack of excitement or interest. 不太兴奋的；不太热情的

a <u>tepid</u> response 不太热情的回答

Unfortunately, when she performed the reception was <u>tepid</u> to say the least. 遗憾的是，在她表演时，观众的反应至少可以说是不冷不热的。

thaw

17.68 If ice or snow **thaws** or something **thaws** it, it becomes warmer and changes into liquid. （使）解冻；（使）融化

汉语用**冰消瓦解**比喻完全消释或崩溃。

If a bad relationship between two or more people or groups of people is **thawing**, it is showing signs of （国家之间）关系变得缓和

improving.
Trade relations between America and EC are <u>thawing</u>.

美国和欧共体之间的贸易关系正在逐渐改善。

17.69 If a person who has been unfriendly or unhelpful towards you **thaws**, he begins to be more friendly, helpful, and positive towards you.

变友好；变亲热

When Peter began to show signs of talent and success, his dad began to <u>thaw</u>.

当彼得开始表露出才能和成功的迹象时，他父亲的态度开始变得温和。

17.70 You can refer to an improvement in the relationship between two countries as **thaw**.

（国家之间）关系缓和

The decision indicates a <u>thaw</u> in relations between the two countries.

这项决定表明，两个国家之间的关系已经解冻。

warm

17.71 Something that is **warm** is in a pleasant temperature.

温暖的；温度宜人的

Warm people, feelings, or actions are friendly and caring.

温情的；热心的；友好的

His smile was <u>warm</u> and friendly.
The speaker was given a <u>warm</u> reception.

他的微笑热情而友好。
演讲者受到热烈的欢迎。

17.72 If you **warm to** someone, you begin to feel friendly, positive feelings towards him.

开始喜欢上（某人）

At first people were afraid of him, then they <u>warmed to</u> him.

最初人们怕他，后来他们开始对他有了好感。

17.73 If you **warm to** something, you become more interested in or enthusiastic about it.

开始喜欢上（某物）

It might take them a while to <u>warm to</u> the idea.

他们可能要过一段时间才会喜欢上这个主意。

warmly

17.74 If you do something **warmly**, you do it with enthusiasm and positive

热情地；友好地；积极地

feelings.
He was <u>warmly</u> congratulated by his five colleagues. 他受到五位同事热烈的祝贺。

He shook my hand <u>warmly</u>. 他热情地和我握手。

warmth

17.75 **Warmth** is the state of being warm. 温暖；暖和

You can refer to the state of being enthusiastic or friendly as **warmth**. 热情；友情

They were touched by the <u>warmth</u> of the welcome. 他们受到了热情欢迎，很感动。

Column 17

This column is adopted to help understand some metaphorical expressions of **temperature** that are unique to Chinese.

爆冷门	(of a contest, etc.) produce an unexpected winner; a dark horse bobbing up
（头脑）发热	be hotheaded; be impetuous
放冷风	spread slanderous rumors
放冷箭	shoot from a hidden position—injure someone by underhand means; snipe
过火	go too far; overdo; go to extremes
寒心	be bitterly disappointed
火并	open fight between factions
火候	level of attainment
火急	urgent; pressing
火坑	fiery pit; pit of hell
火冒三丈	fly into rage; flare up
火烧火燎	feeling terribly hot; restless with anxiety
火速	at top speed; posthaste
泼冷水	dampen the enthusiasm (or spirits) of
冷笑	sneer; laugh grimly
暖流	warm feeling

18 Time

clock

18.1 A **clock** is an object that shows the time.

钟；时钟

If you do something **against the clock**, you do it fast in order to finish before a particular time.

抢时间；争分夺秒

Staffs are working against the clock to meet the deadline.

员工们都在抓紧时间工作，想赶在最后期限前完成任务。

18.2 If you do something **around** or **round the clock**, you do it all day and all night.

日夜不停；夜以继日

汉语用**连轴转**比喻夜以继日地工作，如：工作一忙，我们几个人就得连轴转。

Rescuers worked around the clock to free people trapped in the wreckage.

救生员日夜奋战，解救困在沉船里的人们。

18.3 If you say **the clock is ticking** to someone, you mean that he must do something quickly, because there will soon be no more time left.

时间剩下不多

18.4 If you **put** or **turn the clock back**, you remember a past stage.

倒退；怀旧；回到从前

I wish we could turn the clock back two years and give the marriage another chance.

我但愿时光能倒退两年，再给我们的婚姻一次机会。

The new censorship law will turn the clock back 50 years.

新的审查法令将倒退到 50 年前的状态。

18.5 If you **put** or **turn the clock forward**, you think about a time in the future, and imagine that it is that time.

展望未来

18.6 If you say someone **clocks** a particular time or speed, he reaches it.

达到（某时间或速度）

He *clocked* 10.09 seconds in the 100 meters final.

他 100 米决赛跑出了 10′09″ 的速度。

18.7 If you **clock** the speed at which a person or vehicle is travelling, you measure or record it.

测……速度；给……记时

He was charged with dangerous driving after being *clocked* at 112 mph.

当被测到车速达每小时 112 英里后，他被指控危险驾驶。

clock-watcher

18.8 You can refer to a worker who is always checking the time to make sure he does not work longer than he needs as a **clock-watcher**.

老是看时间等下班的人

dawn

18.9 **Dawn** is the time of day when light first appears.

黎明；拂晓；破晓

汉语用**曙光**比喻已经在望的美好的前景，如：胜利的曙光。

You can refer to the beginning or first signs of something as **dawn**.

开端；曙光；萌芽

the *dawn* of history

历史的开端

Peace marked a new *dawn* in the country's history.

和平使这个国家的历史翻开了新的一页。

18.10 If a day or a period of time **dawns**, it begins.

开始

A new technological age had *dawned*.

新技术时代已经开始。

18.11 If something such as a thought or a feeling **dawns**, you begin to realize, understand, or feel it.

开始明白；开始理解

The realization *dawned* that few of them would survive.

开始意识到他们当中很少人会活下来。

18.12 If something **dawns on** you, you realize it for the first time.

使开始明白；使渐渐领悟；使开始理解

Suddenly it *dawned on* me that they couldn't possibly have met before.

我突然明白他们以前不可能见过面。

day

18.13 A **day** is a period of 24 hours or

一天，一日；白天

the period of time when it is light outside.
You can refer to a particular period of time or history as **days**.
I think my <u>days</u> as a footballer are coming to an end.
She became famous in the early <u>days</u> of television.

时期；时代

我认为我做足球运动员的生涯即将结束。

她成名于电视出现的早期。

18.14 If something happens **day after day**, it happens continuously for a long time in a way that is annoying or boring.
She hates doing the same work <u>day after day</u>.

日复一日地（尤指令人厌烦或不快）

她讨厌日复一日做同样的工作。

18.15 If something happens **day by day**, it happens slowly and gradually.
She's much better now and getting stronger <u>day by day</u>.

一天天地；渐渐地

她现在好多了，正一天天强壮起来。

18.16 If a situation changes **from day to day**, it changes often.
A baby's need for food can vary <u>from day to day</u>.

天天，一天又一天（指经常变化）

婴儿对食物的需要天天都在变化。

18.17 If someone or something **wins** or **carries the day**, he/it is successful in dealing with opposition or an opponent.
Common sense at last <u>won the day</u>.
It was Foster's bowling that finally <u>carried the day</u> for England.

得胜；取得胜利

常识最终获胜。

福斯特的投球最后使英格兰队获胜。

daydream

18.18 A **daydream** is pleasant thoughts that make you forget about the present.
She stared out of the window, lost in a <u>daydream</u>.

白日梦；幻想；空想

她凝视窗外，沉浸在幻想之中。

18.19 If someone **daydreams**, he spends time thinking about something pleasant, especially when he should be

空想；做白日梦

比较汉语中的**黄粱美梦**。

doing something more serious.
I would spend hours <u>daydreaming</u> about a house of my own.
我常常一连几个小时幻想自己有一所房子。

day job
18.20 A **day job** is the paid work that someone normally does.
日常的有薪工作；（白天的）正职

If you say **don't give up the day job** to someone, you tell him that he should continue doing what he is used to, rather than trying something new which he is likely to fail at.
别放弃白天的正职（别放弃老本行去尝试没有把握的新事物）

So you want to be a writer? Well my advice is, <u>don't give up the day job</u>.
这么说你想成为一个作家了？得了，我劝你不要放弃老本行。

day-to-day
18.21 **Day-to-day** jobs or activities are ones that you do every day as a normal part of your life.
日常的

the <u>day-to-day</u> running of the company
公司的日常管理

hour
18.22 An **hour** is a period of time that consists of 60 minutes.
小时

Hour is used metaphorically to talk about a particular point in history or in someone's life or career.
（历史、人生或事业的）某一时刻

This was often thought of as the country's finest <u>hours</u>.
一般认为这是该国最美好的一段时光。

She thought her last <u>hour</u> had come.
她以为她生命的最后时刻到了。

We have lived through our country's darkest <u>hour</u>.
我们经历了我们国家最不幸的时期。

18.23 Something **of the hour** is the most important or popular at the present time.
目前最重要的；目前最受欢迎的

the issues <u>of the hour</u>
当前的问题

hourly
18.24 If you do something **hourly**, you
每小时一次地

do it once every hour.
If you say a situation changes **hourly**, you mean it changes often or all the time.
The situation is changing hourly.

经常；一直
比较汉语的**瞬息万变**。
局势一直在变化。

infancy
18.25 **Infancy** is the time when you are a baby or a very young child.
Something that is **in its infancy** has only just started to develop.
Tourism on the island is still very much in its infancy.

婴儿期；幼儿期

在初级阶段；在早期
该岛的旅游业在很大程度上仍处于初级阶段。

minute
18.26 A **minute** is a period of 60 seconds. You can refer to a very short time as **a minute**.
It only takes a minute to make a salad.
18.27 You can use **by the minute** to refer to something that is changing or developing very quickly.
We became more annoyed by the minute.
18.28 **Not for a/one minute** is used in negative statements for emphasizing what you are saying.
Don't think for a moment that I'll forgive you for this.
18.29 Something **up to the minute** is fashionable and modern or having the latest information.
Her styles are always up to the minute.
The traffic reports are up to the minute.

分；分钟
一会儿；一会儿的工夫

只要一会儿就能做好色拉。
很快地

我们一下子变得愈发恼怒。
根本不；一点儿也不；绝不

绝不要以为我会就此原谅你。

时髦的，紧跟时尚的；包含最新信息的，时时更新的

她的装束总是非常时髦。
交通信息报道是最新的。

moment
18.30 A **moment** is a very short period of time.
Moment is used metaphorically to talk about a particular occasion or a time for

片刻；瞬间

时机；机遇；时光；做某事的时刻

doing something.
I'm waiting for the right <u>moment</u> to tell him the bad news.
That was one of the happiest <u>moments</u> of my life.

18.31 You can use **not for a/one moment** to emphasize that something is definitely not true, or that you would definitely not do or say something.
I have <u>not for a moment</u> suggested that you should leave.

18.32 Something such as a person, a job, or an issue **of the moment** is famous, important and talked about a lot now.
She's the fashion designer <u>of the moment</u>.

month

18.33 A **month** is period of about four weeks.
You can refer to a long time as **months**.
It'll take <u>months</u> to finish the work on the house.

night

18.34 A **night** is the time of darkness between one day and the next.

You can refer to a period of great sadness, failure etc. as **night**.
the dark <u>night</u> of the soul

nightmare

18.35 A **nightmare** is a dream that is very frightening or unpleasant.
Nightmare is used to talk about an experience that is very frightening and unpleasant, or difficult to deal with.
Heavy rain made playing conditions an

我得找个适当的时机告诉他这个坏消息。
那是我一生中最快乐的一段时光。

决不；从来没有

我从来没有暗示过你该离开。

红极一时的；盛行一时的；广为谈论的

她是当前最红的时装设计师。

一个月
参见 3.80
很长一段时间；数月
要完成房子的整修工作将需要很长一段时间。

夜；夜晚
汉语用**夜长梦多**比喻时间拖长了，事情可能发生不利的变化。
悲伤时期；挫败时期；黑暗时期
心灵的伤痛期

噩梦；梦魇

可怕的经历；难以处理之事；噩梦；困境

大雨将比赛条件搞得一团糟。

absolute <u>nightmare</u>.
The new tax has been a bureaucratic <u>nightmare</u>.
The situation on the roads that day was every driver's worst <u>nightmare</u>.
If this computer system fails, this could turn into a <u>nightmare</u> scenario.

新税已经变成了政府部门无法摆脱的困境。

那天的路况是每个司机的梦魇。

如果计算机系统崩溃，情况将异常糟糕。

second

18.36 A **second** is an extremely short period of time that is one of 60 parts in a minute.

You can refer to an extremely short period of time as **a second** or **seconds**.

Just give me <u>a second</u> to put my coat on.
The computer crashed <u>seconds</u> later.

秒

瞬间；片刻

就给我一点儿时间让我穿上大衣。
计算机一下子就瘫痪了。

time

18.37 **Time** is the quality that you measure using a clock.

You can refer to a period in history as a **time**.

Not since Roman <u>times</u> had a single nation been so powerful.

时间

（历史）时期；时代

自罗马时代以来，还没有一个国家如此强大。

year

18.38 A **year** is a period of 12 months.

You can refer to a very long time as **years**.

It wasn't until <u>years</u> later that I realized how foolish I'd been.
He hasn't been back to the country <u>for years</u>.

18.39 You can refer to a particular period of time in history as **years**.

Conditions were very different in the postwar <u>years</u>.

18.40 You can use **not** or **never in a**

年

很久；多年

直到很久以后，我才意识到我有多愚蠢。
他已经好多年没有回到那个国家了。

（历史上的）年代，时代

战后的情况完全不一样。

（用于强调）决不

million years to emphasize that you think something will not happen or is not true.

Column 18

This column is adopted to help understand some metaphorical expressions of **time** that are unique to Chinese.

日积月累	accumulate over a long period
日久见人心	it takes time to know a person
日久天长	after a considerable period of time
日理万机	be occupied with a myriad of state affairs
日暮穷途	approaching the end of one's days
日新月异	change with each passing day
日以继夜	round the clock
日月如梭	time flies
天长地久	forever
朝不保夕	be in a precarious state
朝令夕改	make unpredictable changes in policy
朝秦暮楚	be quick to switch sides
朝三暮四	blow hot and cold
朝思暮想	yearn day and night
朝夕相处	be together from morning to night
只争朝夕	race against time
指日可待	be just around the corner
积年累月	year after year

19 Space and Container

above

19.1 If someone or something is **above** another, the former is at a higher level than the latter or directly over it.
Above is used metaphorically for saying that something is higher than other things in amount or standard.
The company's profits were 23% above the previous year's.
In most subjects the students scored well above average.
19.2 **Above** is used for saying that something is considered more valuable or more important than other things.
We value our independence above anything that you can offer us.
He will be remembered above all as a loving husband and family man.
Above all else, the government must keep the promises it has made.
Don't let them take the children away—I fear that above anything.
19.3 If you are **above** a particular type of behaviour, you are such a morally good person that you would not behave in that way.
Jack was cheating? I thought he was above that sort of thing.
Lady Travers was not above helping

在……上方
比较汉语中的上乘、上等、上品、上策等。
高于；多于；大于；优于

公司的利润比前一年高出23%。

在大部分科目中，这些学生的得分高于平均分。
（在价值或重要性方面）先于

我们认为独立自主比你能提供给我们的任何东西都更有价值。
他首先是作为一个深情的丈夫和喜欢家庭生活的人而被人所铭记。
首先，政府必须恪守它所作出的承诺。

不要让他们把孩子带走。那是我最怕的。
（道德高尚得）不屑于；不至于

杰克在作弊？我想他不至于干那种事。
必要时，特拉弗斯夫人会屈尊帮着做

with the housework when necessary.
家务。

19.4 **Above and beyond** is used for saying apart from something, or outside the normal range of something.
除去；在正常之外

Rescue teams had worked <u>above and beyond</u> the call of duty during hurricane.
飓风时期，救援队所做的远远超过了其职责的要求。

19.5 If you **get above yourself**, you start to think that you are more important than you really are.
自命不凡；自高自大

Ever since they made her assistant manager, she's been <u>getting above herself</u>.
自从他们让她当了助理经理后，她就开始自命不凡了。

ahead

19.6 Something **ahead** is in front of you.
在前方；在前面

Ahead is used when saying what will happen in the future.
在将来；未来；今后

We have a busy day <u>ahead</u> of us.
我们将迎来忙碌的一天。

19.7 If you **look**, **think** or **plan ahead**, you think about the future or plan for the future.
展望、考虑或计划（未来）

<u>Looking ahead</u> to next summer, where would you like to go?
计划一下明年夏天，你想去哪？

19.8 Ideas, achievements etc. that are **ahead of** others have made more progress or are more advanced.
领先

The Russians were now <u>ahead of</u> them in space research.
俄罗斯人目前在太空研究方面领先于他们。

The technology was far <u>ahead of</u> anything available in the West.
这种技术远远领先于西方现有的任何技术。

His ideas were way <u>ahead of</u> his time.
他的思想远远超过了他那个年代。

angle

19.9 An **angle** is the space between two lines or surfaces that join, measured in degrees.
角；夹角

Angle is used metaphorically to talk about a particular way of thinking about something.
We're looking for a new <u>angle</u> for our next advertising campaign.

观点；立场；角度

我们正探索从一个崭新的角度去进行下次广告活动。

beyond

19.10 If one thing is **beyond** another thing, the former is on or to the further side of the latter.

越过；远于

Beyond is used for saying that something is outside the limits of a subject, quality, or activity.

超出……的范围

Our knowledge does not extend much <u>beyond</u> these few facts.

除了这几个事实，其他我们知道的就很少了。

Scott pushed his men <u>beyond</u> the limits of human endurance.

斯科特把他的手下逼迫到了忍无可忍的地步。

19.11 **Beyond** can be used for saying that something cannot be done.

非……力所能及

The situation is already <u>beyond</u> our control.

我们已经控制不了局面。

Martin was living in Brazil, <u>beyond</u> the reach of the British police.

马丁住在巴西，英国警察鞭长莫及。

The centre of Manchester has changed <u>beyond</u> all recognition.

曼彻斯特的中心已经变得认不出来了。

19.12 Something that is **beyond doubt** or **dispute** is so certain that it can not be doubted or argued about.

无疑地；确实地

Brady's guilt had been proved <u>beyond doubt</u>.

布雷迪已被证明确实有罪。

19.13 If something **is beyond somebody**, it is difficult for him to understand or deal with.

对于某人来说难以理解；对于某人来说很难处理

The system <u>was</u> unusually complicated and completely <u>beyond the new trainees</u>.

这个系统异常复杂，对于新学员来说完全无法理解。

It's <u>beyond me</u> why anyone should want

我不理解为什么人人都想嫁给他。

to marry him.

bottleneck

19.14 A **bottleneck** is a place where a road is narrow or blocked, causing traffic to move very slowly.
You can use **bottleneck** to refer to a specific problem that cause delays to the whole process.
bottlenecks in production, resulting from a lack of spare parts

狭窄路段；瓶颈路段
汉语用**瓶颈**来比喻事情进行中容易发生阻碍的关键环节。
妨碍进展的事；障碍；瓶颈

由于缺少零件而导致的生产障碍

bottom

19.15 The **bottom** is the lowest part of something.
Bottom is used metaphorically to refer to the lowest level or position, in status or success.
a football team that is close to the bottom of the league tables
She started at the *bottom* and ended up running the company.

底部；下端；末尾
比较汉语中的**摸底**。
最低水平；底层位置

接近联盟名次表最末尾的一支足球队

她从最底层干起，最后管理了公司。

19.16 You can use **at bottom** when explaining the basic cause or nature of something.
Most of these arguments are, at bottom, motivated by a fear of change.

基本上；实质上

这些争论的大部分实质上是出于对变革的恐惧。

19.17 If something **is at the bottom of** another thing, the former is the true cause of the latter.
His jealousy is at the bottom of most of our problems.

是某事的真正原因

他的妒忌是我们大部分问题的真正原因。

19.18 If you **get to the bottom of** something, you find out the true cause or explanation of a bad situation.
No one has really got to the bottom of this problem.

弄清起因；挖出祸根

不曾有人把这个问题弄个水落石出。

19.19 You can use **the bottom line** to tell someone what the most important part of a situation is, or what the most important thing to consider is.
The bottom line is that he lied to Parliament.
We have to find out what the terrorists' bottom line is.

bottomless
19.20 A **bottomless** well, lake or gorge etc. is extremely deep and seeming to have no bottom.
You can use **a bottomless pit** (of something) to refer to a thing or situation which seems to have no limits or seems never to end.
There isn't a bottomless pit of money for public spending.
the bottomless pit of his sorrow

broad
19.21 A road, river or part of someone's body etc. that is **broad** is wide.

You can say something is **broad** if it includes many different kinds of things or people.
I meet a broad range of people in my daily life.
Our radio station plays a broad spectrum of popular music.
The party is now struggling to maintain a broad political base.
Tropical diseases fall into two broad categories.

最基本的事实（或问题）；要旨；底线

最基本的问题是他对议会撒谎。

我们得了解恐怖分子的底线是什么。

无底的；极深的；深不可测的
汉语中的没底也可用来表示没有把握，没有信心。如：心里没底。
无限度的事物；无休止的状况；无底洞

公共开支并非用之不尽的。

他无尽的悲哀

宽的；广的；阔的
汉语中，宽有使松缓之意，如：宽心、宽限；也有不严厉、不苛求的意思，如：宽容；还可表示宽裕、宽绰。
广泛的；广大的

我在日常生活中遇到各种各样的人。

我们的广播电台播放各种流行音乐。

该党现在正努力保持广泛的政治基础。

热带疾病分成两大类。

19.22 A **broad** strategy, aim or outline etc. is expressed in a general way, without many details. 概括的；粗略的

We need to define a broad strategy for further development. 我们需要为将来的发展确立一个粗略的战略。

We support the broad aims which underlie this Bill. 我们支持构成这一议案基础的大致目标。

This chapter can only give a broad outline of the subject. 这一章只能给出这个主题的大致轮廓。

You made too many broad generalizations about people. 你对人们作了太多粗略的判断。

19.23 If there is **broad** agreement about something, most people agree about it in a general way, even if they do not agree on all its details. 普遍的；大体上的

There is now a broad consensus that the government was right about it. 现在舆论大体上认为政府在这件事上是对的。

19.24 **In broad daylight** is used for saying that a shocking or criminal event happens during the day, when it can easily be seen. 在光天化日之下

They'd robbed the bank in broad daylight. 他们在光天化日之下抢劫了银行。

broaden

19.25 To **broaden** is to become wider or to make something wider. 变宽；加宽；使变阔

If you make something include more things or people, you **broaden** it. 使扩大

If something starts including more things or people, it **broadens**. 扩大

The scope of the book has been broadened to include the history of Eastern Europe. 书的范围有所扩大，包括了东欧历史。

The protest has broadened to encompass other demands. 抗议扩大到包括其他要求。

19.26 If something **broadens** your 开阔视野

horizon, it makes you see a wider range of opportunities and choices.

Spending a year working in the city helped to <u>broaden his horizons</u>. 在城市工作的一年拓宽了他的视野。

19.27 If something **broadens your mind**, it helps you understand the world and make you more able to accept other people's ideas and beliefs. 开阔心胸

Few would disagree that travel <u>broadens the mind</u>. 很少有人会对旅行有助于开阔眼界持有异议。

19.28 If your smile **broadens**, you start to smile in a more obvious way. （笑容）绽开，变明显

If your accent **broadens**, you start to speak with a more noticeable accent. （口音）变重

As he grew angrier, his accent <u>broadened</u>. 他越生气，口音就越重。

central

19.29 The **central** part of a place is the area in the middle. 中心的；在中间的

A **central** idea, aspect, system etc. is one of the main ones that is used or needed. 主要的；首要的

This organization occupies a <u>central</u> role in the development of US economic policy. 这个组织对美国经济政策的发展起着重要作用。

Political life has changed since broadcasting became a <u>central</u> feature of our lives. 自从广播成为我们生活中的焦点后，政治生活就发生了变化。

Listening skills are of <u>central</u> importance to a child's development. 听力技巧对于一个孩子的发展非常重要。

19.30 **Central** control comes from one main organization that usually tells a lot of smaller organizations what they should do. 起领导作用的；为首的

The system is subject to massive and increasing <u>central</u> control. 该制度受制于庞大且日益增强的中央控制。

centre

19.31 A **centre** is the middle of a space or area.

You can use **centre** to refer to an important place for a particular activity.

attempts to make Prague a cultural <u>centre</u>

The town is a major <u>centre</u> for the American book publishing trade.

19.32 **The centre of activities** or **things** is the main area where something is happening.

She rented a flat in town to be at <u>the centre of things</u>.

19.33 **Centre** is used metaphorically to refer to the main subject or cause of something.

an issue that has been the <u>centre</u> of debate in this country recently

He's very shy and hates being the <u>centre of attention</u>.

The prime minister is at the <u>centre</u> of a political row over leaked Cabinet documents.

19.34 If something **centres around** someone or something, or you centre something around him/it, he/it is its main subject of attention or interest. Similar phrases include **centre round**, **centre on** and **centre upon**.

The debate <u>centred around</u> the issue of finance.

State occasion always <u>centred around</u> the king.

（空间或区域的）中央；中间

（某一活动的）中心（地区）

为使布拉格成为文化中心所作的努力

该镇是美国图书出版业的一个主要中心。

活动中心；活动集中的地方

她在城里的繁华地段租了一套公寓。

主题；焦点；中心

近年来成为该国辩论焦点的议题

他很害羞，不喜欢成为人们注意力的中心。

首相成了由内阁文件泄密而引起的一场政治风波的中心人物。

围绕；以……为中心

辩论是围绕财政问题展开的。

国务活动总是以国王为中心。

circle

19.35 A **circle** is a completely round flat shape. 圆；圆形

Circle is used to refer to a group of people who are connected because they have the same interests, jobs, etc. （相同兴趣、职业等的人形成的）圈子；阶层；界

They have a large circle of friends and acquaintances. 他们的交友圈范围很广。

He began to move in the scientific circles centred round Sir Charles Cavendish. 他开始进入以查尔斯·卡文迪什爵士为中心的科学界。

The bank's failure sent shock waves through international financial circles. 这家银行的破产在国际金融界引起了震荡。

19.36 If a situation **comes**, **goes**, or **turns full circle**, it becomes the same again as it was at the beginning. 循环；又回到原处
汉语用兜圈子比喻不照直说话，如：别跟我兜圈子，有话照直说。

close

19.37 Something that is **close** is near in space or time. （在时间、空间上）接近的

If you are **close to** something or **close to** doing something, you are almost in a particular state. 几乎；可能

By the end of the race he was close to collapse. 到赛跑结束时，他几乎都要瘫倒了。

We're closer to signing a contract after today's meeting. 今天的会议之后，我们很快就要签订合同。

19.38 If two people are **close**, they like or love each other very much. 亲密的；亲近的；密切的

Jamal and I have been close friends since we were six. 我和贾梅尔从6岁起就是密友。

She's close to both her parents. 她和父母的关系都很亲密。

He is one of the prime minister's closest advisers. 他是首相最亲信的顾问之一。

19.39 A **close** look, examination, scrutiny etc. is careful and thorough. 细致的；严密的；周密的

On _closer_ examination the painting proved to be a fake.
经过更加仔细的查看，那幅画被证实是件赝品。

The local police kept a _close_ eye on his activities.
当地警方对他的一举一动进行了严密监视。

19.40 A **close** competition, election etc. is one that is won by only a small amount or distance.
旗鼓相当的；势均力敌的

The next election will be a _close_ contest.
下一次选举将是一次势均力敌的较量。

Irvine won the race, with Schumacher a _close_ second.
埃尔文赢得了比赛，紧随其后获得第二名的是舒马赫。

The result is going to be too _close_ to call.
双方实力非常接近，因此结果无法预料。

closed

19.41 If a door, window, lid etc. is **closed**, it is covering an open area, passage, or hole.
关闭的；封闭的

A **closed** society, person etc. is one that is unwilling to accept outside influences or new ideas.
封闭的；闭关自守的；不愿接受新思想的

a _closed_ society
封闭的社会

You can't approach these kind of situations with a _closed_ mind.
你不能以僵化的心态对待这种局势。

deep

19.42 If something is **deep**, it goes a long way from the top to the bottom.
（从顶部向下）深的
比较汉语中的*深谙*、*深奥*、*深层*、*深沉*等。

A **deep** feeling or emotion is very strong.
（感情）深厚的；强烈的

I do feel a very _deep_ sympathy for them all.
我深深地同情他们所有的人。

19.43 Trouble, division, recession etc. that is **deep** is extreme and serious.
极度的；严重的

He's in _deep_ trouble.
他陷入极度困境之中。

The affair had exposed _deep_ divisions
这件事暴露出党内的严重分歧。

within the party.
19.44 A **deep** sound is low.
I recognized George's <u>deep</u> voice on the other end of the phone.
19.45 A **deep** colour is dark and strong.
a beautiful <u>deep</u> red
19.46 If you give a **deep** sigh, breath etc., you take in or give out a lot of air.
He looked at Rose and gave a <u>deep</u> sigh.
19.47 A **deep** sleep is one that you do not wake up easily.
She fell into a <u>deep</u> sleep.
19.48 If a person is **deep**, he hides his real feelings and opinions.
She's always been a <u>deep</u> one, trusting no one.
19.49 Something that is **deep** involves serious thoughts, ideas, or feelings.
We had a very <u>deep</u> conversation about love and death.
19.50 If you are **deep in something**, you are fully involved in an activity or a state.
He is often so <u>deep in his books</u> that he forgets to eat.
The firm ended up <u>deep in debt</u>.
He was <u>deep in thought</u>, oblivious to all the noise around him.
19.51 If you are **in** or **into deep water**, you are in a difficult or serious situation.
I was beginning to feel that I was getting <u>into deep water</u>.
19.52 If you **are thrown in at the deep end**, you are made to deal with something difficult without being prepared

（声音）低沉的
我听出电话另一端乔治低沉的声音。
（颜色）深的
漂亮的深红色
（呼吸）深的

他看着罗茜，深深地叹了口气。
酣睡的

她沉沉地睡去了。
深沉的；摸不透的；城府深的

她这个人一直城府很深，对谁也不相信。
（某事）严肃的

我们进行了一次关于爱与死的严肃交谈。
专心；全神贯注；埋头做某事

他常常专心于读书以致忘了吃饭。

这家公司最后是债台高筑。
他陷入沉思中，没注意到周围的喧闹声。
陷入困境；惹上大麻烦

我开始觉得我正在陷入困境。

（在毫无准备的情况下）被迫解决难题；仓促上阵

for it.
Junior hospital doctors are <u>thrown in at the deep end</u> in their first job.
医院的初级医生们开始工作时会遇上未曾料到的困难。

19.53 If you know or feel something **deep down**, you do know or feel it, although you try to pretend that you do not.
在内心深处；在心底

<u>Deep down</u> I knew that Caroline was right.
我在内心深处知道卡罗琳是对的。

19.54 If you have a particular quality **deep down**, you have that quality, although you try to keep it hidden from other people.
事实上；实际上

<u>Deep down</u> he's really a very thoughtful person.
事实上他确实是一个考虑非常周到的人。

depth

19.55 The **depth** of something is the distance from the top to the bottom of it.
深度；纵深
参见 19.42

Depth is used metaphorically to refer to the quality of knowing or understanding a lot of details about something.
渊博；深刻；洞察力；（想法等的）深度

I was impressed by the <u>depth</u> of his understanding.
他那深刻的理解令我印象深刻。

The newspaper is proud of the <u>depth</u> of its coverage of international affairs.
这家报纸以自己对国际时事的深度报道而感到自豪。

19.56 The **depth** of something is the deepest, most extreme or serious part of something.
最深处；深渊；极限

She was in the <u>depth</u> of despair.
她处于绝望的深渊。

These latest figures have confirmed the <u>depth</u> of the economic recession.
这些最新数字证实了这次经济衰退的严重性。

19.57 If you do something **in depth**, you do it in a very detailed way and give a lot of information.
详细地；深入地

I haven't looked at the report <u>in depth</u>
我还没有细看这份报告。

yet.

19.58 If you feel **out of your depth**, you are in a situation that you cannot deal with because it is too difficult or dangerous.
He felt totally <u>out of his depth</u> in his new job.

非某人所能理解；为某人力所不及

他感到根本不能胜任这份新工作。

dimension

19.59 A **dimension** is the length, height, width, depth or diameter of something.
Dimension is used metaphorically to refer to an aspect, or way of looking at or thinking about.
The strikes had now taken on an important political <u>dimension</u>.
Doing voluntary work has added a whole new <u>dimension</u> to my life.

维；长度；高度；宽度；深度；直径

方面；侧面

这些罢工现在都带有重大的政治色彩。
做志愿者工作已为我的生活增添了全新的内容。

distant

19.60 Something that is **distant** is far away in space or time.
Someone who is **distant** seems unfriendly or does not show his feelings.
Pat sounded very cold and <u>distant</u> on the phone.
19.61 A **distant** look, smile etc. shows you are thinking about something else.
There was a <u>distant</u> look in her eyes; her mind was obviously on something else.

遥远的；远处的；久远的

不友好的；冷淡的；疏远的

从电话里听起来帕特非常冷淡和疏远。

心不在焉的；恍惚的；出神的

她的眼里流露出心不在焉的神情，显然是在想着别的什么事儿。

down

19.62 To go **down** is to go to or towards a lower place or position.
Down is used to show that the amount or strength of something is lower, or that there is less activity.

向下；往下；在下面
参见 20.3
（数量、力量、活动等）减少；减弱；降低

The government is determined to bring <u>down</u> unemployment. 政府决心减少失业。

House prices have come <u>down</u> to a more reasonable level. 房价已经降到了一个更加合理的水平。

The storm had died <u>down</u> by evening. 暴风雨到晚上就变小了。

19.63 **Down** is used for saying that someone has an illness. 病倒

Poor Susan went <u>down</u> with flu just before Christmas. 可怜的苏珊就在圣诞节前感冒病倒了。

19.64 If you say someone is **down**, you mean he is unhappy or sad. 悲哀的；沮丧的；情绪低落的

He's been feeling very <u>down</u> since his wife went away. 他的妻子离开后他一直闷闷不乐。

All these problems are getting her <u>down</u>. 这些问题弄得她很不开心。

19.65 If you say a computer is **down**, it is not working. 停机；停止工作

The system was <u>down</u> all morning. 系统整个上午都无法运行。

front

19.66 The **front** of something is the surface of it that faces forward. 前面；正面

Front is used metaphorically to refer to a particular aspect of a situation. 方面

His main problems were in maths and science, but he has made progress on both <u>fronts</u>. 他的主要问题出在数学和自然科学上，但这两方面他都已经有所进步。

19.67 You can use **front** to refer to an organization or activity that exists to hide an illegal or secret one. （非法或秘密活动的）掩护物；幌子

They kept a shop as a <u>front</u> for dealing in stolen goods. 他们开了家商店为销赃进行掩护。

19.68 You can use **front** to refer to behaviour that is not sincere because you want to hide your real feelings. 假装的样子；伪装

He always pretended he didn't care but we knew it was just a <u>front</u>. 他总是一副满不在乎的样子，但我们知道那只是他装出来的。

She's putting on a brave front, but she's really very worried.
她表面上一副勇敢的样子，但其实她真的很担心。

frontier

19.69 The **frontier** is the outer edge of a country or area that is the furthest point where people have started to live and build towns.

边疆

You can use **the frontiers** to refer to the most advanced or recent ideas about something.

汉语中，**前沿**的本意为防御阵地最前面的边沿，用来比喻科学研究中最新或领先的领域。

（思想的）前沿；（知识的）新领域

Their work was on the frontiers of science.
他们的工作是有关尖端科学的。

We are dedicated to experimentation, to pushing back the frontiers.
我们致力于试验，致力于开拓新的领域。

full

19.70 Something that is **full** has no empty space.

满的；充满的；满是……的

Full is used metaphorically to talk about having or containing a large number or amount of something.

（有）大量的；（有）许多的；丰富的
比较汉语中的**满不在乎、满怀、满口、满心**等。

Life is full of coincidences.
生活中巧合很多。

She was full of admiration for the care she had received.
她对所受到的关怀照顾赞叹不已。

He was full of his new job and everything he'd been doing.
他滔滔不绝地谈他的新工作和所做的一切。

19.71 A **full** day, life etc. is busy.

忙碌的；繁忙的

Her life was too full to find time or hobbies.
她的生活太忙，无暇顾及业余爱好。

further

19.72 If you go **further**, you go a longer distance.

较远；更远

Further is used for saying that something exists or happens more, or to a greater degree.

进一步；在更大程度上
汉语中类似的隐喻表达方式包括**差得远、远远超过**等。

Her health may worsen even further if 她如果不动手术，健康状况会更加恶

she doesn't have the operation.
The party was moving *further and further* away from its socialist principles.
化。
该政党越来越偏离其社会主义原则。

high
19.73 Something that is **high** is large in size from the top to the ground.
A **high** amount, number, or level is large, or larger than usual.
This is an area of <u>high</u> unemployment.
The risk of the disease spreading is <u>high</u>.

高的
汉语中的**高**可用来表示等级在上的。
数量大的；高的
这是个高失业率地区。
这种疾病传染的风险很高。

19.74 A **high** standard, quality etc. is very good.
They're known for the <u>high</u> quality of their products.

极佳的；出色的
他们以其产品的高质量而著称。

19.75 A **high** opinion, regard, praise etc. shows strong approval of someone or something.
I have the <u>highest</u> regard for him.

极佳的；出色的

我最敬重他。

19.76 If someone or something has a **high** position, status, rank etc., he/it is more important than the others.
Both parties are giving a <u>high</u> priority to education in their campaigns.

重要的；高级的

在总统竞选中两党都把教育置于优先考虑。

19.77 You can use **high** to refer to a feeling of great happiness or excitement.
They've experienced both the <u>highs</u> and the lows of married life.

幸福感；兴奋感

他们经历了婚姻生活的种种幸福和痛苦。

horizon
19.78 The **horizon** is the line in the distance where the sky seems to meet the earth.

地平线

Horizons are used metaphorically to refer to the limits of your experience.
Travelling has really helped to expand

阅历的范围；眼界

旅行确实有利于开阔她的视野。

her <u>horizons</u>.
19.79 Something **on the horizon** seems likely to happen in the future.
I've got some job possibilities <u>on the horizon</u>.
 See also **broadens horizon: 19.26**

即将来临的

我找工作已经有点眉目了。

inner
19.80 The **inner** part of something is inside or further towards the centre of it.
Inner thoughts or feelings are ones that you feel strongly but do not always show to other people.
Read closely and you will discover an <u>inner</u> meaning to her words.
19.81 You can refer to a small group of people who have a lot of power or influence within a larger group as **inner circle**.
the <u>inner circle</u> of the Imperial Court

内部的；里面的；接近中心的

内心的；个人的；隐秘的

仔细阅读，你会发现她言辞中的隐秘含义。

核心集团；核心组织

皇家法庭的核心集团

inside
19.82 To be **inside** is to be within the inner part or area of something.
If something happens **inside** you, or inside your head or mind, it is part of what you think and feel, especially when you do not express it.
He was silent, but Elizabeth could sense the anger burning <u>inside</u> him.
I knew how stubborn he could be once he'd got an idea <u>inside</u> his head.
19.83 Someone who is **on the side** works in the organization or is a member of the group that you are talking about.
If you want to know what is really happening in a company, ask the people

内部的；里面的

在内心；在心中

他沉默不语，但伊丽莎白能感觉到他正怒火中烧。

我知道他头脑中一旦有了主意就会变得多么固执。

在（组织或集团）内部

如果你想了解某公司内真实发生的事，就要问在公司内部工作的人。

on the side.

19.84 If you **know** someone or something **inside out**, you know him/it very well.
He _knows_ that computer program _inside out_.

对……了如指掌

他对那个电脑程序了如指掌。

19.85 If you **turn** something **inside out**, you search a place very thoroughly and quickly so that you make a mess, or you cause large changes.
The police _turned the place inside out_ looking for the stolen money.
The new manager _turns the old systems inside out_.

把某处翻得底朝天；引起巨大变化

警方为寻找被盗的钱财把这个地方翻了个底朝天。

新任经理对旧体制进行了彻底的改革。

low

19.86 Something that is **low** is small in size from the top to the ground.

矮的；低的

A **low** amount, number, or level is small, or smaller than usual.
The bigger shops are able to keep their prices _low_.

数量小的；低的

大商店能够把价格压低。

19.87 A **low** standard, quality etc. is very bad.
The standard of housing in some areas is very _low_.

（质量或水平）低的

某些地区的居住条件很差。

19.88 Someone who is **low** feels unhappy and does not have much hope or confidence.
It was unlike her to be in such _low_ spirits.
It's the kind of illness that leaves you feeling _low_ for a few days.

不快活的；消沉的

她情绪如此低落，这可不像她。

正是这种病让你萎靡不振了好几天。

19.89 **Low** is metaphorically used about someone's negative attitudes.
Sandra's problem is she has really _low_ expectations.

（态度）消极的

桑德拉的问题是她的期望太低。

Morale is really <u>low</u> in the office.

19.90 You can refer to a bad time in your life as a **low**.

He's experienced all the highs and <u>lows</u> of an actor's life.

办公室里的士气低落。

（人生的）低谷

一个演员一生中的起起落落他都经历过了。

middle

19.91 If something is in the **middle,** it is nearest to the centre and furthest from the edge, top, end etc.

A **middle** way of doing something is a way of doing it that is not as extreme as two other ways of doing it.

The party is seeking to find a <u>middle</u> way between extreme right-wing and left-wing policies.

中部（的）；中间（的）；中央（的）

中庸的；折中的

该党派正在寻求走一条既不极左也不极右的中间路线。

narrow

19.92 Something that is **narrow** is small in width, especially when compared to how high or how long it is.

Narrow is used metaphorically to talk about being limited in range, thinking, meaning etc.

We are left with a relatively <u>narrow</u> range of options.

The book takes a rather <u>narrow</u> view of what we mean by civilization.

the court's <u>narrow</u> definition of a criminal act

19.93 A **narrow** victory, escape, defeat etc. is achieved with difficulty, in a way that shows how close the result is.

Our resolution passed with the <u>narrowest</u> possible majority.

狭窄的；狭长的；狭小的

（范围）有限的；（思想）狭隘的；狭义的；精确的

我们只余下相对有限的选择范围。

这本书对于我们所指的文明采取了一种非常狭隘的观点。

法庭对犯罪行为的精确定义

勉强的；（成败）差距很小的

我们的决议以微弱多数票获得通过。

open

19.94 An **open** space or area is not

空旷的；开阔的；无遮盖的

covered or enclosed, or does not have many buildings, trees etc. in or on it.
Open is used about someone who is honest and does not keep things secret.

坦率的；坦诚的

Everyone in the group is honest and <u>open</u>.

组里的每个人都很友善而坦率。

The president promised an <u>open</u> dialogue.

总统许诺进行一次开诚布公的对话。

He has always been <u>open</u> about his drinking problem.

他对自己的酗酒问题一直很坦率。

19.95 Something that is **open** is not hidden or secret.

公开的；不隐藏的

Their relationship has deteriorated to the point of <u>open</u> hostility.

他们的关系已经恶化到公开敌对的地步。

19.96 If you **are open to** something, you are willing to consider many different possibilities.

愿意考虑的

I have some ideas about where to go, but I <u>am open to</u> suggestion.

对于去哪儿我有几个想法，但我乐意接受各种建议。

19.97 **Open** is used for saying a situation that has at least two results.

尚未决定的；悬而未决的

His contract keeps <u>open</u> the possibilities that he might return to the series.

他的合同为他重回剧中演出留下了余地。

Shall we leave it <u>open</u> for now, and decide at the meeting?

我们现在不作决定，到会上再决定好吗？

parallel

19.98 Lines that are **parallel** are the same distance apart at every point along their whole length.

平行的

Parallel is metaphorically used to talk about being similar and happening at the same way.

同时发生的；不约而同的

There will be <u>parallel</u> announcements from both governments.

双方政府将会同时发表公告。

<u>Parallel</u> efforts by many groups aim to research how to use the Internet more

许多团体不约而同地打算研究如何更成功地利用因特网。

successfully.

19.99 You can refer to similar features between two or more things as **parallels**. 相似之处；共同点

There are many parallels between the two attacks. 两次袭击有许多相似之处。

The parallels with developments in the software industry are clear for all to see. 与软件产业的相似之处显而易见。

A number of books at that time tried to draw parallels between brains and computers. 当时有一些书试图把人脑和计算机进行比较。

19.100 If someone or something has **no parallel** or is **without parallel**, he/it is greater, better, worse etc. than anyone or anything else. 无与伦比的

There is no parallel in modern history for the military superiority the United States currently has. 美国当前的军事优势在现代史上还无人可比。

Woods is a golfer without parallel in terms of talent. 伍兹打高尔夫球的天赋无与伦比。

19.101 If two or more things happen **in parallel**, they happen at the same time and are connected. 同时；同步

Advertising has developed in parallel with modern industry and the mass media. 广告一直以来都与现代工业和大众传媒同步发展。

remote

19.102 Something that is **remote** is far away in space or time. （空间或时间）遥远的

If a chance or possibility of something happening is **remote**, it is not very likely to happen. 不可能的

You have only the remotest chance of winning the lottery. 中彩票的机会是微乎其微的。

The possibility of kidnapping is <u>remote</u>, but be careful.
被绑架的机会是很小，但还是谨慎为妙。

I don't have the <u>remotest</u> idea what you're talking about.
你在说什么我一点儿都不懂。

19.103 If you say someone or his behavior is **remote**, you mean that he is not friendly or not interested in other people.
冷淡的；不很友好的；孤高的

His eyes were melancholy and <u>remote</u>.
他的眼神哀伤而又漠然。

She is a silent girl, cold and <u>remote</u>.
她是个沉默寡言的姑娘，态度冷漠而孤高。

shallow

19.104 Something that is **shallow** is with only a short distance from the top or surface to the bottom.
浅的

If a person, comment etc. is **shallow**, he/it does not show serious thought, feelings, etc. about something.
浅薄的；肤浅的

His arguments seemed <u>shallow</u> and tedious.
他的论点显得肤浅乏味。

I was too young and <u>shallow</u> to understand love.
那时我太年轻无知，不懂得什么是爱情。

19.105 A **shallow** breathing takes in only small amounts of air.
（呼吸）浅的；微弱的

Her breathing was very <u>shallow</u>.
她的呼吸很微弱。

sphere

19.106 A **sphere** is an object that is round like a ball.
球；球体；球形

Sphere is used metaphorically to refer to a particular area of interest, activity, work etc. that is one of many parts of life.
（兴趣、活动、工作等的）范围

Let's take this debate out of the political <u>sphere</u> and into the public arena.
让我们把辩论从政治范畴转移到公众领域。

Women were beginning to take
妇女们开始担负起家庭之外的责任。

responsibility for things outside the domestic sphere.
19.107 You can use **sphere** to refer to a group in society.
They moved in different cultural spheres.
19.108 A person's, country's, organization's etc. **sphere of influence** is the area where he/it has power to change things.
The economic boom has greatly expanded the US's sphere of influence.

社会阶层

他们生活在不同的文化圈子里。

势力范围；权力范围

经济的增长极大地扩大了美国的势力范围。

spiral
19.109 A **spiral** is a shape that looks like a set of circles inside each other, made by one line curving inside itself.
Spiral is used metaphorically to refer to a process, usually a harmful one, in which something gradually but continuously gets worse or better.
the endless spiral of violence and hatred
a downward economic spiral
19.110 If a situation **spirals**, it gets worse, more violent etc. in a way that cannot be controlled.
Crime has begun to spiral out of control in the capital.
The economic crisis could spiral into a political disaster.
The news sent share prices spiraling down to a five-year low.

螺旋；螺旋形

逐渐加速上升（或下降）

暴力和仇恨无休止的恶性循环
经济的螺旋式下降
不断地恶化

首都的犯罪现象开始急剧增多，到了失控的地步。
经济危机不断加剧会导致政治灾难。
该新闻使股票价格急剧下跌到五年来的最低点。

top
19.111 The **top** is the highest place, point, part, or surface of something.
You can use **the top** to refer to the highest status within a group or organization, or the person in this

顶端；顶部；上端；上面

（团体或组织的）最高职位；处于最高职位者

position.
She started as an administrative assistant and worked her way to <u>the top</u>. 她从行政助理做起，一直做到最高层。

19.112 Something that is **at the top of the list** is of greatest importance. 最重要的；居首位的
Sports were not <u>at the top of the list</u>. 体育运动不是排在第一位的。

19.113 If you do something **from the top to the bottom**, you do it completely and thoroughly. 完全地；彻底地；从头到脚
We cleaned the house <u>from top to bottom</u>. 我们彻底打扫了屋子。

19.114 If a problem or difficult situation **gets on top of** you, you become unable to deal with it effectively. 某事物使某人受不了
Things are really <u>getting on top of</u> me at home. 家里的事情真的越来越让我吃不消了。

up

19.115 To go **up** is to go to or towards a higher place or position. 从下往上地；向上地
Up is used when an amount increases. 上升；增加
Total new car sales were <u>up</u> £3 million over last year. 新汽车销售总额比去年增加了 300 万英镑。
Net advances in August were £1.13 billion, marginally <u>up</u> on July's figure. 8 月份净增 11.3 亿英镑，略多于 7 月份。
Competition between the production groups is hotting <u>up</u> rapidly. 生产小组之间的竞争很快日趋激烈。

19.116 A computer system that is **up** is working properly. （计算机系统）正常工作的
By ten o'clock we had the computers <u>up</u> again after the power cut. 到 10 点钟，我们在断电后又使计算机恢复正常工作了。

19.117 You can use **ups and downs** to refer to the mixture of good and bad experiences that happen in life or in a particular situation or relationship. 沉浮；兴衰；荣辱
汉语用**沉浮**来比喻起落或盛衰消长，如：官海**沉浮**。
The company has had its share of <u>ups</u> 公司经历了兴衰起伏，但现在似乎经

and downs, *but it seems to be doing well now.* 营得很好。

Column 19

This column is adopted to help understand some metaphorical expressions of **space** & **container** that are unique to Chinese.

半半拉拉	incomplete; unfinished
半吊子（半瓶醋）	dabbler; smatterer
半响	a long time; quite a while
饱经沧桑	have experienced many vicissitudes of life
饱经风霜	weather-beaten
饱学之士	an erudite person; a man of learning
饱眼福	enjoy to the full (watching a scene, show, etc.)
鞭辟入里	incisive
不出所料	as expected
不知分寸/进退	lack tact; have no sense of propriety
恶贯满盈	be steeped in evil and deserve damnation
里出外进	irregular; uneven
（行家）里手	expert; old hand
没底	unsure
摸底	know the real situation
内行	be expert at; master; professional
内忧外患	internal disturbance and foreign aggression
内外交困	beset with difficulties both at home and abroad
充耳不闻	go in one ear and out the other
浅尝辄止	stop after gaining a little knowledge
浅显	plain; easy to read and understand
浅谈	brief talk
全才	a versatile person; all-rounder
深入浅出	explain the profound in simple terms
外道（儿）	over-polite
外行	layman; nonprofessional
外柔内刚	outwardly yielding but inwardly firm

外史	unofficial history; informal history
外心	unfaithful intentions
外圆内方	outwardly gentle but inwardly stern; easygoing in manners but strict on matters of principle

20 Movement

climb

20.1 To **climb** means to use your hands and feet to move up, over, down, or across something.
If a temperature, price, or the level of something **climbs**, it becomes higher.
Temperatures <u>climbed</u> into the 90s.
Unemployment <u>has climbed</u> steadily over the past year.

20.2 You can use **climb** to describe the action of moving to a higher level in job, social position, list or competition.

He began working at eighteen, determined to <u>climb</u> the career ladder.
The book <u>climbed</u> steadily to number one on the New York Times bestseller list.

爬，攀爬
汉语用**爬升**来比喻逐步提高。

（气温、价格或水平）增长，上升

气温升高到九十几度。
去年以来失业率稳步上升。

晋升；提高；上升
汉语用**爬坡**来比喻克服困难和阻力，向好的方面努力或向着更高的目标前进。

他18岁开始工作，并下决心要取得事业上的成功。
这本书稳稳上升到《纽约时报》畅销书排行榜的第一位。

dip

20.3 To **dip** means to move down, or to make something move down, usually for just a short time.
If an amount or level **dips**, it becomes less, usually for just a short time.
Public support for the project <u>has dipped</u> sharply.

20.4 You can refer to a reduction in the amount or level of something as a **dip**.
The <u>dip</u> in the share price wiped £36.8

下降；落下；降下
汉语中类似的隐喻表达方式包括：下浮、下滑、下落等。
减少；下降

公众对这个项目的支持率已急剧下降。

减少；下降

昨天股票价格下跌使公司的价值缩水

million off the value of the company yesterday. 了3 680万英镑。

The President's popularity took a <u>dip</u> before the election. 总统的声望在选举前有所下降。

dive

20.5 To **dive** means to jump into deep water with your head and arms going in first. 跳水

If numbers, prices etc. **dive**, they suddenly become much lower than before. 汉语用**跳水**来比喻证券价格、指数等急速下跌。

突然下降；暴跌

The share price <u>dived</u> from 49p to an all-time low of 40p. 股价从49便士暴跌到40便士的历史最低位。

20.6 You can refer to a sudden fall in the amount, value, or success of something as a **dive**. 突然贬值；暴跌

The share price took a 30% <u>dive</u> last year. 股票价格去年暴跌了30%。

drain

20.7 If you **drain** something or a place, you let liquid flow away from it. 使排走；使流出

比较汉语中的**排解、排忧解难、抽取**等。

If something **drains** you, it uses so much of your energy or strength etc. that you feel very tired or weak. 耗尽（精力或气力）

My mother's hospital expenses were slowly <u>draining</u> my income. 我母亲的住院开销把我的收入渐渐耗光了。

The experience left her emotionally <u>drained</u>. 这段经历使她委靡不振。

20.8 You can refer to something that continuously uses a lot of time, money etc. as a **drain**. 消耗；耗竭；耗费

Military spending is a huge <u>drain</u> on the country's resources. 军费开支是对国家资源的巨大耗费。

20.9 **Drain** is used metaphorically to refer to a situation in which a lot of （国家或机构中大量的人或物的）外流，流失

people or things leave a country or organization.

The government pledged to stop the <u>drain</u> of capital overseas.

政府承诺制止资金流往海外。

drop

20.10 If you **drop** something, you deliberately let it fall. If something **drops**, it falls to the ground or into something.

使落下
参见 20.3
落下

If you **drop** something such as price, you reduce it to a lower amount or value. If something such as price **drops**, it falls to a lower amount or level.

使减少；使降低；使下降
（数量、价格）下降，降低

We had to <u>drop</u> the price of our house to sell it.

为了把房子卖掉，我们只好降低价格。

In winter the temperature often <u>drops</u> below freezing.

冬天温度经常降到零度以下。

gallop

20.11 If a horse **gallops**, it runs at its fastest speed.

（马）飞跑；飞奔
汉语用**白驹过隙**形容时间过得飞快。

If something **gallops**, it moves, passes, or develops very quickly.

飞速移动；极快发展

The year has just <u>galloped</u> by.

这一年飞逝而过。

That is very low by the standards of the mid 1980s, when China's economy <u>galloped</u> ahead.

按 20 世纪 80 年代中期中国经济向上腾飞时的标准来衡量，这个速度是非常低的。

The <u>galloping</u> inflation of the previous two years seemed to have been brought under control.

这两年急剧上升的通货膨胀率看来已经得到控制。

jump

20.12 To **jump** means to move your body off the ground using your legs.

跳；跳跃
汉语中类似的隐喻表达方式包括：跃进、跃升、跃增等。

Jump is used metaphorically to talk about the action of increasing or

激增；暴涨

improving.
Profits jumped by 15% last year.   去年利润激增了 15%。
Williams jumped from 39th to 5th in the world rankings.   威廉姆斯从世界排名第 39 位蹿升到第 5 位。

leap

20.13 To **leap** means to jump high or a long way.   跳；跳跃；跳越
参见 20.11

If something **leaps**, it suddenly improves, increases, or progresses.   猛涨；激增

Sales have leapt 43% this quarter.   这个季度销售量猛增了 43%。

20.14 You can refer to a big change in the way you think or in what you do as a **leap**.   （思维方式或行为的）骤变

Most publishing companies have made the leap into multimedia.   绝大部分出版公司已作了重大调整，转而采用多媒体出版。

Moving to a place where I knew no one was a big leap for me.   搬到一个举目无亲的地方对我来说是人生的一大转折。

20.15 If something increases, develops, grows etc. **by leaps and bounds**, it does it very quickly.   突飞猛进地；迅速地

Murray has been working hard at his game and has progressed by leaps and bounds.   默里在自己的行当里一直都很努力，并且也取得了相当大的进展。

lurch

20.16 To **lurch** means to move suddenly in a way that is not smooth or controlled.   蹒跚而行；颠簸着行进
汉语用磕磕绊绊来形容事情遇到困难、挫折，不顺心，不顺利。

If something such as a government or economy **lurches** from one bad condition or state to another, it keeps having serious problems, usually caused by a lack of judgment.   （常指由于缺乏判断力致使）重大问题不断出现

The government seems to lurch from one crisis to another.   该政府看来好像危机重重。

plummet

20.17 To **plummet** means to fall straight down very quickly from a high position.
If something such as an amount, rate, or value **plummets**, it suddenly becomes much lower.
Share prices <u>plummeted</u> today to a three-month low.
The president's popularity <u>has plummeted</u> since the war began.

快速落下；垂直坠落
参见 20.3

（数量、价格、价值等）骤跌，暴跌

股票价格今天骤跌至三个月以来的最低点。
战争爆发以来，总统的支持率直线下降。

plunge

20.18 To **plunge** means to move, fall, or be thrown suddenly forwards or downwards.
If a price, rate etc. **plunges**, it suddenly decreases by a large amount.
The temperature is expected to <u>plunge</u> below zero degrees overnight.
20.19 If you **plunge in** or **into** something, you suddenly start doing it with energy and enthusiasm, but sometimes without thinking about it first.
Your help will not always be appreciated at first, but <u>plunge in</u> anyway.
She was about to <u>plunge into</u> her story when the phone rang.

迅速下落；跌落
参见 20.3

（数量或水平）骤然降低，骤跌

估计一夜之间气温会陡然下降到零度以下。

（有时未加思考便）投身（某事中），冒进

最初你的帮助并不都会得到感激，但是不管怎样，投身进来吧。
她刚要开始大谈她的经历，电话响了。

runaway

20.20 A **runaway** vehicle or animal is moving fast without anyone controlling it.
Runaway is used metaphorically to describe things such as system or price increases that seem to be developing in a way that no one can control.

（车辆或动物）失控的

迅速增加的；飞涨的

In just six months, the country's <u>runaway</u> inflation has been brought under control.

仅用了 6 个月时间，这个国家似乎不可遏止的急升的通货膨胀已经得到控制。

skip

20.21 To **skip** means to move forwards by jumping first on one foot and then the other.

蹦跳；蹦跳着走

To **skip** something means to avoid doing it or having it.

不做；略过；跳过

It's not a good idea to <u>skip</u> breakfast.

不吃早餐不是个好主意。

Let's <u>skip</u> to the final item of business.

我们跳到最后一项交易吧。

slide

20.22 To **slide** means to move smoothly and quickly across a surface.

滑动；滑行

汉语用滑坡来比喻下降。如：质量滑坡。

If prices, amounts, rates etc. **slide**, they become lower.

数量减少

Profits <u>have been sliding</u> over the last few years.

在过去几年里利润一直在下降。

20.23 If a situation **slides**, it gradually becomes worse, or begins to have a problem.

衰落；逐渐陷入

The company <u>slid</u> further into debt last year.

去年公司进一步陷入债务中。

He got depressed and began to let things <u>slide</u>.

他意志消沉，得过且过。

20.24 You can use **slide** as a noun to refer to a state or condition which is gradually getting worse, in a way that will be difficult to reverse later.

降低；衰落

The company was hit by a <u>slide</u> in profits last year.

公司利润去年有所下滑。

talks to prevent a <u>slide</u> into civil war

旨在避免陷入内战的谈判

slump

20.25 If you **slump**, you suddenly fall

（由于劳累或失去知觉而）突然倒下，

or sit because you are very tired or unconscious. 突然坐下
参见 20.18

If the level, amount, or value of something **slumps**, it falls suddenly and by a large amount. 暴跌；剧减

The organization's profits slumped to under $250 million. 这个机构的利润剧降到不足 2.5 亿美元。

20.26 You can refer to a sudden large reduction in amount as a **slump**. 暴跌；剧降

a slump in profits 利润的锐减

20.27 You can refer to a period when a country's economy or a business is doing very badly as a **slump**. 萧条期；衰退

Housing sales are finally coming out of a three-month slump. 房屋销售终于走出了一连三个月的萧条期。

The toy industry is in a slump. 玩具业现在不景气。

soar

20.28 To **soar** means to fly high in the sky. 高飞；翱翔

If the value, amount or level of something **soars**, it rises quickly. 猛增；剧增

Air pollution will soon soar above safety levels. 空气污染会很快突破安全标准。

Unemployment has soared to 18%. 失业率猛升到了 18%。

20.29 If your spirits or hopes **soar**, you suddenly feel very happy and hopeful. （精神或希望）高涨

Her spirits soared. 她情绪高涨。

stagger

20.30 If you **stagger**, you walk in an uncontrolled way, as if you are going to fall over. 蹒跚；摇摇晃晃地行走

If something such as an organization or system **staggers** or **staggers on**, it continues working despite great difficulty. 顽强继续

He *staggers on* as president, despite his increasing frailty.
The museum *is staggering* under debts of nearly £5 million.

尽管过失越来越多，他依然在总统的位置上硬撑着。
博物馆在将近 500 万英镑债务的重压下顽强地坚持着。

stride

20.31 A **stride** is one long step.

大步；阔步

Stride is used metaphorically to refer to an improvement in a situation or in the development of something.

进展；进步；发展

We're making great *strides* in the search for a cure.

在探索治疗办法方面，我们正不断取得重大进展。

20.32 If you **get into** or **hit your stride**, you begin to do something confidently and well.

开始上轨道；开始满怀信心地做

He soon *got into his stride* and produced several more books.

他很快就上了轨道，又接着出版了几本书。

20.33 If you **put someone off his stride**, you upset or trouble him.

使某人不安；使某人分心

He wasn't going to let a bit of heckling *put him off his stride*.

他不会因为一点点诘难就让自己乱了阵脚。

20.34 If you **take something in your stride**, you are not upset or troubled by it.

从容处理某事

I told her what had happened and she *took it all in her stride*.

我告诉了她发生的事情，她完全从容地去应对。

stumble

20.35 If you **stumble**, you fall or almost fall while you are walking or running.

绊倒；绊了一下
汉语用**摔跟头**来比喻遭受挫折或犯错误。

If you make a mistake when you are trying to achieve something, you **stumble**.

出岔子；出错

There are plenty of young rivals to take his place if he *stumbles*.

如果他出了差错，有许多年轻的竞争对手会取而代之。

The company *stumbled* in the late 1980s when it rushed a new machine to market and allowed costs to soar.

20 世纪 80 年代后期，这家公司因匆忙将一种新机器推向市场并任凭其成本急速增加而铸成大错，几乎导致生

20.36 If you **stumble across, on** or **upon** something or someone, you find it/him by accident.
A journalist finally <u>stumbled on</u> the truth.
偶然发现（某物）；邂逅（某人）
一位新闻记者最终在无意间发现了真相。

tumble
20.37 If someone **tumbles**, he falls to the ground.
摔倒；跌倒
参见 20.35

If a price or value **tumbles**, it suddenly becomes much lower.
Unemployment <u>tumbled</u> to 5.6% in November.
（价格或价值）猛跌，暴跌
11 月的失业率猛降到 5.6%。

20.38 You can say that something such as a price or value **takes a tumble** if it falls suddenly.
The dollar <u>took its biggest tumble</u> in over two years.
（价格或价值）猛跌，暴跌
美元创下了两年来的最大跌幅。

Column 20

This column is adopted to help understand some metaphorical expressions of **movements** that are unique to Chinese.

绊脚石	stumbling block; obstacle
飞黄腾达	make rapid advances in one's career; have a meteoric rise
滑坡	① landslide; landslip ② be on the slippery slope; decline; come down; drop
磕磕绊绊	(of a road) bumpy; (of a person) limping
爬坡	experience a difficult stage
漂泊	lead a wandering life; drift
摔打	① beat; knock ② rough it; temper oneself
摔跟头	① tumble; trip and fall ② trip up; come a cropper; make a blunder
跳槽	① (of a horse, etc.) leave its own manager to eat at another ② throw up one job and take on another

词条英文字母顺序索引

above 在……上方 19.1-19.5
access 通道；入口 6.1
acid 酸的；酸味的 5.1
acidly 尖刻地 5.2
advertise（为……）做广告；登广告宣传 9.1
afford 买得起 9.2，9.3
ahead 在前方；在前面 19.6-19.8
ailing 生病的；体弱的 2.1
also-run（赛跑中）未获名次的马 12.1
anaemic 贫血的；患贫血症的 2.2
angle 角；夹角 19.9
angling 垂钓 12.2
animal 动物 3.2-3.4
ape 猿；类人猿 3.106，3.107
artificial 人造的；人工的 9.4，9.5
asset 资产；财产 9.6
attack 攻击，进攻，袭击 13.1-13.3
avalanche 雪崩 14.1
avenue 大道；（尤指）林阴大道 8.9
backbone 脊骨；脊柱 1.1，1.2
back door 后门；旁门 6.2
back seat（汽车的）后座 8.54，8.55
backyard 后院 6.3
bait（钓鱼、捕鸟或猎兽用的）饵 12.3，12.4
bake 烘，烤，焙（面包、蛋糕等）5.3
bankrupt（人或企业）破产的；倒闭的 9.7
bankruptcy 破产；倒闭 9.8
bargain 讨价还价；洽谈；谈判 9.9
battle 战役；战斗 13.4-13.7

battlefield 战场 13.8
bear 熊 3.108
bearish（股市）行情下跌的 3.109
beast 动物，兽 3.5-3.7
beastly 野兽般的；野蛮的；贪欲的 3.8，3.9
belt 腰带；皮带 11.1，11.2
bend（尤指道路或河流的）拐弯，弯道 8.41
besiege 包围；围困 13.9
beyond 越过；远于 19.10-19.13
bitch（侮辱性用语）坏女人；淫妇；狗婆娘 3.46-3.49
bite 咬；咬断 1.77
bitter 有苦味的；苦的 5.4-5.7
bitterly 愤怒地；苦恼地；失望地 5.8，5.9
bitter-sweet 又苦又甜的 5.10
black 黑色 15.1-15.4
blacken（使）变黑 15.5
bland 清淡的，无味的 5.11，5.12
blaze 熊熊燃烧 17.1-17.4
blazing 激烈的争吵 17.5
blitz 闪电战；闪击战；突然袭击 13.10
blood 血；血液 1.3-1.5
-blooded（和某些形容词连用构成形容词）表示"有……特征的" 1.9，1.10
bloom 花 4.15-4.17
blossom（尤指果树或灌木的）花朵，花簇 4.18
blue 蓝色 15.6
body 身体，躯体 1.11-1.14
boil 沸腾；烧开；煮沸 5.13-5.17
boiling point 沸点 5.18，5.19
bombard 轰炸；炮击（某地） 13.11
bone 骨；骨头 1.15-1.17
bottleneck 狭窄路段；瓶颈路段 19.14
bottom 底部；下端；末尾 19.15-19.19
bottomless 无底的；极深的；深不可测的 19.20
brake 制动器；刹车；车闸 8.56
branch 树枝 4.19-4.21

breeze 微风；和风 14.2-14.4
breezy 通风良好的；有微风的 14.5，14.6
bridge 桥；桥梁 6.4，6.5
bright 明亮的；光亮的 16.1-16.6
brighten 发亮；发光 16.7，16.8
brilliant 明亮的；鲜亮的 16.9，16.10
broad 宽的；广的；阔的 19.21-19.24
broaden 变宽；加宽；使变阔 19.25-19.28
brown 棕色 15.7
bruise（人体受击打或碰撞后的）伤痕，青肿 2.3
bruising（身体的）伤痕，青肿 2.4，2.5
brute（大而强壮的）兽 3.10，3.11
bud 芽；花蕾 4.22
budding 开始发展的；崭露头角的；刚开始的 4.23
build 建筑；建造 6.6-6.10
bull 牛；公牛 3.71-3.74
bull-headed 固执的 3.75
bullish（金融市场价格）看涨的 3.76，3.77
burn 燃烧；烧 17.6-17.8
burner 燃烧器；炉子 5.20，5.21
burning 强烈的 17.9，17.10
burn-out 筋疲力尽的；疲惫不堪的 17.11
buy 买；购买 9.10，9.11
byway 旁道；偏僻小路 8.10
cabbage 卷心菜；甘蓝 4.1
cancer 癌症 2.6
cap（有帽舌的）帽子 11.3-11.6
card 扑克牌 12.5-12.10
carrot 胡萝卜 4.2，4.3
cat 猫 3.14-3.22
catty 恶毒的；恶意的；刁钻刻薄的 3.23
ceiling 天花板；顶棚 6.11
cement 水泥 6.12，6.13
central 中心的；在中间的 19.29，19.30
centre（空间或区域的）中央；中间 19.31-19.34

chain 链子；链条；铁链 7.1-7.7
cheap 便宜的；廉价的；劣质的 9.12
checkmate （国际象棋中的）将死，将军 12.11
chess 国际象棋 12.12
chew 嚼碎；咀嚼 1.78，1.79
chick 雏鸟 3.52，3.53
chicken 懦夫；胆小鬼 3.54-3.62
chill （使）变冷；冰镇 17.12，17.13
chilling 令人胆寒的；令人担心的；令人沮丧的 17.14
chilly 寒冷的 14.7
circle 圆；圆形 8.42-8.46，19.35，19.36
climb 爬，攀爬 20.1，20.2
clock 钟；时钟 18.1-18.7
clock-watcher 老是看时间等下班的人 18.8
clockwork （玩具等上面的）发条装置 7.8，7.9
close （在时间、空间上）接近 19.37-19.40
closed 关闭的；封闭的 19.41
cloud 云；云雾 14.8-14.15
coast （汽车或自行车）靠惯性滑行 8.57
coat 外套 11.7，11.8
cock 公鸡 3.63
cocky 趾高气扬的；过分自信的 3.64
cog 齿轮 7.11
cold 冷的；寒冷的 17.15，17.16
coldly 冷淡地；冷漠地；不友好地 17.17
coldness 冷淡；冷漠；不友好的举止 17.18
colour 色；颜色 15.8-15.11
colourful 色彩丰富的，引人注目的 15.12-15.15
colourless 无色的 15.16
conquer 征服；占领；攻克 13.12，13.13
construct 建造；修筑 6.14
consume 吃；喝；消费 9.13，9.14
consuming 使人全神贯注的；强烈的 9.15
consumption 消费 9.16
contagion 接触传染 2.7

contagious（疾病）接触传染的 2.8
cook 烹调；煮；烧 5.22
cool 凉爽的；凉快的 17.19-17.25
corner（道路的）拐角；街角 8.47，8.48
cornerstone 基石；奠基石 6.15
corridor 走廊；通道 6.16
cost 价钱；价格；成本 9.17
course 方向 8.1，8.2
cow 母牛 3.78
cripple 残疾人；（尤指）跛子，瘸子 2.9-2.11
crippling 使残疾的；（尤指）使跛的 2.12
crop 收成；产量 4.45，4.46
crossfire 交叉火力 13.14
crossroads 交叉路口；十字路口 8.49
cultivate 开垦；耕作；栽培；种植 4.47，4.48
cultivated（土地）耕种的；耕作的 4.49
cure（有效的）药，疗法 2.13-2.15
curtain 幕，幕布 10.1-10.4
dark 黑暗的；无光的 16.20-16.27
darken（使）变暗；（使）变黑 16.28
darkly 威胁地；险恶地；负面地 16.29
dawn 黎明；拂晓；破晓 18.9-18.12
day 一天，一日；白天 18.13-18.17
daydream 白日梦；幻想；空想 18.18，18.19
day job 日常的有薪工作；（白天的）正职 18.20
day-to-day 日常的 18.21
dazzle（强光）使目眩，使眼花 16.11
dazzling 耀眼的；眩目的 16.12
dead end 死路；死胡同 8.50，8.51
deadlock 单闩锁 7.30
deadly 致死的；致命的 2.16
debt 债务；欠款 9.18
deep（从顶部向下）深的 19.42-19.54
defuse 拆除（炸弹的）引信 13.15
deluge 暴雨；大雨 14.16，14.17

demolish 拆毁 6.17-6.20
demolition 拆毁，毁坏 6.21，6.22
depth 深度；纵深 19.55-19.58
diet 食物；饮食 5.23
digest 消化（食物） 1.80
dilute 稀释；冲淡 5.24
dim （光）暗淡的；昏暗的 16.30-16.32
dimension 维；长度；高度；宽度；深度；直径 19.59
dinosaur 恐龙 3.110
dip 下降；落下；降下 20.3，20.4
discount 打折扣；打折出售 9.19
disease 病；疾病 2.17
dissect 解剖 2.18
distant 遥远的；远处的；久远的 19.60，19.61
dive 跳水 20.5，20.6
dog 狗 3.29-3.44
dogged 坚持不懈的；顽强的 3.45
donkey 驴 3.79-3.81
door 门 6.23
down 向下；往下；在下面 19.62-19.65
drain 使排走；使流出 20.7-20.9
drama 戏剧；电视剧 10.5-10.7
drily 枯燥地；干巴巴地；冷冰冰地 5.25
drive 驾驶；驾车 8.58-8.61
driving seat 驾驶座 8.62
drop 使落下 20.10
dry 脱水的；没有脂肪的；没有汁的；干的 5.26，5.27
duck 鸭；鸭子 3.66，3.67
dynamite 炸药 13.16
ear 耳；耳朵 1.18，1.19
edifice （雄伟的）大厦 6.24
engine 发动机；引擎 7.11
engineer 设计（公路、铁路、桥梁或机械） 7.12
epidemic （疾病的）传播，流行 2.19
export 出口；输出 9.20

eye 眼睛 1.20-1.24
face 脸；面部 1.25-1.33
fatal 致命的；致死的 2.20
favourite 最有可能赢得比赛的马 12.13
ferret （猎兔或猎鼠用的）白鼬，雪貂 3.111，3.112
fester 化脓；溃烂 2.21
fever 发烧；发热 2.22
feverish 发烧的；发热的 2.23
fiery 如火的；似火的 17.26，17.27
fish 捕鱼；钓鱼 12.14
fire 开火；发射 13.17
　　火 17.28，17.29
firestorm （炸弹爆炸引起的）风暴性大火 13.18
flame 火焰；火舌 17.30，17.31
flare 突然烧旺；闪耀 17.32-17.36
flavour 味道；滋味 5.28-5.30
flicker （火焰、灯光）摇曳，闪烁 17.37，17.38
flourish 茂盛；兴盛；茁壮成长 4.63
flourishing 繁盛的；欣欣向荣的；蒸蒸日上的 4.64
flower 花，花卉 4.24
flowering 兴盛时期；成熟期 4.25
fog 雾 14.18，14.19
foggy 多雾的；有雾的 14.20，14.21
forge 锻造 7.31，7.32
foundation 地基；地脚 6.25
fox 狐狸 3.113-3.115
foxy 狡猾的；奸诈的；精明的 3.116，3.117
freeze 结冰 14.22，14.23
front 前面；正面 19.66-19.68
frontier 边疆 19.69
front line （战争的）前线 13.19
front-line 前线的 13.20
frosty 霜冻的；严寒的 14.24
fruit 水果；果实 4.26，4.27
fruition （计划或想法的）实现；完成；取得成果 4.29

fruitless 无结果的；无收益的；徒劳的 4.30
full 满的；充满的；满是……的 19.70，19.71
fund 资金；基金；专款 9.21
further 较远；更远 19.72
gale 大风；强风 14.25
gallop （马）飞跑；飞奔 20.11
gamble 打赌；赌博 12.15，12.16
game 游戏 12.17-12.19
gateway 出入口；门口 6.26
gear （排）挡 8.63-8.65
germinate （使）发芽 4.65
gloom 昏暗；阴暗 16.33
gloomy 阴暗的；幽暗的 16.34，16.35
goal 球门；球篮 12.20，12.21
goalpost 球门柱 12.22
goat 山羊 3.82，3.83
goose 鹅 3.68-3.70
grass 草 4.4-4.6
green 绿色 15.17-15.19
green light （交通）绿灯 8.52
grey 灰色 15.20，15.21
grill （在烤架上）炙烤 5.31
grind 磨碎；把……磨成粉状 7.33-7.36
grinding 极端的（用于强调形势的恶劣） 7.37
gust 一阵强风；一阵狂风 14.26
guts 内脏；（尤指）肠胃 1.34-1.37
hail 冰雹 14.27
halfway 中间的；中途的 8.4-8.7
hammer 锤击；把……锤进 7.38-7.44
hand 手 1.38-1.41
hare 野兔 3.118，3.119
harvest 收割；收获；收成 4.50-4.52
hat 帽子 11.9-11.11
haze 薄雾；霾 14.28
hazy 雾蒙蒙的；烟雾弥漫的 14.29

head 头；头部 1.42，1.43
headache 头痛 2.24
health 健康（状况） 2.25
healthy 健康的；健壮的 2.26-2.28
heart 心；心脏 1.44-1.52
heartbreaking 使人悲伤的；令人心碎 1.53
heartbroken 极度伤心的；心碎的 1.54
heart-warming 暖人心扉的；温馨感 1.55
-hearted （和某些形容词连用构成形容词）表示"有……性格的，有……感情的" 1.56-1.60
heat 热；热度 17.39-17.44
heated 温的；暖的 17.45，17.46
heatedly 愤怒地；激动地；情绪激烈地 17.47
hen 母鸡 3.65
high 高的 19.73-19.77
highway 公路 8.11
hog 阉公猪 3.84-3.86
horizon 地平线 19.78，19.79
horse 马 3.92-3.96
hot 热的；烫的；温度高的 17.48-17.53
hotly （情绪）强烈地；激动地 17.54，17.55
hound 猎狗 3.50，3.51
hour 小时 18.22，18.23
hourly 每小时一次地 18.24
hunt 打猎；射杀（猎物） 12.23
hunted （表情）焦虑的，十分惊恐的 12.24
hurricane 飓风 14.30，14.31
hurt （使）疼痛；（使）受伤；感到疼痛 2.29
icily 冷冷地；冷漠地 14.32
icy 寒冷的，冰封的 14.33
ignite 使……燃烧；点燃 17.56，17.57
ill 不健康的；有病的 2.30
ills 问题；困难 2.31
infancy 婴儿期；幼儿期 18.25
infectious （疾病）传染性的 2.32

ingredient（烹调用的）原料，配料 5.32
inject 注射 2.33，2.34
inner 内部的；里面的；接近中心的 19.80，19.81
inside 内部的；里面的 19.82-19.85
instrument 仪器；器具 7.45
invade 武力入侵；侵占；侵略 13.21，13.22
invasion 入侵；侵略 13.23，13.24
jaundiced 黄疸（病） 2.35
journey（尤指长途）旅行；行程 8.3
juicy（食物）多汁的 5.33-5.35
jump 跳；跳跃 20.12
key 钥匙 7.46，7.47
kill 杀死；弄死 13.25，13.26
kitten 小猫 3.24，3.25
kittenish（忸怩或卖弄风情地）嬉耍的 3.26
labyrinth 迷宫；曲径 6.27
ladder 梯子 7.48
lamb 羔羊；小羊 3.87，3.88
lame（动物）跛的，瘸的 2.36，2.37
lane 车道 8.12，8.13
launch 发射（导弹、太空飞行器、人造卫星等） 13.27-13.29
laurel 月桂树 4.7-4.9
leap 跳；跳跃；跳越 20.13-20.15
legacy 遗产；遗赠财物 9.22
lever 杠杆；撬棒 7.49
leverage 杠杆作用；杠杆力量 7.50
light 光；光线；光亮 16.13-16.15
lighten（使）变亮；（使）明亮；点亮 16.16
lightening 闪电 14.34，14.35
lily 百合花 4.10
link（链的）一环 7.13-7.16
limp 一瘸一拐地走；跛行 2.38
line（移动或注视的）方向，路线 8.14-8.18
lion 狮子 3.120，3.121
lip 嘴唇 1.61

lock 锁；锁住 6.28
lottery 抽彩给奖（筹款法）；彩票游戏 12.25
low 矮的；低的 19.86-19.90
lukewarm 不冷不热的；微温的 17.58
lurch 踉跄而行；颠簸着行进 20.16
machinery 机器；机械 7.17
manufacture （大量）生产；制造 9.23
marathon 马拉松（长跑） 12.26
mechanical 机械操作的；机械的 7.18
mechanics 机械学；力学 7.19
mechanism 机器；机械装置；机件 7.20
melt （使）融化；（使）熔化 17.59
mend 缝补；修补 11.12-11.15
middle 中部（的）；中间（的）；中央（的） 19.91
minute 分；分钟 18.26-18.29
mist 薄雾；雾气 14.36，14.37
moment 片刻；瞬间 18.30-18.32
monkey 猴子 3.122，3.123
month 一个月 18.33
mouse 鼠；老鼠 3.124
mousy 安静害羞的 3.125
mushroom 蘑菇 4.11
nail 钉牢；钉住；把……钉上 7.51-7.54
narrow 狭窄的；狭长的；狭小的 19.92，19.93
neck and neck （赛马比赛中）并驾齐驱 12.27
needle 针；缝衣针 11.16
nettle 荨麻 4.12，4.13
neutral （汽车的）空挡位置 8.66
night 夜；夜晚 18.34
nightmare 噩梦；梦魇 18.35
nose 鼻子 1.62，1.63
odds 投注赔率 12.28，12.29
open 空旷的；开阔的；无遮盖的 19.94-19.97
outsider 不大可能获胜的赛马 12.30
package 包装；把……打包；把……装箱 9.24，9.25

词条英文字母顺序索引

pain 痛；疼痛 2.39-2.41
painful 疼痛的 2.42，2.43
parallel 平行的 19.98-19.101
paralyse 使瘫痪；使麻痹 2.44
paralysis（通常因受伤或疾病而引起的）瘫痪（症） 2.45
path（人走出来的）小径；（人走的）小道 8.19-8.21
pave（用砖、石块、水泥等）铺，铺砌 6.29
pawn（国际象棋中的）卒 12.31
peppery 胡椒味的；似胡椒的 5.36
pet 宠物 3.12，3.13
pig 猪 3.97-3.104
pink 粉红色；淡红色 15.22
plant 种；植；栽种 4.54-4.58
play 扮演，饰演（角色） 10.8-10.10
　　　参加（体育运动或比赛） 12.32-12.38
player 选手 12.39
playing field 球场 12.40
plummet 快速落下；垂直坠落 20.17
plunge 迅速下落；跌落 20.18，20.19
polish 磨光；擦亮 7.55
powder keg 火药桶；危险的局面；一触即发的情势 13.30
prelude（乐曲的）前奏，过门 10.11
pressure cooker 压力锅；高压锅 5.37
product 制品；产品 9.26，9.27
property 所有物；财产 9.28
prune 修剪；修整（树木） 4.53
pump（尤指用泵）抽取；抽吸；注入 7.21-7.25
puppet 木偶 10.12
purple 紫色 15.23，15.24
pussy 猫咪（尤为儿语） 3.27
pussyfoot 蹑手蹑脚 3.28
rail 铁轨 8.22-8.24
rain 雨，雨水 14.38
rash 皮疹 2.46
rat 老鼠 3.026-3.028

reap 收割（庄稼） 4.60，4.61
recipe 食谱；烹饪法 5.38
red 红色的 15.25-15.29
rehearsal 排演；排练 10.29
remote（空间或时间）遥远的 19.102，19.103
road 路；道路；（尤指）公路 8.25-8.29
roast 烤；烘 5.39
roasting 燥热的，灼热的；严厉批评 17.60，17.61
roof 屋顶；房顶 6.30，6.31
root（植物的）根；根茎 4.31-4.36
route 路线；航线 8.30
ruin 废墟；遗迹 6.32
runaway（车辆或动物）失控的 20.20
running 一马当先 12.41
sail（船只）航行 12.42，12.43
salty 含盐的；咸的 5.40
salvo（火炮或其他武器）齐射，齐发，齐鸣 13.31
scalding 灼热的；滚烫的 17.62
scar 伤疤；疤痕；伤痕 2.47，2.48
scene（戏剧、书、电影等的）片断，场面，情节，镜头 10.13-10.18
second 秒 18.36
seed 种子；籽 4.37-4.40
sell 卖；出售 9.29
shadow 阴影；暗影 16.36，16.37
shallow 浅的 19.104，19.105
sharpen 使锋利；削尖 7.56-7.59
sheep 羊；绵羊 3.89，3.90
sheepish 羞愧的；不好意思的；困窘的 3.91
shine（太阳）发光；照耀 16.17-16.19
shoe 鞋；鞋子 11.17，11.18
shoot 嫩芽；秧苗；新枝 4.41
shot 射击；开枪 13.32
shoulder 肩；肩膀 1.64，1.65
show 假装；演戏 10.19-10.21
show your hand 亮出底牌；摊牌 12.44

shower 阵雨；阵雪 14.39-14.41
shrivel （植物）枯萎；皱缩 4.66
sick （感觉）不适的，生病的 2.49-2.51
sickness 问题；疾患 2.52
simmer 煨；用文火炖 5.41，5.42
skate 滑冰 12.45，12.46
skeleton 骨骼；骨架 1.66，1.67
skip 蹦跳；蹦跳着走 20.21
slice （切下的食物）薄片，片 5.43-5.48
slide 滑动；滑行 20.22-20.24
slump （由于劳累或失去知觉而）突然倒下，突然坐下 20.25-20.27
smoulder （无明火地）慢慢燃烧；闷燃 17.63
snake 蛇 3.129
snow 下雪；降雪 14.42
soar 高飞；翱翔 20.28，20.29
sock 袜子 11.19
sour 酸的 5.49-5.51
sourly 气愤地 5.52
sourness 愤怒、痛苦 5.53
sow 播（种） 4.59
spark 火花 17.64-17.66
sphere 球；球体；球形 19.106-19.108
spine 脊椎；脊柱 1.68
spineless 没有勇气的；没有骨气的 1.69
spiral 螺旋；螺旋形 19.109，19.110
spit 吐唾沫；吐痰 1.81
sport 运动；体育比赛 12.47，12.48
sporting 可能成功的机会 12.49
springboard 跳板；踏板 7.60
sprout 发芽；萌芽；抽条 4.67
stage 舞台 10.27，10.28
stagger 蹒跚；摇摇晃晃地行走 20.30
stake 赌注；赌金 12.50-12.54
stalemate （棋局的）僵棋，和棋 12.55
steer 掌舵；驾驶 8.67-8.69

stem（植物的）茎；柄；梗 4.42
stew 炖；煨；焖 5.54-5.56
stomach 胃 1.70-1.72
storm 暴风雨 14.43-14.49
stormy 有暴风雨的；风暴的 14.50
stride 大步；阔步 20.31-20.34
string 细绳 10.22-10.26
stumble 绊倒；绊了一下 20.35，20.36
suit 一套衣服；服装 11.20，11.21
sunny 阳光充足的；阳光明媚的 14.51
swallow 吞下；咽下 1.82
sweet 甜（味）的 5.57，5.58
sweetly 可爱地；亲切地；温柔地 5.59
swine 猪猡；下流坯 3.105
sword 剑；刀 13.33
symptom 症状 2.53
symptomatic 显露症状的；症状性的 2.54
syndrome 综合症状；综合症 2.55
tempest 暴风雨 14.52
tempestuous（情绪）强烈的，骚动的，狂暴的 14.53
tepid 温的；不够热的 17.67
thaw（使）解冻；（使）融化 17.68-17.70
thorn 刺 4.43
thorny 带刺的；多刺的 4.44
thread 线 11.22-11.25
thunder 雷；雷声 14.54-14.56
thunderous 雷鸣般的 14.57
tick over（汽车引擎）空转；慢转 7.25
tie 领带 11.26-11.29
time 时间 18.37
time bomb 定时炸弹 13.34
tone 声调；腔音；语气 10.30-10.33
tongue 舌头；舌 1.73-1.75
tool 工具；用具 7.61
tooth 牙；牙齿 1.76

top 顶端；顶部；上端；上面 19.111-19.114
tower 塔 6.33
towering 高耸的；参天的；屹立的 6.34
toy 玩具 12.56
track 粗糙不平的小路；铁轨 8.31-8.39
transport（通常指用车辆）运输，运送，搬运 8.70
travel（长途）旅行 8.80
troop 部队 13.35
trump（牌戏中的）一套王牌 12.58，12.59
trump card 王牌 12.60
tumble 摔倒；跌倒 20.37
tunnel 隧道；地道 8.40
unhealthy 有病的；不健康的 2.56，2.57
unlock 打开 6.39，6.40
unsavoury（食品）难闻的，看起来很糟糕的 5.60
unsporting 无体育道德的；自私的；不公平的 12.61
up 从下往上地；向上地 19.115-19.117
U-turn（车辆的）掉头 8.53
veer（尤指车辆等）突然转向 8.71
vegetable 蔬菜 4.14
vehicle 机动车辆 8.72
vermin（引起破坏或疾病的）害兽，害虫，寄生虫 3.130
wall 墙，墙壁 6.35-6.37
war 战争 13.36-13.38
warm 温暖的；温度宜人的 17.71-17.73
warmly 热情地；友好地；积极地 17.74
warmth 温暖；暖和 17.75
water down 掺水冲淡；加水稀释 5.61
wear 穿戴；佩带 11.30-11.37
weasel 鼬；黄鼠狼 3.031
weed 野草 4.62
weld 锻接，焊接（金属） 7.62
well-rehearsed 计划周密的 10.32
wheel 轮子；车轮 7.27-7.29
whirlwind 旋风 14.58

white 白色 15.30-15.33
wilt （植物）枯萎；凋谢 4.68
wind 风 14.59
window 窗；窗户 6.38
wither （使）枯萎；凋谢 4.69
withered （植物）枯萎的；干枯的 4.70
withering 使人感到愚蠢的；使人难堪的 4.71
wolf 狼 3.132-3.134
wolfish 凶残的；狡诈的 3.135
wound 伤；伤口 2.58-2.61
year 年 18.38，18.39
yellow 黄色 15.34

附录

英语常用概念隐喻

achievement	An achievement is like a **building**, and the process of achieving is like the process of building.
angry	Being angry is like being **hot** or **on fire**.
argument	An argument is like a **fight** or **war**, with people attacking each other's opinions and defending their own.
busy	Being very busy at work is like being **covered with things** or **surrounded by** something such as water or the ground, so that you cannot move easily.
confused	Being confused is like being **lost** or **in the wrong place** or **position**.
conversation	A conversation is like a **journey**, with the speakers going from one place to another.
criticize	Criticizing someone or speaking in an angry and unpleasant way to them is like **hitting** or **injuring** them.
discover	Discovering things such as facts and information is like **finding** them by **digging** or **searching in the ground**.
effort	When you put a lot of effort into doing something, it is like **using a part of your body**.
enthusiasm/excitement	Enthusiasm and excitement are like **heat** and a lack of enthusiasm and excitement are like **cold** or **wet**.
feeling	When something has an emotional effect on you, you feel as if you have been **hit hard, shaken, touched,** or **injured**.
force	Forcing someone to do something is like putting **physical pressure** on them, or **pulling** or **pushing** them.
guilty	Being guilty is like being **dirty**, and being innocent is like being **clean**. Becoming more moral or getting rid of guilt is like **washing**.

continued:

happy/hopeful	Feeling happy and hopeful is like being **high up** or like **moving upwards**.
help	Helping people is like **supporting** them **physically**, for example with your body or with something that you build.
honest	Being honest and moral is like being in a **high** position. Being dishonest and immoral is like being **low down**.
idea/theory	An idea or theory is like a **building** or **structure**. Developing an idea is like building something, and destroying an idea is like destroying a building.
important	Being important is like being **large** or **heavy**.
intelligence	Intelligence is like a **light**. The more intelligent someone is, the brighter the light.
knowledge	Getting knowledge about something is like **making a map of a place** or like **traveling** there. Teaching someone is like showing them how to **reach a place**. When you have some knowledge about something, it is as if you are **shining a light** on it. Not having knowledge is like **being in darkness**.
life	Life is like a **journey**, and your experiences are like different parts of a journey. Dying is like traveling to another place.
method	The methods that you use to do something are like **tools** and **machines**. The process of doing something is like using a machine.
mind	Your mind is like a **container** or **area**, with thoughts being stored there or going in and out.
mistake	Making a mistake is like **falling over**, or like being **clumsy** and **dropping things**.
money	Money is like **food**, which gets eaten or is shared out. The same idea is used to talk about other types of resource.
opportunity	Having an opportunity to do something is like having a **door** or **way of getting into a building**.
organization	An organization is like a **body**, and its different sections are like different parts of a body.

continued:

power	Having power and controlling someone is like being in a **higher position** than them. Not having power is like being **low down**.
problem	Problems and troubles are like **illness**. When things get better, people think of the problems as being cured.
quantity	Changes in quantities and amounts are like **movements up and down**. People think of large quantities as being in a high position and small quantities as being in a low position.
relationship	Relationships between people or groups are like **physical connections**. Having a good relationship is like being joined to the other person or group, and ending a relationship is like breaking it.
responsibility	Having responsibilities is like **carrying** something. Responsibilities that cause you problems and make you worried are like heavy loads.
sad	Feeling sad and unhappy is like being **low down** or like **falling**.
search	Searching for something is like **hunting** an animal, or like one animal hunting another.
secret	To keep something secret is like **covering it**, or **putting it in a container**, so that other people cannot see it.
situation	Situations and states are like **places**. A pleasant/happy situation is safe, like your home, and a bad situation is like an unhappy or dangerous place.
success	Being successful is like being **high up**. Failing is like **falling** or being **low down**.
time	Time is like **money**, or like something that you **buy** and **use**.
understand	Understanding something is like **seeing** it. If it is easy to understand, it is easy to see.
unimportant	Being unimportant is like being **small** or **light**.
want	Wanting something is like being **hungry** or **thirsty**, and doing or having something that you want is like eating it.
win	Winning a competition or game is like **hitting** or **killing** your opponent. Losing is like being injured.

参考书目

1. 北京外国语学院英语系词典组. 汉英成语词典. 北京：商务印书馆，1982.
2. 陈文伯. 英语成语与汉语成语. 北京：外语教学与研究出版社，1982.
3. 惠宇. 新世纪英汉大词典. 北京：外语教学与研究出版社，2003.
4. 陆谷孙. 英汉大词典（第二版）. 上海：上海译文出版社，2007.
5. 麦克米伦出版公司编. 杨信彰等译. 麦克米伦高阶英汉双解词典. 北京：外语教学与研究出版社，2005.
6. 商务印书馆辞书研究中心编. 应用汉语词典. 北京：商务印书馆，2002.
7. 任绍曾主编. 丁建民译. 英语语法系列：7.隐喻. 北京：外文出版社，2001.
8. 萨默斯（Summers, D.）. 朗文英语理想活用词典（第二版）. 上海：上海外语教育出版社，2006.
9. 辛克莱（Sinclair, J.）.《柯伯英汉双解词典》编译组译. 柯伯英汉双解词典. 上海：上海译文出版社，2002.
10. 辛克莱（Sinclair, J.）. 柯林斯COBUILD英语词典. 上海：上海外语教育出版社，2000.
11. Wehmeier, Sally. 石孝殊译. 牛津高阶英汉双解词典（第六版）. 北京：商务印书馆；香港：牛津大学出版社，2004.
12. 中国社会科学院语言研究所词典编辑室编. 现代汉语词典（第五版）. 北京：商务印书馆，2005.
13. 中国社会科学院语言研究所词典编辑室编. 现代汉语词典（2002年增补本）. 北京：商务印书馆，2002.
14. Agnes, Michael. ed. *Webster's New World College Dictionary*, 4th ed. Cleveland Ohio: Wiley Publishing, Inc, 2002.
15. Deignan, Alice. ed. *Collins COBUILD English Guides 7: Metaphor*. London: Harper Collins Publishers, 1995.
16. Sinclair, J. ed. *Advanced Learner's English Dictionary*, 4th ed. Glasgow: Harper Collins Publishers, 2003.
17. Summers, Della. ed. *Longman Dictionary of Contemporary English*, 4th ed. Edinburgh Gate: Pearson Educational Limited, 2005.